The Diplomacy of the American Revolution

MIDLAND BOOKS

SAMUEL FLAGG BEMIS

THE
DIPLOMACY
OF THE
AMERICAN
REVOLUTION

INDIANA UNIVERSITY PRESS
Bloomington & London

EIGHTH PRINTING 1975

COPYRIGHT 1935 BY THE AMERICAN HISTORICAL ASSOCIATION

COPYRIGHT © 1957 BY INDIANA UNIVERSITY PRESS

ALL RIGHTS RESERVED

LIBRARY OF CONGRESS CATALOG CARD NO. 57-7878

MANUFACTURED IN THE UNITED STATES OF AMERICA

pa. ISBN 0-253-20006-7

To
J. FRANKLIN JAMESON

PREFACE

Hitherto no one with access to a full abundance of foreign as well as American sources has attempted to write the diplomatic history of the American Revolution. Mr. William Henry Trescot's notable essay, published in 1852,[1] and the notes in the first volume in Francis Wharton's *Revolutionary Diplomatic Correspondence of the United States* (Washington, 1889) depended pretty exclusively on American sources and records. The monumental publication of Mr. Henri Doniol,[2] besides being out of reach of the average reader or student, is too dominantly French in its point of view and its presentation of selected documents, voluminous as they are, from the archives of the French foreign office. Back of the printed records still lies a great quantity of manuscript material. I have perused essential portions of the American, British, French, and Spanish sources, printed and unprinted, and have made use of notable monographs by scholars who have exploited parts of these and also Dutch, Scandinavian, Russian, Prussian, and Austrian archives.[3] My endeavor has been to present, I think for the first time, a balanced and somewhat condensed narrative of the diplomacy of American independence, that is to say, the diplomatic history of the American Revolution. In doing so details have been subordinated to the significant factors and to the broad movements.

The achievement of American independence depended on European diplomacy and international politics. Through France, the cumbersome government of the Continental Congress availed itself of bitter European rivalries and found an ally to help bring to its knees the British Empire, never defeated before or since. Through France and the allies of France the United States became

---

[1] *The Diplomacy of the Revolution, an Historical Study* (New York, 1852).

[2] *Histoire de la participation de la France à l'établissement des Etats-Unis d'Amérique; correspondance diplomatique et documents* (5 vols., Paris, 1886–1892).

[3] See Bibliographical Note at end of this volume.

involved in the entanglements of European diplomacy. The perspicacity of Franklin, Jay, and Adams perceived this in great degree, though not in such large measure as the historian of to-day can envisage it. While preserving the letter of the alliance with France, these bold plenipotentiaries broke their instructions and cut loose from French advice and control. To clinch their own country's advantage and independence, they took advantage of Europe's rivalries and distresses. Thanks to decades of European convulsion which followed, the United States was able to preserve that independence safe and uncudgeled, to secure its national domain, to expand from sea to sea, to make good its territorial basis as a world power of to-day fronting on two oceans. Further, because of Europe's divisions and prostrations after 1815 American statesmen, one of them the great son of the Adams of 1782–1783, were able to formulate and to proclaim in 1823 the Monroe Doctrine to hold away from American shores for future decades these bitternesses and these conflicts from which the United States had loosed itself by its separation from the British Empire.

These later chapters of the Foundations of American Diplomacy I hope to make the subject of a sequent volume covering the period from 1783 to 1823. But nowhere in those interesting years shall we find a diplomatic victory to equal the American triumph recorded a century and a half ago.

I wish to acknowledge assistance and encouragement from many institutions and people. First should be mentioned the Library of Congress. While Director of the European Mission of that library, from 1927 to 1929, I was able to visit the state archives of western and central Europe and to provide for the photocopying of masses of material illustrative of American diplomacy (a small portion of a much greater quantity of manuscripts illuminating American history in general), a volume of documentary intake which has since continued to flow under the able and scholarly management of Dr. Worthington C. Ford. This, added to the already comprehensive material which the Library had already assembled for the period of the American Revolution, to its rich collections of original manuscripts, and to other bodies of sources in Washington, makes that institution, in effect if not in name, a national library, cer-

tainly the best place in the world to study the diplomatic history
of the United States. These tangible resources are by no means all
that the Library of Congress has to offer to the scholar. Under the
direction of its eminent Librarian, Dr. Herbert Putnam, with his
close to forty years' of most constructive service, that institution
has become in spirit as in fact an unrivaled workshop. Nowhere
is there a more sincere and eager devotion, from chief down to
deck attendant, to serve the search for knowledge.

Truly the international spirit is strongest and kindest in the
domain of scholarship. To make acknowledgment to these facilities, and to this spirit of the Library of Congress, does not lighten
my gratitude to other libraries, in this country and abroad: the
British Museum, the *Bibliothèque Nationale,* the *Staatsbibliothek*
in Berlin, the *Biblioteca Nacional* in Madrid, the Widener Memorial Library of Harvard University, the William L. Clements
Library at the University of Michigan, the Carnegie Institution
of Washington. No less important are the archives: the Department of State, the British Public Record Office, the Archives du
Ministère des Affaires Etrangères in Paris, the Archivo Histórico
Nacional in Madrid, the Archivo General de Simancas, near Val-
ladolid, and the Archivo General de Indias in Seville. To the chiefs
and to the staffs of these institutions I make my respectful and
grateful acknowledgments.

Dr. John Franklin Jameson has been of continued assistance and
inspiration to me. On many occasions during several years I have
discussed questions of the diplomacy of the Revolution with that
thoughtful man, Dr. James Brown Scott. Dr. Scott has read a
draft of the entire manuscript. So has Dr. Burton J. Hendrick.
Dr. Worthington C. Ford has sustained me with the wisdom and
grace of a veteran scholar and worker. Dr. Edmund C. Burnett,
of the Division of Historical Research of the Carnegie Institution
of Washington, so model an editor of the letters of the members
of the Continental Congress, has given me unstintedly of his time
and counsel. Colonel Lawrence Martin, Chief of the Division of
Maps of the Library of Congress, has helped me greatly with his
unrivaled knowledge of maps in general and his quite esoteric
acquaintance with Mitchell's Map, the most important map in the

diplomatic history of the United States. I have profited from many discussions with Dr. Hunter Miller, Historical Adviser of the Department of State, who mingles with his great legal erudition an unequaled mastery of the history of the treaties of the United States and who carefully read my manuscript. Dr. John C. Fitzpatrick, the authority on George Washington, and Miss Grace Gardner Griffin, the enthusiastic and indefatigable bibliographer of American history, have helped me. Miss Edna Vosper, specialist in manuscripts at the W. L. Clements Library, has kindly read the chapters on the peace negotiations, and I have profited greatly from her suggestions. Mr. H. P. Biggar, of Ottawa, kindly read the introductory chapter and gave me the advantage of certain corrections. And how many other persons, so keen and so kind, have helped me and other investigators. I have to add that I alone must be responsible for the shortcomings in this volume.

A grant-in-aid from the American Council of Learned Societies has enabled me to have drafted the maps in this volume and has helped in other practical ways.

S. F. B.

PREFACE TO SECOND PRINTING

I have this opportunity to correct a few small errors in the original publication.

S. F. B.

New Haven, Ct.
March 3, 1937

FOREWORD TO 1957 EDITION

I started writing this book, in a log cabin in the woods, by the shore of little Sunapee Lake, in New London, New Hampshire, on the Fourth of July, 1926, the 150th anniversary of the Declaration of Independence. It was also the centenary of raising the Meeting House in the village, while John Adams and Thomas Jefferson were breathing their last at Quincy and Monticello, July 4, 1826. John Adams and Thomas Jefferson played parts in the following narrative of the diplomacy of the Revolution, which brought this nation into sovereign existence. Benjamin Franklin, whose 250th anniversary we have been celebrating this year, in 1956, played an even greater part.

Since the first edition in 1935, very little has appeared which would require me to change the original text. However, I am able in this edition to incorporate the discovery of Professor John J. Meng in the archives of the French Foreign Office, which enabled him to redate as of April 1776 Vergennes's secret memorandum on policy, entitled *"Réflexions,"* as drawn up by his secretary, Gérard de Rayneval. Dr. Meng demonstrated that it followed rather than preceded the memorandum entitled *"Considérations."* Consequently in this edition I have rearranged pages 20 to 28 so as to place the *"Réflexions"* before the *"Considérations."* I have also added on page 90 some details from Professor John W. Caughey's published *Bernardo de Gálvez in Louisiana* (University of California Press, 1934) not noticed by me in the first edition of this book. To both of these accomplished scholars I acknowledge my indebtedness.

The original edition contained five large folding maps, of interest chiefly to scholarly specialists, which have been omitted from this edition in order to keep the price as low as possible. But I have not deleted the occasional references to these maps in the footnotes, in case any student of the period should wish to consult them in the original edition, which is now out of print but is available in most large libraries.

Originally this book was intended as the first volume of a trilogy on "The Foundations of American Foreign Policy, 1775-1823." I have since deserted that original concept in favor of a volume on *John Quincy Adams and the Foundations of American Foreign Policy* (Alfred A. Knopf, Inc., 1949).

S. F. B.

December 7, 1956
New Haven, Connecticut

CONTENTS

The Diplomacy of the American Revolution

CHAPTER I

INTRODUCTION

After a preliminary glimpse of America as a factor in European diplomacy from the discovery to the eve of the revolution of the English Colonies it will be the task of this volume to describe and to interpret the diplomatic history of the American Revolution and the establishment of the independence of the United States. It is a chronicle of momentous import to the modern world.

For nearly three centuries after 1492 North America was increasingly the stakes of European diplomacy. The maritime powers of western Europe never accepted the single-handed award by which the Pope had immediately divided up the lands and seas just discovered, and to be discovered, between Spain and Portugal, nor the treaty by which those two crowns in 1494 had complacently marked off and agreed upon each other's new and spacious overseas sovereignties. During the sixteenth, seventeenth, and eighteenth centuries the vulnerable Spanish claim of monopoly to the New World offered to European enemies and rivals a mighty panorama of spoil, inviting dispute and war. The sparsely settled continents could not be preserved from French, English, and Dutch interlopers. France, England, and the Netherlands successively challenged Spain's impossible monopoly and established their colonies in North America and the Caribbean. As these colonies grew in importance and trade expanded with them, North America, at first only incidentally the spoil of European controversies and wars, became more and more the principal cause of them—the real stakes. Spain's rivals began to quarrel and to fight among themselves over what they had taken from her, and to erect against each other and the world colonial monopolies like that of Spain. To political thinkers of the eighteenth century, expansive colonies and a control of trade with them had become the touchstone of national prosperity, pride, and power.

Even France, inheritor of the classic policies of Richelieu, succumbed to the allurements of the mercantilists, and herein lies a fact of vital importance to the establishment of American independence. These thinkers explained, perhaps accurately enough, the growth of British power and prestige after the War of the Spanish Succession (1701–1713), and of the Austrian Succession (1740–1748) as due to the new colonies and the sea power which was based on them. They finally persuaded French statesmen that in order to rival England it was necessary to strengthen the resources of France by building up a great colonial empire which would equal or overshadow the British. For a brief period France accordingly reoriented her foreign policy. Before the Seven Years' War (1756–1763) France's policy had been mainly a European one, to which overseas adventures were incidental, if important; that is to say, it had been the traditional policy of preventing the rise of any large political entity in the Germanies and of expanding her own frontier toward the Rhine. In the previous war, of the Austrian Succession, it had been the interest of France to ally herself with Frederick the Great of Prussia after his seizure of Silesia; and it had been England's interest to side with Maria Theresa, in order to keep France balanced by Austria on the eastern flank—thus making France less capable of coping with England on the seas. In the new contest for colonial supremacy (1756), Louis XV's Government allowed itself to be maneuvered by the Austrian Foreign Minister, Kaunitz, into that dramatic reversal of alliances which resulted in the combination of France, Austria, Russia, Saxony, and Poland against Prussia, now supported only by her new ally Great Britain, for the recovery of Silesia and the partition of the dominions of Frederick the Great. Traditional enemies thus became for a bloody decade friends and allies. Traditional allies were transformed into bitter enemies. The Seven Years' War proved to France the folly of this diplomatic revolution, this desertion of her traditional European policy. She was drained of her resources and troops for the bootless purpose of protecting her Austrian ally from the assaults of Frederick, while on the sea and in America and India she weakened and eventually succumbed to Great Britain. Safe behind the Channel, the English eagerly sent men and money to abet and assist the Prussian King.

Important as these features of the European balance of power may be for the international relations of the Old World, it is the overseas and not the European phase of this war which forms the background for the diplomatic history of the future United States. The rivalry of the powers of western Europe for the possession of America had now become so pronounced that it precipitated in 1754 the first world conflict of modern times, the Seven Years' War (dated in Europe, 1756–1763). The general features of this war, popularly known in America as the French and Indian War, are familiar to the average reader of American history. It was the first war which witnessed the maneuverings of European armies on territory now within the present United States, and which illustrated on the North American continent the application of the principles of higher strategy. The French were embarrassed by the feeble resources of a small colonial population from which to recruit their local forces, and could not spare many troops from Europe. Nor, at the critical moment, could they get forces to Canada. The officialdom of New France was honeycombed with corruption (except for Montcalm). Under these fatal conditions France resisted the superior fleets and man-power of Great Britain longer than might have been expected, even considering the divided counsels and energies among the English Colonies, which so weakened British campaigns. At the last moment Spain, which hitherto had refused to regard France's war with Great Britain as a defensive one, became alarmed at the stupendous successes of the English. By a rewriting of the Family Compact [1] Charles III

---

[1] During the eighteenth century there were three so-called Family Compact treaties of alliance, by which the crowns of Spain and France professed to present a united front in war and peace against their enemies. The two compacts of November 7, 1733, and October 3, 1743, were directed against the Hapsburgs in Italy as well as against British maritime and colonial ambitions. The third Family Compact, of August 15, 1761, was ostensibly general in character and not in its main text applicable specifically to the existing Seven Years' War then raging. It contained a reciprocal guaranty of all territories of every party, as they should be fixed following the general European peace, under the principle that who attacks one crown attacks the others. Spain was not bound to intervene in France's purely continental wars arising out of the provisions of the treaty of Westphalia. To this pact the kings of Naples and Parma subsequently

of Spain promised to come into the conflict if France should not make a satisfactory peace by May 1, 1762. William Pitt, the British Prime Minister, heard of this while engaged in peace negotiations with France. He wanted to reply by a sudden declaration of war before the Spanish treasure fleet could get home from Mexico, but George III intervened. Pitt resigned over this issue, but his successor, Lord Bute, the rubber-stamp of George III, was soon forced to declare war. British forces immediately seized Cuba.

For Great Britain the Seven Years' War was as decisive a victory as the great struggle with Napoleon or the more recent one with the German Empire. The Peace of Paris, 1763, which signalized that victory, forms the immediate setting, from both the provincial and the international point of view, of the situation which brought forth the independence of the United States. Its articles reach deep into our diplomatic history.

In that epochal peace settlement France transferred to Great Britain Canada and all French territory east of the Mississippi River, or her claims thereto, with the exception of New Orleans (which remained attached to French Louisiana west of the Mississippi) and the surrounding plot of low, marshy land south of the Iberville River,[2] on which the city stands; and with the exception also of the two small islands of St. Pierre and Miquelon, south of Newfoundland, which were retained as a base for the

adhered. In a secret convention separate from the above treaty, but dated simultaneously, Charles III agreed to declare war on Great Britain on May 1, 1762, if by that date peace had not been reëstablished; in turn France was to place Spain in possession of Minorca on that date. To mask Spain's hostile motives against England, Grimaldi caused the secret convention to be rewritten, re-ratified, and redated to February 4, 1762, after the English declaration of war! A. I. Aiton, "A Neglected Intrigue of the Family Compact," *Hispanic Am. His. Rev.*, XI, 387–393. See L. Blart, *Les rapports de la France et de l'Espagne après le Pacte de Famille* (Paris, 1915), p. 214 for text.

Great Britain having anticipated things by declaring war on Spain, January 4, 1762, Spain and France ratified another particular military and naval convention on February 4, 1762, further binding them to offensive and defensive alliance.

[2] The name applied in the eighteenth century to a bayou-like creek which connected the waters of the Mississippi, but not the main channel, with Lake Maurepas, and thus with Lakes Pontchartrain and Borgne and with the Gulf of Mexico to the east of New Orleans, which city is thus left on what was called an "island."

Newfoundland fisheries, with the provision that they should never be fortified. Fishing liberties on the coasts of Newfoundland, according to the thirteenth article of the treaty of Utrecht, were reserved to France, a stipulation which was to be the source of much diplomatic controversy until finally adjusted in the Entente Cordiale of 1904. All French military and naval works at the Channel port of Dunkerque were dismantled and razed, and an English commissioner was placed there to see that no new ones be erected under any guise. In addition Great Britain retained the French islands which had been conquered in the West Indies,[3] with the exception of Guadeloupe and its two small dependent

[3] Great Britain had crushed France completely on the seas and overseas, and Spain would soon have been at the mercy of British sea power organized for victory under the genius of the elder Pitt had not George III, who came to the throne in 1760, been more anxious to restore his personal government in England and to control his own ministry than to push through the traditional policy of Great Britain to complete victory. The peace allowed France to retain two important West India Islands, which had been conquered by Great Britain, and which with the prosperous, unconquered French portion of Santo Domingo, became an important factor in the regeneration of French maritime power.

In these negotiations the question arose whether it would be better to keep Canada, or Guadeloupe and Martinique. The economy and politics of the times esteemed the sugar islands as the basis of French commercial prosperity and potential maritime strength, and therefore more valuable than the vacant snowy acres of a northern continental colony. But through the influence of Pitt and the advice of Benjamin Franklin, then a colonial agent in London, and of English manufacturing interests, opinion in the Government and Parliament slowly matured in favor of keeping Canada rather than the French islands (once it was decided to make a choice to hasten peace) on the theory that the future value of Canada was greater than that of Martinique and Guadeloupe. Doubtless the opposition of those factions in Parliament which represented the West India trading elements to admitting Martinique and Guadeloupe into the competition for the imperial market made it easier to choose for Canada. This was a piece of far-sighted wisdom. It was not many decades before the markets of Canada began to justify all that had been expected of that region by Franklin and the negotiators of 1763. Particularly with the advent of the Industrial Revolution in England, with its demand for big English-speaking consuming markets, Canada proved of great value, especially during the Napoleonic contest.

For the question of Canada versus the sugar islands in the peace negotiations, 1763, see the contemporary English account, *A Complete History of the Late War, or Annual Register of Its Rise, Progress and Events, in Europe, Asia, Africa, and America* (London, 1765), pp. 383, 549–552. The pamphlet literature of the time has been analyzed by Professor W. L. Grant, "Canada versus Guadeloupe, an Episode of the Seven Years' War." *A.H.R.*, XVII (July, 1912), 735–743. See also the significant work of C. W. Alvord, *The Mississippi Valley in British Politics* (Cleveland, 1917), I, 45–75, and the still more recent study of L. B. Namier, *England in the Age of the American Revolution* (London, 1930), I, 317–327.

islets, Marie Galante and Desirade; Martinique; and Santa Lucia.[4] France also gave up her fortifications in India, abandoning the rôle of a colonizing and conquering power there and accepting that of trader pure and simple. By the same treaty Spain ceded to Great Britain, Florida and all Spanish possessions east of the Mississippi, in return for British relinquishment of Cuba; and recognized the right of the ancient British log-cutting settlements "on the Bay of Honduras and other places of the territory of Spain in that part of the world" to peaceful existence, with demolition of all fortifications.

The navigation of the Mississippi River, which south of the Iberville still flowed between French banks for some 200 miles to the sea, was declared "equally free, as well to the subjects of Great Britain as to those of France, in its whole breadth and length, from its source to the sea, and expressly that part which is between the said island of New Orleans and the right bank of the river, as well as the passage both in and out of the mouth." The ink was scarcely dry on the treaty when France transferred to Spain all of Louisiana west of the Mississippi, together with the "island" of New Orleans on the east bank. Though of great potential value, Louisiana till then had been a profitless province. French ministers, anxious for peace, were able to justify its cession. Furthermore the Family Compact had provided that France and Spain should share all profits and losses in the war against Great Britain. France had already lost more territory than Spain, but, professing that it was compensation for the Spanish loss of Florida, Louis XV made the province over to his cousin Charles III. In this way the Spanish Government was induced to accept a quick peace. Reluctantly the Spanish King accepted what his ministers had arranged with Choiseul, the French Minister of Foreign Affairs. The peace and the cession pleased the Spaniards. They were made to feel that Louisiana would henceforth be a buffer of protection between the outposts of New Spain and the aggressive English provinces in Canada and on the

---

[4] The four "neutral" islands of St. Vincent, Dominica, Tobago, and Santa Lucia were partitioned, France receiving only the last.

Mississippi.[5] This peace settlement was the beginning of that Mississippi navigation question which bulked so large in later American history. It is also the first chapter in that sequence of events which led to the procurement of Louisiana by the United States in 1803.

The treaty of Paris marked the end of France's history as a territorial power on the continent of North America.[6] The dreams and labors of Colbert, the controller-general of the finances (1662–1683), and the mercantilist school which succeeded him, for the establishment of a great French colonial empire in America, were abandoned after 1763—except for a brief revival under Bonaparte's régime—and France reverted to her traditional European policy, so disastrously upset by the Diplomatic Revolution of 1756.

It was to a different Europe that French diplomatists turned after 1763 to salvage the ruined prestige of their monarch's former sway. From the first power in Europe, France had collapsed to a condition of profound humiliation and enfeeblement. Her client states were at the mercy of avaricious neighbors. She was forced to stand by helpless at the first partition of Poland (1772) and the dismemberment of Turkey at the treaty of Kutchuk-Kainardji (1774). On ceremonial occasions at the courts of Europe, the British diplomatic representatives demanded and received, as a result of the Seven Years' War, precedence over the French, a practice which sometimes led to exceptionally humiliating exhibitions. The loss of prestige was a measure of the loss of power, of influence, and of potential wealth. In addition to this, French morale was badly shattered, a fact revealed in the subdued tone of French diplomacy from 1763 to 1776.[7]

As we approach the decade of the American Revolution, it is

---

[5] A. I. Aiton, "The Diplomacy of the Louisiana Cession," *A.H.R.*, XXXVI (July, 1931), 701–721, adds new light to the text of W. R. Shepherd, "The Cession of Louisiana to Spain," *Pol. Sci. Quar.*, XIX, 439–458.

[6] Except during the few days in 1803 when France repossessed the province before turning it over to the United States.

[7] H. Doniol, *Histoire de la participation de la France à l'établissement des Etats-Unis d'Amérique* (hereinafter cited as Doniol), I, 11.

possible to lay down certain generalizations as to the natural and traditional foreign policy of the several powers of western Europe whose rivalry decided the political destiny of the American continents.

Spain and Portugal claimed their overseas dominions by virtue of a contract of partition between themselves in the treaty of Tordesillas (1494) based on the precedent of the papal bulls of 1493, which shut out the other European powers from half the globe before those vast seas and lands that lay behind the Bahamas had ever been discovered or surveyed. To maintain this preposterous claim against the rest of the world and to protect and exploit these expansive dominions proved a task so beyond the resources [8] of either of the Iberian kingdoms that, coupled with perverted economic policy, and unskilful European diplomacy, it brought about their downfall as great powers. In questions arising over American trade and dominions—that is to say, in matters pertaining to the Indies—Spanish statesmen after the sixteenth century shrank from putting them to the risk of discussion or the test of force. By discussing the right of any other power to sail to the Indies, or to make settlements there, or to trade with Spanish settlements there, Spain had something to lose, nothing to gain. In war Spain consistently lost. Hence her diplomatists habitually sought to keep these matters off the carpet. This explains the traditional procrastination so characteristic of Spanish foreign policy, a technique so exasperating to American representatives in the later diplomatic relations between that monarchy and the United States.

Portugal at first fell within the orbit of Spanish policy, because her prosperity rested so exclusively on her overseas commerce and because the rulers of that nation, realizing that Spain had given equally rich hostages to fortune in commerce and colonies depending for their inviolability on the same partition principle of Tordesillas, felt that Spain could not safely stand aside and see Portuguese colonies and monopolies attacked by other maritime

---

[8] For reflections on the significance of the Indies to the Spanish Empire, see R. B. Merriman, *Rise of the Spanish Empire* (New York, 1918–1925), II, 236–237.

powers.[9] Spain championed Portugal's monopoly not only because of principle but with the hope of some day absorbing it. This she did, at least during the years 1580 to 1640. Thereafter Portugal sought the alliance of whosoever might free her from the fatal protection of her stronger neighbor. To get such assistance, to secure her independence at home on the peninsula, Portugal bartered away her legacy of Tordesillas. When England emerged from the arena as the greatest maritime power, Portugal fixed her alliance there in order to find support against the everlasting Spanish menace. The present Anglo-Portuguese affinity dates consistently from 1654.

England's foreign policy after Elizabeth needs little comment. Except for the paralyzing interval of the Civil War, it was steadily one of aggressive expansion in commerce and colonies overseas, at the expense of powers with weaker navies or Continental liabilities.

The bellicose overseas activities of the Dutch yielded, like those of the Portuguese, after 1676 to the necessity of sacrificing their overseas wealth to protect their vulnerable land frontiers from the attacks of neighboring armies. For this defense they also accepted, during the first three quarters of the eighteenth century, what seemed to be the lesser evil of British patronage.

The policy of France was primarily a European one—breaking apart the Hapsburg vise that threatened to press her to death between its jaws; next, the political pulverization of the Germanies. This achieved, France under Louis XIV embarked on a career of aggrandizement by land which was halted by the combination of most of Europe against her. The overseas activity, which had been incidental to a primarily European policy, in the eighteenth century became for a brief and almost fatal period a paramount object, under the mercantilist persuasion that only thus would France be able to maintain her position as a great power in the new age of trade and colonies. This led to the fateful reversal of alliances and the collapse of 1763. France then abandoned the colonial dream and reverted to the traditional Con-

---

[9] A. Rein, *Der Kampf Westeuropas um Nordamerika im 15. und 16. Jahrhundert* (Stuttgart-Gotha, 1925), pp. 106–110.

tinental policy. But she did not abandon the conviction that Britain's strength came from colonies and that the mighty rival might yet be struck a fatal blow, such as Spain had suffered by the intervention of the maritime powers in the Dutch and Portuguese revolts.

Before 1776 the American colonies of England were automatically involved in every war in which the mother country was engaged, even though in most instances the colonists themselves had no concern with the Old-World questions which made war, rather than peace, the normal condition of European politics. They understood little of these questions. They called the wars King William's War, Queen Anne's War, King George's War, the French and Indian War. It is to-day a matter of some wonderment that this involvement *ipso facto* in European wars, which was a consequence of the colonial condition, was not itself the cause of the Revolution. Some thoughtful Americans had vaguely sensed that peace was a more normal condition of American life than of that of the Old World,[10] but in 1775 the revolting colonists did not think of separation for such a reason. They looked upon such involvement as a matter of course, an ineluctable turn of fate, like tide and time and death. The Declaration of Independence, with its formidable list of grievances, does not mention this particular burden of British allegiance. It does not appear in the political expositions of the Revolution until the publication of Tom Paine's *Common Sense,*[11] a few months before the Declaration. That famous pamphlet awakened American statesmen to a realization that one of the most significant things which they might hope for in independence was comparative disentanglement from European international convulsions.[12] Such was the

[10] Max Savelle, "Colonial Origins of American Diplomatic Principles," *Pacific Historical Review,* III (Sept., 1934), 334–350.

[11] ". . . any submission to, or dependance on Great Britain, tends directly to involve this Continent in European wars and quarrels. As Europe is our market for trade, we ought to form no political connection with any part of it. 'Tis the true interest of America, to steer clear of European contentions, which she never can do, while by her dependance on Britain, she is made the make-weight in the scale of British politics." *Common Sense,* 1st. ed. (Philadelphia, 1776), pp. 37–38.

[12] In his old age John Adams wrote in his *Autobiography* that on the question of independence Thomas Paine's *Common Sense* presented only "a tolerable

ultimate significance to America, from the international point of view, of the war that followed the Declaration of Independence. Before we turn to the significance to Europe of the War for American Independence we should observe the practice of contemporary European statecraft.

European diplomacy in the eighteenth century was no gentle craft. The chancelleries of the powers acted according to the unblushing principles of Machiavelli—that the attainment of a good end justified the use of any means, however dirty. What the monarchs of Europe and their advisers defined as a good end was the interest and welfare of their own as against the interest and welfare of other states. It was a world of the survival of the strongest, or of the weak only with the assistance of the strong bought at a heavy price, a price such as the Portuguese and Dutch paid for British aid. Between wars the battles of diplomacy went on continuously and unmercifully, often with less sense of honorable treatment of adversaries than obtained in the conflicts of open warfare. The rape of Silesia by Frederick the Great, the counter-plots of Russia and Austria for the partition of Prussia, the actual partition of Poland and the attempted partition of Sweden, the dismemberment of Turkey, these were only outward manifestations of a rotten, corrupt, and perfidious system of international dealings. No ruler trusted another, not even a blood relative and treaty ally. No government could rely on the fulfilment of a treaty, unless by calculating it to be to the interest of the obligated party. Montesquieu himself in the quiet of his study justified the principle of preventive wars. It was not only deemed excusable to begin a war in order to avoid danger; it was considered necessary to spring it suddenly in order thus to get the better of the chosen enemy. The prospect of success or failure,

---

summary of the arguments which I had been repeating again and again in Congress for nine months." The notes in E. C. Burnett's *Letters of Members of the Continental Congress,* I (see index under J. Adams), (Washington, D. C., Carnegie Institution, 1921) enable one to check Adams's *ex post facto* views with the dates of discussions in Congress to which they would correspond, all of which would appear to have taken place after the appearance of *Common Sense* in January, 1776. It is nevertheless quite possible and likely that Adams independently developed a reasoning against involvement in European wars and politics, even before Paine. He was a consistent advocate of it throughout his life.

and that alone, decided the aggressions of European rulers. "A great power which has a grand design," Louis XV said to his secret adviser the Count de Broglie, "begins by executing it, notwithstanding the clamor that may be raised against it. It takes its neighbors into consideration, and the calculation is always favorable to itself." There were no such things as national boundaries or race limits. Witness how portions of Italy were exchanged between non-Italian sovereigns at the treaty of Utrecht and after, how the Belgian Netherlands passed from Spanish to Austrian possession, and would have gone to France had France been able to defy Europe and take them; how the dominions of Spain were coolly partitioned in the unsuccessful treaties that preceded the War of the Spanish Succession; how Poland was divided among three alien monarchs. In all this the statesmen did not consult or even think of the wishes of the peoples concerned in the transfers. They cut and pared states like Dutch cheeses, wrote the Spanish minister Alberoni, a process which, remarks Professor Hassall, was pursued with brutal consistency by all the great powers from the treaty of Utrecht to that of Vienna in 1815. We will not carry the thought to a later date! [13]

These grosser crimes obscure the continual contemptuous trickery by which the diplomacy of the eighteenth century was conducted. The capitals of Europe were full of international spies. The technique of deciphering intercepted despatches attained a high degree of perfection. Corruption was the conventional instrument of diplomatic success. The art of dissimulation and deception was a necessary part of the equipment of any minister of foreign affairs, no matter how clean a character and upright a gentleman he might be in the purlieus of his own social group, or in the intimacy of family life. To be otherwise in his official dealings was impossible, as impossible as disarmament by example

[13] "No high-minded man would think of doing as an individual what he seems perfectly ready to do as a representative of a State. It has been thought entirely legitimate to lie, deceive, and be cruel in the name of patriotism. I endeavored to point out that we could not get very far toward a proper international understanding until one nation treated another as individuals treat one another." *Intimate Papers of Colonel House,* Charles Seymour, Ed. (New York, 1926), I, 295.

has been in the twentieth century. Diplomatic immunity was good only when matters reached no vital issue. Diplomatic couriers were waylaid and even assassinated, by official orders, in order to get at the contents of their despatch pouches. The person of an ambassador himself was not safe under all circumstances.[14]

It was this cynical and brutal international world of the eighteenth century into which the United States of America was to be delivered as a living state. To the superficial observer there would seem never to have been an age less propitious for the birth of a new nation. The tendency of the times was altogether for the aggrandizement of big states and the consolidation of their territory at the expense of the little ones, for the extinction of the weaker nations and governments rather than for the creation of new ones. Nevertheless it was this bitter cut-throat international rivalry which was to make American independence possible.

[14] For a magisterial sketch of diplomatic morals and manners in the eighteenth century, see A. Sorel, *L'Europe et la révolution française* (Paris, 1885), I, 1–81.

CHAPTER II

FRANCE'S OPPORTUNITY

That Choiseul and his successors at Versailles were determined to undo the prostration of their country in 1763 by getting revenge on Great Britain as soon as the proper opportunity should present itself is the basic explanation of French foreign policy from 1763 to 1783. The American Revolution presented that opportunity.[1]

Though France immediately after the Peace of Paris reconciled herself to a renunciation of colonial interests on the continent of North America,[2] she never accepted, except by *force majeure,* the status of a cipher in European international politics—and France was as near a cipher after 1763 as such a power can be. No sooner had the Peace of Paris been settled than Choiseul turned his attention and energy to that necessary rebuilding of military and naval power and of the finances, so indispensable if the monarchy were to retrieve its position as a great power, and to a study of ways and means to bolster the diplomatic position of France *vis-à-vis* England. There is no evidence that he had purposely ceded Canada to Great Britain, as some historians once guessed, in order to remove the need of the English colonies in America for protection against the French on their northern frontier.[3] But it is certain that he realized the political significance of the cession of Canada in the development of an independent spirit in

---

[1] "M. de Maurepas, M. de Vergennes, and all their colleagues served the descendant of Louis XIV in policies truly imbued with their country's past, but penetrated with the necessities which the moment imposed." Doniol, I, vi. "Almost immediately after the peace of 1763 it [the French Government] had sought in the tendency of the English Colonies to revolt against their metropolis the occasion by which we could avenge ourselves on England and tear up the treaty of Paris." *Ibid.,* I, 4.

[2] The project of reviving a French colonial empire in North America did not appear until after the inauguration of the Directory, in Talleyrand's time.

[3] Doniol, I, 5.

America and that he began to study the American situation most attentively, with the definite hope that Britain's troubles with the colonies might be France's opportunity.

Choiseul sent secret observers to the English Colonies in America in 1764 and thereafter to report on the military resources of Great Britain and the political temper of the colonists.[4] England herself was overrun by his spies. These persons found much more preference in their employer's favor when they reported what he wanted to believe—that an American rebellion was close at hand—than they did when they reported (as did the cool-headed de Kalb, who visited the Colonies after the Stamp Act had been repealed) that there was little immediate likelihood that discontented Americans would seek French assistance to settle grievances with England. Choiseul fell from power in 1770, convinced that insurrection in America and consequent independence were sure in the future, though not in his generation. Before he quitted office he had already diverted his attention to a study of the chance of combating Great Britain in the field of strictly European diplomacy, but he left the French Foreign Office full of reports and memoranda on the colonial difficulties of Great Britain and France's prime interest therein. This material served for useful reference when, four years later,[5] the Count de Vergennes became Minister of Foreign Affairs under the new king Louis XVI, in the year 1774, on the eve of the American Revolution.

Vergennes [6] was a methodical thinker with the habit—so illumi-

[4] See C. H. Van Tyne, "French Aid before the Alliance of 1778," *A.H.R.*, XXXI, 23–28, and documents published by Abel Doysié, *ibid.*, XXVI, 726–747; and XXVII, 70–89.

[5] From 1770–1774 the Ministry of Foreign Affairs was under the administration of d'Aiguillon, a dissolute courtier, who owed his appointment to the protection of Louis XV's favorite, Mme. du Barry. He had no experience in foreign affairs and showed little ability in the conduct of his office. The real diplomacy of France under d'Aiguillon's ministership was conducted by Louis XV's secret unaccredited agents, whose operations were masked to the foreign minister. D'Aiguillon showed no sympathy for, nor grasp of, Choiseul's principles—he declared against the Austrian alliance and weakened the bonds of the Family Alliance with Spain. See article in *Biographie Universelle* (Michaud), I, 270; and Louis Bonneville de Marsagny, *Le Comte de Vergennes, son ambassade en Suède, 1771–1774* (Paris, 1898), pp. 87–95.

[6] Charles Gravier de Vergennes, born, of *noblesse de robe,* Dijon, 1717; ap-

nating for the historian—of crystallizing his ideas on paper. When he assumed office in 1774 he mapped out the principles on which French diplomacy was to operate: maintenance of the Family Compact with Spain as the essential mainstay of France's military and naval support against England; holding to the Austrian alliance of 1756 in a purely defensive sense only—it might prevent England from setting Prussia against the Rhine again, in case of Anglo-French troubles; [7] eventual war with England only when France could envisage such a contingency with a sure chance of success; in short, the policy of Choiseul in the hands of a more circumspect and prudent man. To Vergennes was to come France's opportunity, for which Choiseul had waited in vain.

prenticeship in diplomacy as protégé of a relative, Chavigny, ambassador to Portugal, to whom he served as clerk and secretary, later fulfilling the same function at Frankfort, and at Munich; minister of Louis XV at Trèves, then Hanover; ambassador at Constantinople during the Seven Years' War; recalled, 1768; ambassador to Sweden, 1770–1774; Minister of Foreign Affairs, 1774 until his death, 1787. Vergennes was a typical diplomatist of the eighteenth century with more than the average level of moral enlightenment, but descriptive of his subtle and highly subjective mind and type of argument is the following quotation from one of his despatches to Choiseul from Constantinople: "The surest method to succeed in a negotiation being that of entering as much as possible into the genius and inclination of those with whom one is negotiating, it seems to me that we should be careful to hide from the Turks the real end toward which we are driving them. If we present war to them as something inevitable we shall frighten them and discredit ourselves. Let us enlighten them as to their true interests; let us appear to be occupied only with what concerns them, without reference to ourselves. . . ." L. Bonneville de Marsagny, *Le Chevalier de Vergennes, son ambassade à Constantinople* (Paris, 1894), II, 313. His correspondence, particularly with his allies, the United States and Spain, properly to be understood, should be read in the light of this philosophy. Said Vergennes, in his instructions to Gérard, the first French minister to the United States, April 22, 1778: "You will show them that we are making war only for them, that it is only because of them that we are in it, that consequently the engagements we have undertaken with them are absolute and permanent, that our causes are now common causes never to be separated." (Doniol, III, 281.) Vergennes organized the Foreign Office so that it became the model for all later modern chancelleries. See P. M. Hennin's memoirs, published by H. Doniol, in *Le Comte de Vergennes et P. M. Hennin, 1749–1787* (Paris, 1898), pp. 53–69. Despite the studies of Bonneville de Marsagny on Vergennes's missions at Constantinople and Stockholm (*op. cit.*), there is no adequate complete biography of him. Marsagny used the papers of the Foreign Office. Note also Gaston de Bourges, "Le Comte de Vergennes; ses débuts diplomatiques en Allemagne auprès de l'électeur de Trèves et de l'électeur d'Hanover," in *Revue des questions historiques*, XLIV, 92–166.
    [7] Doniol, I, 12–24.

Vergennes's first reaction to the news of the American troubles of Great Britain was one of perspicacious but cautious interest. The alert French chargé at London, Garnier, pointed out the international significance of Britain's predicament. He reported, as early as December 19, 1774, that friends of the insurgents had approached him with suggestions of an alliance, or at least the secret assistance of France. They had mentioned the precedent afforded by the British in supplying munitions to the Corsicans, in their insurrection against France a few years before. To French observers in 1774, however, the American insurrection appeared at first merely as the reflection of issues in English party politics, which might cease at any time with the fall of the actual ministry. In that way the earlier troubles over the colonial Stamp Tax had abruptly ended. In such an overturn Vergennes and every Frenchman feared a possible return of Lord Chatham to leadership of the British Government. The correspondence of the French Foreign Office for 1774 and the first half of 1775 was full of alarm as to this contingency.[8]

It was well known that the former prime minister had considered the Peace of Paris too lenient. In Paris they really feared that if Chatham came back to power he might heal the breach with the Colonies and then, uniting American and assembled British forces, descend on the French West India Islands and the colonial possessions of Spain. This possibility undoubtedly speeded French and Spanish military and naval preparation, but it lost its real horror when the British prohibitory acts and proclamations were announced to the world and made it apparent that the American Revolution would become a long and bitter contest.[9] After that Vergennes reverted to this danger when it suited his purpose to argue to the King of France or of Spain for a policy of intervention in American affairs. The predicament of England became so involved after 1775 that it is impossible to believe that he was really afraid of any immediate danger from a British attack in American waters.[10] Had the French and

[8] Doniol, I, 43, 70, 81, 188.
[9] Doniol, I, 174–178.
[10] E. S. Corwin, *French Policy and the American Alliance* (Princeton, New

Spanish powers cared to remain passive spectators of the American Revolution, they could have had adequate assurances and guaranties from England for the security of their American possessions. They were in no real danger. It is significant that Vergennes carefully avoided any opportunity for an understanding with the British as to the safety of French and Spanish possessions and rejected British offers for mutual limitation of armaments on the ground that any such arrangement would leave the British forces superior to those of the French and Spanish.[11] What Vergennes wanted was not the continuance of peace with Great Britain but a chance to meet that power, on better than even terms, in a war for the recovery of French power and prestige.

Realization that the opportunity for reversing the balance of British power was imminent began to dawn on Vergennes in the summer of 1775 after promptings from the adventurous courtier and dramatist Caron de Beaumarchais. It was in these very summer months that the young author of *The Barber of Seville,* now a French political agent in London who had developed abundant contacts with English and American radicals in that city, began to send in to Vergennes observations on the course of contemporary

Jersey, 1916), pp. 121-149; C. Tower, *The Marquis of Lafayette and the American Revolution* (Philadelphia, 1894, and 1901), I, 115.

11 Vergennes advised the Comte de Guines (French Ambassador at London), May 9, 1775, against demanding assurances from Great Britain which not only might be worthless but which also would give ground for reciprocal British demands from Spain and France. For Vergennes's refusal of Lord Rochford's suggested tripartite understanding, with mutual guaranties by France, Spain, and Great Britain in America, see J. F. Yela Utrilla, *España ante la independencia de los Estados Unidos,* 2 vols. (Lérida, 1925), I, 55-56. For British proposals in April, 1777, for limitation of armaments in European waters, involving disarmament respectively of eight ships-of-the-line, and Vergennes's opposition to it, see Doniol, II, 155, 208-210; Stevens, *Facsimiles,* Nos. 1525, 1544. For other evidence that Vergennes had no fear of any real danger of an attack by Great Britain on French or Spanish possessions, and for his consistent policy of avoiding any understanding with Great Britain, see Doniol, II, 2, 450. In September, 1777, the British Ministry requested France not to send troops then about to be dispatched to Santo Domingo and in return offered, for the purpose of preserving peace between the two powers, a formal assurance for the safety of French colonial possessions. Vergennes, in a statement approved by the Council and by the King, rejected the proposal. *Ibid.,* II, 528, 539.

English politics,[12] particularly on the American question. We do not know what the text of these earliest reports was, and because of this we cannot trace precisely the initiative behind them or the exact measure of their influence on French policy; at any rate Beaumarchais crossed to France in September, 1775, and had long conferences with Vergennes and Sartine, the Minister of Marine, on the matter of establishing some sort of understanding with the American insurrectionists.[13] It was on this occasion that he drew up for the King's perusal his first memorial on the American crisis. He pictured it as likely to produce great political turbulence in England, even a civil war, if the North Ministry should be overthrown. "It is indispensable to have a superior and vigilant man in London at present," he said, reflecting on the ineptitude of the regular ambassador there.[14] Equipped with a supply of secret service money, and understanding that he was in no way to compromise anybody,[15] he went back to London, as he wrote Vergennes, "well informed of the King's intentions and your own." These intentions are not revealed, but Beaumarchais alludes, in another letter, to "the necessity of undertaking, the facility of doing, the certainty of succeeding, and the immense

---

[12] In a letter of July 14, 1775, from London, relating to the d'Eon affair (in which Beaumarchais was employed to buy off d'Eon, who threatened to publish documents incriminating Louis XV in plans to invade England) Beaumarchais wrote: "I would return at once to give the details of what I have accomplished if I were only charged with one object; but I am charged with four. . . ." Elizabeth Kite, *Beaumarchais and the War of American Independence* (Boston, 1918), II, 31-32, calls this "the earliest written allusion" to any definite commission of Beaumarchais in regard to the American Revolution. For the best works on Beaumarchais's extraordinary career see Kite, and above all the classic biography by Loménie, *Beaumarchais and His Times* (New York, 1857). Loménie used Beaumarchais's private papers.

[13] Doniol, I, 134.

[14] The Comte de Guines, who showed himself unable to distinguish the real trend of affairs, was frequently beguiled by British ministers and went so far as to favor a triple alliance of England, France and Spain. Vergennes took advantage of an excuse to remove him in February, 1776. Doniol, I, 263. He was succeeded by the Marquis de Noailles, who though immediately designated, did not take up his duties until October 24. This delay was successfully calculated to incite the temporary recall of the too vigilant and energetic British Ambassador to France, Lord Stormont.

[15] Beaumarchais to Vergennes, Paris, September 23, 1775, Loménie, *op. cit.*, p. 266.

harvest of glory and repose which this little sowing of seed will yield to his reign." [16]

Coincident with Beaumarchais's urgings Vergennes in September, 1775 sent to the English Colonies a secret observer, who had previously traveled in America and therefore knew something of the country and language. This officer, Achard de Bonvouloir, had verbal instructions to assure colonial leaders that France did not want to get back Canada and was far from being unfriendly to the independence of the old English Colonies. On the contrary, she admired the greatness and nobleness of their efforts. "Without any interest to harm them we would be pleased to see fortunate circumstances enable them to frequent our ports; the facilities which they would find there for their commerce would soon prove the esteem which we hold for them." Bonvouloir was not to make any official representations. He must not commit the French Ministry to anything.[17]

Thereafter Beaumarchais, again in Paris, addressed another letter, December 7, 1775, to the King, the purpose of which was to overcome royal personal scruples which revolted at "the proposed expedient." "The objection, then," wrote Beaumarchais, "has no bearing on the immense utility of the project, nor on the danger of carrying it out, but solely on the delicate conscientiousness of your Majesty. . . . But, Sire, the policy of governments is not the moral law of their citizens. . . . It is the English, Sire, which it concerns you to humiliate and to weaken, if you do not wish to be humiliated and weakened yourself on every occasion."[18]

The project alluded to was that of assisting the American insurrectionists by supplying them with munitions, and even money, in so secret a way as not to compromise the French authorities.

While Vergennes was watching the situation and standing ready to present his American policy to the King for approval, Bonvou-

---

[16] Kite, *op. cit.,* II, 46.

[17] Vergennes to Guines, Aug. 7, 1775, Doniol, I, 155-157. The instructions were conveyed verbally by Guines to Bonvouloir. Vergennes was astonished by the ease with which, at such a crisis, the British Government allowed foreigners to embark from England for Philadelphia.

[18] Kite, *op. cit.,* II, 47, 48.

loir's report from Philadelphia arrived, February 27, 1776, assuring the French Government that the revolted Colonies were rapidly preparing to assert their independence and to fight for it, and telling of the hopes he had given—without committing the French Ministry—to expect shelter for their trade in French harbors, perhaps even more material assistance. It was immediately following reception in Paris of Bonvouloir's communication that Beaumarchais sent his famous "Peace or War" memoir "to the King alone," which first went to Vergennes unsealed. Perhaps Beaumarchais had read Bonvouloir's report, but most likely his new memoir was based rather on representations made to him by an American in London, Arthur Lee, the correspondent of the Secret Committee of Correspondence of the Continental Congress. These he reported to be to the effect that if the American insurrectionists should become too discouraged at the futility of their efforts to obtain from the French Ministry aid in the shape of powder and munitions, they might in exasperation join forces to those of England and fall on the French sugar islands. After analyzing the British colonial situation, Beaumarchais put the question to the King:

"What shall we do in this extremity to win peace and save our islands?

"Sire, the only means is to give help to the Americans, so as to make their forces equal to those of England. . . . Believe me, Sire, the saving of a few millions to-day soon may cause a great deal of blood to flow, and money to be lost to France.

"If it is replied that we cannot aid the Americans without drawing upon us a storm, I reply that this danger can be averted if the plan be adopted which I have so often proposed, to aid the Americans secretly." [19]

The fact that Vergennes allowed this memoir to go up to the King is revealing of his new decision as to policy, as is the fact that on March 1 Vergennes sent a despatch to Grimaldi, the Spanish Foreign Minister, asking if Spain would be prepared to

[19] Loménie, *op. cit.*, p. 270.

join France in rendering secret assistance to the Americans.[20] Beaumarchais's arguments are generally credited with having overcome the scruples of Louis XVI.

Vergennes himself now prepared a statement for submission to a committee of ministers, for the purpose of persuading the French King's government of the efficacy and necessity of the policy of secret assistance, even though this might lead later to war with England. This statement is entitled *"Considérations,"* to which the Foreign Office archivist has added the label: "on the matter of the English Colonies in America." The *"Considér-ations"* recommended: (1) military preparations by both courts, Spain and France, against all contingencies with Great Britain; (2) studied friendly assurances to the British Government, calculated to deceive it as to France's relations with the Colonies; (3) the furnishing of secret assistance, in the way of munitions of war, to the Colonies, "without making any convention with them until their independence be established and notorious."[21] The paper was submitted to Maurepas, the aged Principal Minister, to Turgot, Controller General of Finances, to Sartine, Minister of Marine, and to the Count de Saint-Germain, Minister of War. That all except Turgot would approve the policy seems to have been a foregone conclusion. The purpose of the *"Considérations"* was to win over Turgot by a professedly objective exposition of the question, but the arguments did not convince him that France ought to fight a war with Great Britain on account of the American Colonies. All American colonies of all powers, including France, were inevitably destined to be free anyway, thought Turgot; it was unnecessary to go to war to secure American independence. As for Vergennes's alarmist arguments as to the safety of the French West Indies, they did not disturb his colleague; the French colonies would sometime be free, and it was

[20] Yela, *op. cit.*, I, 97; Grimaldi replied, Mar. 14, 1776, agreeing in principle to secret assistance: "It is certainly desirable to us that the revolt of these people keep up, and we ought to want the English, and them, to exhaust themselves reciprocally." He stated that "the King is ready and offers to join reasonably in all expenses." Doniol, I, 370.

[21] Doniol, I, 284.

not worth the cost of a preventive war with Great Britain to protect them against some future danger. Somewhat reluctantly the Minister of Finance agreed to a policy of secret assistance only.[22]

Turgot's ideas were absolutely sound. The finances of France were uncertain. The burden of expenditures which he foresaw to be inevitable from any war with Great Britain finally did prove to be more than the monarchy under the ancient régime could stand. The financial question was what brought on the meeting of the Estates General in 1789; the assembly of the Estates General precipitated the French Revolution. It is not contended that there would have been no French Revolution had there been no American Revolution and French intervention; but we are safe in saying that the financial question, aggravated by the expenditures in the American war, had a direct influence in bringing about the French upheaval in the year 1789, and that if Louis XVI had followed the advice of the far-seeing Turgot, instead of that of Vergennes and Beaumarchais, he might not have lost his head in 1793.

The King on the contrary accepted the recommendations presented by Vergennes. The *Considérations* had outlined a definite policy, which was adopted by the King's Council against the advice of Turgot. The first aim, that of persuading Great Britain that France and Spain desired peace, was already being attempted by French diplomacy. A royal command of April 22, 1776, ordering the rebuilding of the navy and the supplying of new equipment for the army, would organize French military resources for the second aim. The third objective, outlined in the *Considérations*, was to encourage the revolting American colonies by furnishing secret aid in munitions and money. To implement this proposal, Vergennes had another memoir prepared, in April, 1776.[23]

[22] His long written answer to the *"Considérations"* is summarized somewhat disdainfully by Doniol, I, 283. It is more cogently paraphrased by Corwin, *op. cit.*, pp. 74-78, and has been frequently printed under the title: *Mémoire sur la manière dont la France et l'Espagne devraient envisager les suites de la querelle entre la Grande Bretagne et ses colonies.*

[23] *Note to 1957 Edition.* Professor John J. Meng's discovery, in the archives of the French Foreign Office, of a draft of this memoir, the *Réflexions,* missed

by his principal Secretary, Joseph Mathias Gérard de Rayneval, presumably from his chief's dictation, entitled *Réflexions*, to which was added, when the document was filed in the Foreign Office archives, the words: "on the Present Situation of the English Colonies, and on the Conduct which France ought to hold in Regard to Them." These "reflections" followed the suggestions of Beaumarchais's insistence. The youthful playwright who dabbled in diplomacy, or, perhaps better said, the diplomatist who dabbled in dramatics, and the older professional Foreign Minister who specialized in wars, worked hand in hand, mind in mind, to swing French policy into secret aid to the revolted Americans. We find Beaumarchais's inimitable phrases in the Minister's state papers for the King. The correspondence of Beaumarchais from London in 1775 and 1776 resembles that of an actual ambassador much more than a buyer of old coin, which was then his ostensible mission.

The *Réflexions* began by summarizing the colonial controversy and stating that matters appeared to have reached a pass where the Colonies would take the resolution to free themselves from all dependence on their mother country and to form a nation or republic. He declared that Great Britain was making great exertions to subdue them because (1) of their value for trade and revenue, and (2) of their military resources for the Empire, exhibited so abundantly in the Seven Years' War. Despite the cost of victory to Great Britain, such a triumph would keep up her manufactures and her navy and prevent the loss of the Colonies. In whatever manner Great Britain might preserve her Colonies, they would always be of considerable advantage, whilst by losing them, that empire would suffer immeasurable damage. Since England was the natural enemy of France, "a rapacious, unjust and faithless enemy," possessed of an invariable policy for

by Cornelius DeWitt, Doniol, and scholars who followed them, has dated the document as "April, 1776." In "A Footnote to Secret Aid in the American Revolution," *Am. Hist. Rev., XLIII* (July, 1938), 791-795, Dr. Meng seems to me to have proven that the *Réflexions* followed and implemented the *Considérations,* rather than the *Réflexions* preceding the *Considérations.* This discovery, briefly noted in Note 20, p. 23, of the second printing of this book, has caused me to rearrange pages 20-28 in this new edition.

the abasement of France, it became the duty of France to seize every possible opportunity to weaken the power of England. The present condition and disposition of the Colonies presented the opportunity for this. French assistance to them would offer the following advantages: "First, it will diminish the power of England, and increase in proportion that of France. Second, it will cause irreparable loss to English trade, while it will considerably extend ours. Third, it presents to us as very probable the recovery of a part of the possessions which the English have taken from us in America, such as the fisheries of Newfoundland and of the Gulf of St. Lawrence, Isle Royale, etc. We do not speak of Canada."

The paper then proceeded to dismiss any fear that the independence of the Colonies would result in an aggressive action by them in the New World; the war would tire them out for a long time to come, and it was to be presumed that they would set up a republican form of government, "or even as many small republics as there are now provinces,"—and republics rarely had the spirit of conquest. What the Colonies most needed in the way of assistance was arms and munitions, and the author recommended that these be supplied by the government under the mask of private commercial transactions.[24]

This was a definite program. It was one thing for the Foreign Minister to outline a program; it was another to get it adopted by the French Council and the King. It was in the efforts to win the King and Ministry over that Beaumarchais's labors and arguments were valuable accessories to Vergennes.

The King followed the advice of Vergennes and Beaumarchais, with results so fatal to that young monarch, so beneficial for America. He decided for secret assistance to the Colonists and directed, May 2, 1776, that one million *livres* be supplied to them, in the shape of munitions, through Beaumarchais, disguised as a private trader under the fictitious name of Roderigue Hortalez and Company. Turgot resigned May 12,

---

[24] Doniol, I, 243-249. All except the last paragraphs of the memoir are reproduced in facsimile of Rayneval's handwriting in Steven's *Facsimiles*, No. 1310.

leaving Vergennes as the dominating influence in the government. Thus, before an American agent had set foot on the soil of France, the French Ministry, actuated by coolly calculated motives of European international policy connected with the principle of the balance of power, had decided to offer secret assistance to the Colonies and was looking to a war with Great Britain as soon as the opportune moment should arrive. Informed by Louis XVI of his recent gift of a million, "under the title of a loan," Charles III of Spain matched it with another million, to be distributed to the Americans through the same source, according to an understanding already reached between the two courts.[25] It was the first of a series of loans and subsidies from both powers which enabled the United States to go forward with the rebellion.[26]

[25] Doniol, I, 370-372; Yela, *op. cit.*, I, 97-105; II, 7-15.
[26] See below, p. 92, n. 28.

CHAPTER III

In our effort to approach the War of American Independence as an event in the international history of Europe, we have said nothing of the beginning of the foreign relations of the United States itself. It is proper at this point to turn to the revolted Colonies and to notice the way in which they opened contact with European governments.

When the French agent Bonvouloir arrived at Philadelphia in December, 1775, the insurrection already had assumed the proportions of a continental revolution, and the "illegally" assembled Congress of the Colonies had been brought face to face with the hard problem of securing supplies wherewith to furnish its troops to fight its battles. The first tactics of protest, the forming of non-importation and non-exportation associations against British trade, as a means of securing parliamentary redress of grievances, had failed; this was countered in England with the King's proclamation of August 23, 1775, declaring the Colonies in rebellion, and by an act of Parliament cutting off all trade with them, December 22, 1775. One of the purposes of such a prohibition of trade was to prevent the rebels from getting munitions of war from the outside world. This was forbidden not only by act of Parliament, but by the Articles of Association—the boycott agreement—of the Continental Congress. It soon became apparent that if military supplies were to be secured, some relaxation of these self-imposed restrictions on foreign trade would have to be allowed.[1] Throughout 1775 the Congress stood firm against declaring American ports open to foreign trade and foreign ships, because that seemed tantamount to a declaration of

---

[1] *Journals of the Continental Congress,* Hunt and Ford, Eds. (Washington, 1904–1931), III, 477.

independence, to which the delegates at that time were unable to agree; and they hesitated to let down the bars of their own boycott and embargo for fear of the political damage that it might do to their cause.

The necessity of getting munitions soon led to special permissions by Congress to export produce to pay for them. The inevitable gun-runners who flock to the shores of every revolutionary country were not slow to put in appearance. French ships loaded with powder began to come into American harbors. It is difficult to trace the operations of such clandestine trade,[2] but in the early months of 1776 members of Congress were reporting that foreign goods had begun to come in and that French ships were arriving at Philadelphia.

The idea of independence and trade with all nations of the world, as well as the possibility of foreign alliances, was early in the minds of a few men in Congress, particularly Benjamin Franklin and John Adams, though the movement did not gain effective momentum in that body until December, 1775. One of the powerful arguments for independence was this necessity of opening up a foreign trade. "Can we hope to carry on war without having trade and commerce somewhere?" wrote a North Carolina delegate from Philadelphia, February 14, 1776. "The consequence of making alliances is perhaps a total separation with Britain and without something of that sort we may not be able to provide what is necessary for our defense."[3] Franklin on February 26, 1776, made a formal proposal for the opening of the Colonies to the commerce and ships of all nations for a minimum period of two years beginning from July 20, 1776,[4] but his motion was not carried.

Not until the Colonies were ready to consider an actual declaration of independence did the Congress venture, April 6, 1776, as a step in that direction, to open trade with the rest of the world,

[2] Doniol makes frequent allusions (I, 133, 373) to trade connections of this kind which Franklin had established in the Netherlands and France in 1774 before his return to America; but they are unsupported by documentary evidence.

[3] John Penn to Thomas Person, Philadelphia, Feb. 14, 1776. E. C. Burnett, *Letters of Members of the Continental Congress,* I, 349.

[4] *Ibid.,* I, 364.

other than Great Britain, against which the non-importation and non-exportation agreements remained in effect. The "three great measures"—that is, a declaration of independence, the preparation of a plan for a treaty to be proposed to France, and the study of a system of American confederation for the Colonies —went hand in hand in the proceedings of Congress.[5] Total independence was resolved on July 2, and the famous Declaration proclaimed to the world July 4, 1776. This made possible, under a new sovereign government, the making of war and peace and the maintenance of diplomatic relations, as well as the contracting of treaties and alliances with foreign powers.

The first representatives whom the American Colonies had on the other side of the Atlantic were those agents which it had been the custom of individual colonies to establish in London, to represent at the capital of the Empire their interests in the measures of King and Parliament. There were six of these men there in 1775. None had any experience in the field of international diplomacy; for that purpose, however, their political experience in London was helpful in some degree. Outside of the native ability of that man of the world and human marvel, Benjamin Franklin, the American Revolution at the outset had no experienced diplomatists, and even Franklin's experience was limited to that of men and measures, and the diplomacy of human nature in general, —he had had none in the international field. Two of the colonial agents [6] were members of Parliament who had incidentally taken upon themselves the agencies. Franklin and Arthur Lee, among the three native-born American agents, had traveled much in Europe and had a tolerable knowledge of the politics or languages of other than their mother country. Lee in particular, though lacking Franklin's wisdom, tact, ability, and experience, had traveled widely on that continent, spoke fluent French, Italian, and Spanish, and had a fairly wide acquaintance. Franklin had taught himself, through a long lifetime, to read these languages, and Latin too, and in his old age he learned to speak French reasonably well.

[5] John Adams's *Autobiography*, Burnett, *op. cit.*, I, 514.
[6] Edmund Burke and Charles Garth.

It was to the care of these colonial agents that Congress had entrusted its petitions to the King for the redress of grievances, and its addresses to the people of Great Britain—a sort of diplomatic function within the Empire. Only two of them, Franklin and Lee, proved adaptable to the higher agency of the greater constituency, the Continental Congress.[7] Franklin returned home in 1775, to become an active member of Congress, particularly in directing the movement which resulted in the opening of diplomatic contacts, leaving Lee as the sole quasi-representative of the United Colonies in London.

Several months before the opening of the colonial ports, there had been created by Congress, November 29, 1775, a secret committee "for the sole purpose of corresponding with our friends in Great Britain, Ireland *and other parts of the world.*"[8] This was really the embryo from which the "foreign office" of the United States developed, for as a result of it, after some committee evolution there was created in 1781 a "Secretary of Foreign Affairs for the Continental Congress" and, eventually in 1789, the present Department of State. The original members of this first "Committee of Secret Correspondence" were Benjamin Franklin and John Dickinson of Pennsylvania; John Jay of New York; Thomas Johnson of Maryland; and Benjamin Harrison of Virginia. Franklin and Jay were at first the most influential personages. After the departure of Franklin on his mission to France, the Committee's membership fluctuated both in number and personnel; one of the most energetic members was James Lovell of Massachusetts. At first this committee did not concern itself exclusively with foreign affairs. It occasionally handled war and other business. Special committees *ad hoc* also dealt with various aspects of relations with foreign countries. Nor was the name of the committee invariable. After April 17, 1777, it be-

---

[7] William Bollan, agent for the Massachusetts Council, joined with Franklin and Lee in presenting the petitions. Bollan presently drops out of sight and had nothing more to do with the Congress. Paul Wentworth became a Loyalist and subsequently served as a British spy in Europe. See Wharton, *Revolutionary Diplomatic Correspondence of the United States,* 6 vols. (Washington, G.P.O., 1889), II, 3; *A.H.R.,* XXIX, 474–475.

[8] *Journals,* III, 392. Italics mine.

came known as the Committee for Foreign Affairs. A Secretary of Foreign Affairs, acting under the direct control of Congress, supplanted the Committee in 1781. Under the constant advice and oversight of Congress this officer conducted the diplomacy of the nation until the new Department of State was created in 1789 under the Constitution of 1787. The first Secretary of Foreign Affairs was Robert R. Livingston, Jr., who held the office from 1781 to 1783. In the middle of that year John Jay took over the office and administered it until the new Department of State was set up in 1789. He was Secretary of State *ad interim* for a few months until Thomas Jefferson arrived from abroad to become Secretary of State in 1790.[9]

The wonder is that a committee of so much fluidity and changing personnel as the Committee of Secret Correspondence functioned as well as it did. On December 12, 1775, the Committee began the diplomatic correspondence of the United Colonies by directing Arthur Lee, in London, to furnish it with secret information in regard to the disposition of foreign powers toward them and remitted to him a small sum of money for his expenses.[10] At about the same time Franklin wrote to an old friend of his at The Hague, Charles William Frederick Dumas, saying that the Committee requested him, as a person resident at The Hague where there were ambassadors from all courts, to use any opportunity to discover "if possible, the disposition of the several courts with respect to assistance or alliance, if we should apply for the one or propose for the other." [11] Dumas subsequently

[9] Gaillard Hunt, *The Department of State* (Yale University Press, 1914), and Royden J. Dangerfield, *In Defense of the Senate, a Study in Treaty-Making* (University of Oklahoma Press, 1933), describe the origin of the offices of foreign affairs and Department of State. The relation of the committee system in Congress to the administration of foreign affairs is detailed in G. C. Wood, *Congressional Control of Foreign Relations during the American Revolution, 1774–1789* (Allentown, Pennsylvania, 1919). See also M. L. Bonham, Jr.'s sketch of Livingston in *The American Secretaries of State and Their Diplomacy* (New York, 1927), Vol. I.

[10] Wharton, II, 63. There is also an unsigned draft to Lee of Nov. 30, 1775, which is the first official diplomatic instruction of the Continental Congress. Burnett, I, 265.

[11] Dec. 19, 1775. Wharton, II, 64. Much of Dumas's correspondence is therein printed. For Dumas, see below, pp. 125–126.

became a regular correspondent of Congress, a sort of official observer, under salary. Thus did the Committee establish its first political contacts abroad.

It was to this Committee that Bonvouloir had made his informal assurances in that same month.[12] During the last week of the year 1775, two private French commercial agents, named Penet and Pliarne, appeared in Philadelphia from Washington's camp at Cambridge, with letters of introduction from the General. With these men [13] Congress made a contract for the purchase of munitions and powder, to be paid for by exports in American produce; and this was the beginning of the agitation for special export licenses, and finally for open trade.

The Secret Committee of Correspondence, which convinced Bonvouloir that Congress was determined for independence, was somewhat at a loss whether to dispatch an American agent to the Court of France at once, on the basis of his assurances. There was also the question of whether it would be worth while to send such a person before the independence of the Colonies should be declared, or the ports of the country opened to the trade of the world. On March 3, 1776, however, they decided to send an agent, Silas Deane, recently a delegate to Congress from Connecticut.[14]

When Silas Deane in the guise of a merchant arrived in Paris July 7, 1776, seeking French assistance in the way of permissions

[12] Bonvouloir's report is dated Philadelphia, Dec. 28, 1775. For text see Doniol, I, 287.

[13] For Penet and Pliarne, see *Journals of Continental Congress*, III, 466n.; Burnett, *Letters*, I, 291, 299n., 304; Force, *American Archives*, 6 vols. (Washington, 1837–1846), 4th Ser., IV, 235, 261, 262, 264, 447, 660; VI, 771–782; Ford's *Writings of George Washington*, 14 vols. (New York, 1889–1893), III, 274; Wharton, II, 113, 178, 248, 268; VI, 136; Doniol, I, 377, 482, 489, 499, 505; Stevens, *Facsimiles*, Nos. 566, 568, 890. On May 31, 1776, Dubourg, a Paris correspondent of Penet and Pliarne, who in vain wished himself, instead of Beaumarchais, to be the medium of supply to the American Colonies, wrote to Vergennes: "You have seen the contract with the Secret Committee of the Colonies and ratified by the General Congress on the one hand and Messrs. Pliarne and Penet on the other." I have not been able to find the text of this contract. Vergennes denied that he had any connection with these two men, but was very complaisant toward their correspondent at Nantes. See Doniol, I, 373, 377n., 378.

[14] One of Deane's duties was to purchase goods suitable for the Indian trade, for the purpose of securing the favor of the aborigines against England. Charles Isham, Introductory note in *N. Y. Hist. Soc. Collections, 1886, Deane Papers*, I, x.

to buy military and other supplies on credit, and inquiring about
the possibilities of French support of a political as well as a
military nature, Beaumarchais had already been closeted with
Arthur Lee, former colonial agent and now secret correspondent
of Congress in London. The creator of *Figaro* had been unsuc-
cessfully beseeching Vergennes to let him promise Lee some of
the assistance which that agent had been soliciting, unauthorized
by any powers of the Continental Congress so far as our documents reveal.[15] Soon afterwards the King accepted the American
policy of Vergennes, that of secret assistance. Beaumarchais had
some interviews with Lee on the subject in London in May,
1776.[16]

We would like to know, though we cannot for lack of satisfactory documentary evidence, just what assurances Beaumarchais did give Lee, particularly whether he told him that French
supplies were to be given to the Colonies, with only nominal pay-
ments in American produce, merely for the purpose of disguising
the business as a commercial transaction; or whether Beaumarchais insisted that eventual real payment must be made by the
Colonists. It must be borne in mind that the French Government
itself had no expectation of reimbursement. The exchanges of
letters which passed between Beaumarchais and Lee, following
the interview, between May 23 and July 26, 1776, leave the matter
no clearer. They show Beaumarchais asking for eventual payment in kind and Lee acquiescing, but stating that "the want of
tobacco ought not to hinder your sending out your supplies to
the Americans; for tobacco is so weighty an article, that it will
greatly impede the sailing of the ships, and the essential object is
to maintain the war"; and begging Beaumarchais to "consider
above all things that we are not transacting a mere mercantile
business, but that politics is greatly concerned in this affair." Lee
sent home despatches to Congress describing this interview, but

[15] Doniol, I, 384, 402–419.
[16] We can place the date (1) because the King did not approve Vergennes's
policy until May 2 (Doniol, I, 372–377) and (2) because Beaumarchais and
Lee were corresponding on the subject, after the former's return to Paris, from
May 23 to July 26, 1776. See U. S. House of Representatives Report, No. 220,
20 Cong., 1 Sess.

they were sunken at sea to avoid capture, and the courier delivered only an oral report, "that the Duke de Vergennes had sent a gentleman to Arthur Lee, who informed him, that the French Court could not think of entering into a war with England, but that they would assist America by sending from Holland this fall £200,000 sterling worth of arms and ammunition, to St. Eustatius, Martinique, or Cap Français; that application was to be made to the governors or commandants of those places, by inquiring for Monsieur Hortales, and that, on persons properly authorized applying, the above articles would be delivered to them." This was repeated eighteen months later by Lee in a communication to Congress complaining about Silas Deane's having made a contract to *pay* for goods furnished by Hortalez and Company.[17]

The oral message was delivered December 1, 1776, to the Committee of Secret Correspondence, was entered in its secret journal—which valuable source has since disappeared—and prudently not divulged to Congress at that time by the Committee.[18] Months before this Silas Deane had landed in France. Vergennes had received him, treated him most considerately, and referred him to Beaumarchais, for the matter of the *purchase* of munitions, which Deane had requested permission to buy; adding that Deane might consider himself perfectly free to carry on any kind of commerce in France, as the Court had decided that its ports should be open equally to both parties.[19]

Upon Vergennes's request Deane gave him a copy of that clause of his instructions which related to the procuring of arms. He later sent a copy to Beaumarchais, who had now turned from

[17] It was confirmed at that time by a statement made by one Laraguais, a Frenchman whom Vergennes was employing as an observer in London, and who said that he was present at the interview between Lee and Beaumarchais. See note 18.

[18] The oral message is printed, apparently from the journal of the Committee, in *American Quarterly Review*, I (March, 1827), 132–133; also in Sparks's *Diplomatic Correspondence of the American Revolution*, 12 vols. (New York, 1829–1830), II, 16, in part only; and Wharton, II, 151. For this extract, and the correspondence between Beaumarchais and Lee, statement of Laraguais, and further correspondence of Lee, see U. S. House of Representatives Report 220, 20 Cong., 1 Sess., 1827–1828.

[19] For the interviews see Doniol, I, 493–495; Wharton, II, 113–146.

Lee to Deane as a person vested with more specific authority by Congress. If Beaumarchais had any doubts whether to insist on payment for military supplies furnished by his secretly subsidized fictitious house, those hesitations vanished when he saw that Deane had instructions *to purchase* military stores on terms of liberal credit, payable in American produce. Why try to give the Congress the supplies which were furnished through him by the French Government, when Deane was specifically instructed to buy them, and when Vergennes and Beaumarchais had read his instructions to that effect? Beaumarchais proceeded to draw up an agreement with Deane for the sale of supplies, which was subsequently put into the form of a written contract and signed by Congress on the one hand and the agent of Beaumarchais on the other. The supplies were to be furnished to Congress, at its risk, f.o.b. France, and to be paid for later—the date not fixed —in produce or money. Beaumarchais also advanced credit to charter vessels to carry the munitions to America.[20] Other, and genuine, French mercantile firms also sold much goods on credit to the Colonies. The secret subsidy of two million *livres* from the kings of France and Spain was thus used to set this vast "commercial" business of Roderigue Hortalez in motion. Beaumarchais supplied goods to the Colonies on credit many times the value of the two million *livres*. Much of this came directly to him from French arsenals.[21]

[20] Wharton, II, 171.

[21] In a memorial dated October 10, 1776, to Aranda, Spanish Ambassador at Paris, Beaumarchais summarized what had been done by him up to that date with the two millions. The first shipment, he stated, consisted of 300 "thousands" of powder for cannon, 30,000 guns, 3,000 tents, 200 cannons with full train, 27 mortars, 100,000 balls (*boulets*), 13,000 bombs (*bombes*); the chartering of eight ships; utensils and three months' subsistence for thirty officers who went out to assist the insurrectionists; and clothing for 30,000 men, which goods he enumerates in detail.

He then recapitulates the finances of this operation:

Shipment of clothes	*livres*	2,500,000
War munitions, and vessels to carry		2,500,000
Advances in money for officers, and for the ships' crews		600,000
		5,600,000
Of these 5,600,000 *livres,* France and Spain have each furnished one million		2,000,000
Due to the banker of both courts [Hortalez & Co.]		3,600,000

Closely connected with the new policy of furnishing secret assistance to the American Colonies was the decision of the French Government as to what should be its attitude toward American vessels seeking its ports, and toward its own neutral rights in face of the action of British cruisers on the high seas. Vergennes defended, against British protest, the reception of American merchant ships in the ports of France along with those of all other flags. He instructed the French chargé at London, in June, 1776, that the right of British cruisers to search French ships for contraband would be admitted on the high seas, but not in French territorial waters; British naval vessels had been tempted to search them in the West Indies, where French ports had become the basis for the commerce in munitions. Vergennes also laid down the principle that British vessels of war could not interfere with any kind of commerce between France and the French colonies, otherwise France would be prevented from preparing the defense of its own dominions.[22] This position greatly assisted the clandestine contraband commerce with the American States, a commerce which frequently set out disguised as a shipment to Cap Français,[23] the French possession in Haiti, for transference there to the American flag. The doctrine of continuous voyage, perfected nearly a century later by the prize courts of the United States during the American Civil War to stop contraband from reaching its ultimate belligerent destination under such circumstances, happily had not been conceived by Great Britain in 1776. To discourage too close a scrutiny of French roadsteads for arrivals of American vessels and depar-

---

This left a balance, he pointed out, of 1,800,000 (*sic*) for each court to pay. He asked that Spain grant an amount in cash equal to the munitions furnished by France (2,500,000), to reimburse him, and to allow him to expand his credit and his operations. Spain refused to grant any more assistance through Beaumarchais. See Yela, *op. cit.,* I, 99–108; II, 7–21.

It is interesting to reflect whether, if Beaumarchais had received this sum requested from Spain, he would have insisted upon payment for the munitions by the United States. The memorial is published by Yela, *op. cit.,* II, 19.

Other French firms than Beaumarchais may have been subsidized by the French Government. Wharton, I, 372.

[22] Doniol, I, 462, 467–469.

[23] American agents were established at Cap Français and Martinique in 1776, for the purpose of assisting this traffic.

tures of contraband commerce, a French naval squadron of polite observation was stationed off the Channel ports, and in May, 1776, another squadron was sent to the French West India Islands with instructions to protect "insurgent" vessels which, pursued by British cruisers, should seek asylum under the French flag.[24] The attitude taken by France was tantamount to what would be termed to-day, or would have been during the period of the American Civil War, a recognition of belligerency. It was the result, not of Deane's mission, but of the adoption in May, before Deane's arrival, of the policy of secret assistance.

There may be doubt as to whether the arrangement, originally discussed between Beaumarchais and Arthur Lee in London, meant that the Congress would have to pay ultimately for all the military supplies furnished to it out of French arsenals, and out of the French treasury, under the guise of trade with Hortalez and Company. There can be no doubt about the agreement made at Paris by Deane, and subsequently ratified by Congress in the form of a contract. That contract called for eventual payment. After the war Beaumarchais claimed 3,600,000 *livres*. In 1835 his heirs received only 800,000 *francs* out of monies due the United States for Napoleonic spoliations, under the treaty of July 4, 1831. This repudiation of a contract was due to the fact that Arthur Lee[25] made Congress see that Beaumarchais was being given these goods secretly by the French Court for the United States, and hence he had no right to charge anything for them, and that the commercial contract was meant only for the purpose of hiding French violations of neutrality.[26] That Beaumarchais himself referred to this business of furnishing supplies

[24] Doniol, I, 426; II, 53.

[25] A. Lee to Committee of Foreign Affairs, Paris, Oct. 6, 1777, Wharton, II, 401. It is significant that in a joint despatch of the three commissioners, dated Oct. 7, 1777, they say that they have been assured "that no repayment will be required from us of what has been already given us, either in money or military stores." *Ibid.*, II, 405. A *livre* equals a *franc*.

[26] For history of the Beaumarchais claim and the "lost million" see C. J. Stillé, "Beaumarchais and the Lost Million," in *Pa. Mag. Hist. and Biog.*, XI, 1–36; Wharton, I, 371–386; Loménie, *Beaumarchais and His Time*, Ch. XIX; E. S. Kite, *op. cit.*, II, 184–212; A. Fliniaux, *Quelques précisions sur les dettes des États-Unis envers la France ou des Français pendant la guerre de l'indépendance et sur leur remboursement* (Toulouse, É. Privat, 1922).

to the Americans as a "politico-commercial transaction," [27] that he sought to get the King of Spain also to pay for what he had contracted with the Americans to pay, as the student knows to-day; and that at the worst he probably lost nothing except profits on the enterprise,[28] does not altogether excuse the stingy action of Congress, particularly when we realize, as we do to-day, that it was with these supplies that the Saratoga campaign was won.[29]

[27] Doniol, I, 486.

[28] His biographer Loménie, examining Beaumarchais's accounts from Oct. 1, 1776 to Sept. 30, 1783, found 21,044,191 *livres* disbursements, 21,092,515 *livres* receipts.

[29] O. W. Stephenson, "The Supply of Gunpowder in 1776," *A.H.R.*, XXX, 271–281.

CHAPTER IV

FRANCE AND SPAIN IN 1777

While Deane and Beaumarchais were directing the stream of munitions from Rodrigue Hortalez and Company across the Atlantic to Washington's army, the diplomatic situation in Europe was rapidly developing to a crisis which invited a French and Spanish declaration of war on Great Britain. We must keep in mind that up to the very eve of the signature of the Franco-American alliance of 1778, French policy depended on Spain. Louis XVI of France and Charles III of Spain were allies. To each monarch the Family Alliance had been the pole-star of his foreign policy. The attitude of the Spanish Government toward the American Revolution, under the minister Grimaldi, the Genoese, had been one of exultant rejoicing, because the conflict now broken out in America would weaken both the English and the Colonists. As centuries of her overseas history had proven, it was greatly to the advantage of Spain to have these aggressive sea and land forces separated, their strength sapped by war between themselves. To pour oil on the flames of insurrection Charles III furnished the million *livres* to Beaumarchais in the summer of 1776, and subsequently issued independently further secret succors, taking great care to conceal the operation and to avoid the appearance of assistance to colonies rebelling against a European dominion.[1] Spain had too many colonial hostages of her own on the other side of the Atlantic to allow her to champion American independence. Throughout the war Spanish policy was consistently opposed to that. The revolted North American Colonists were merely a tool in Spain's European international combinations, a tool with sharp and dangerous edges, to be handled with greatest care and caution.

[1] Yela, *España ante la independencia de los Estados Unidos,* 95–113, 371–375. For summary of Spanish subsidies, see below, p. 92.

Spain nevertheless was willing to go to war against Great Britain, during 1775 and 1776, with the alliance of France. Grimaldi eagerly listened to Vergennes's warning of the danger that Great Britain, win or lose in America, might attack the French and Spanish possessions in the New World, in order to recoup the expenses of pacification of her own colonies or to secure compensation for their loss in case of defeat. In his turn, he made these warnings the occasion of urging upon the French Ministry to hasten military and naval preparations, particularly to send a division to protect the island of Santo Domingo, where the colonial possessions of both powers were most vulnerable to English attack. The Spanish Ambassador in Paris, the Count de Aranda, flamed with zeal for a joint war with England. He believed that either a united British Empire or an independent United States would menace Spain's own American colonies in the future, but that an independent United States would be the lesser danger; and this danger could be mitigated by now making with the new republic a defensive alliance to guarantee the territorial integrity of each party's possessions in America.[2]

Vergennes found Spain responding with such alacrity to his suggestions of war that he repeatedly fell back, and even argued that after all there was little to fear in the way of an attack from Great Britain, at least while the actual ministry remained in power in London.[3]

The bellicose inclinations of Spain during these early months of the American Revolution were due to her hope of conquering Portugal in any war with Great Britain. Trouble had been brewing between the two peninsular kingdoms in regard to the disputed boundary of their dominions in the La Plata River region of South America. Portuguese detachments had possessed themselves of some Spanish outposts and had taken advantage of their military superiority in that part of the world to threaten the Spanish garrisons still more. Another Portuguese attack occurred in 1776 while the two courts were engaged at home in diplomatic

[2] R. Konetzke, *Die Politik des Grafen Aranda* (Berlin, 1929), pp. 142–144; Yela, *op. cit.*, p. 336.
[3] Doniol, I, 308.

conversations for the settlement of the issue. Vergennes up to this time had been urging Spain to adjust the dispute by diplomacy and to restrict to South America any military operations which might come out of a failure to settle it. He had participated even in some efforts to present to the two disputants a joint Anglo-French mediation, a maneuver which never reached a definite formal proposal because of the mutual suspicions of France and Great Britain. He knew that, in any war with Portugal, Spain would aim at the conquest of that neighboring country, to the throne of which the Catholic King still nursed remote but aggressive dynastic claims. Since Great Britain and Portugal were allies, any invasion of Portugal was bound to be a *casus foederis*. War between Great Britain and Spain over Portugal would oblige France to come to the defense of Spain. Grimaldi offered to France the Portuguese possessions in South America in return for French help in conquering Portugal, but Vergennes had not been ready to spend French military and naval strength in any war to conquer Portugal.

Nor was it expansion which Vergennes sought for France herself; rather he wished to retrieve her position in the European balance. To take the field with Spain directly on the Portuguese question was not certain to break up the British Empire, unless the revolted English Colonies were in an exceptionally strong military position beforehand. At one moment in 1776 such a prospect invited him. The Portuguese aggression of February 19 became known in Versailles shortly after the arrival there of news of the Declaration of Independence. The latter event, together with the evacuation of Boston by Howe's army several weeks before, impressed Vergennes with the favorable position of the Colonies. In August, 1776, it seemed to him that the time had come to consider a joint Franco-Spanish war against England, and the chances for success appeared so good that he was willing to let the war begin with a Spanish invasion of Portugal. No convention was to be made with the American Colonists, but they were to be given every aid and encouragement. He read another of his memoirs recommending this step, to the King in Council. The memoir as read was forwarded to the Spanish Court and it is safe to assume it would not have been transmitted to Spain without the approval of King and Council.

At a meeting of the Spanish Council of State the question was debated, war or peace with England; they decided easily and unanimously that plenty of righteous excuses existed for a declaration of war against Portugal, and for a preventive war against Great Britain—preventive by reason of future attacks said to be feared. Three of the six ministers, including those of war and navy, were for taking up the French proposal and going to war against England. The Minister of Finances was against letting any Portuguese war in South America spread to Europe. Grimaldi opposed an attack on Portugal in Europe before France and Spain had carefully inventoried their military and naval resources and arranged a plan of campaign against Great Britain. The Minister of the Indies agreed with this, adding that the Americans ought meanwhile to be animated and encouraged by holding up to them the possibility of a diversion of England's forces in Europe. The result of the deliberations was that Grimaldi wrote a long reply to the French Court, approving in principle the proposal for war with Great Britain but insisting, as a condition precedent for such a conflict, that the two powers agree on a military and naval convention, and that it should be perfectly understood that Portugal and Minorca (nothing was said about Florida or Gibraltar, on this occasion) should go to Spain in the final peace arrangement. The Spanish note added, with proper caution, that it was desirable to know what the decision of Louis XVI's Council had been on Vergennes's proposal when submitted to it, since of this there had been no mention.[4]

The two courts were now in almost perfect harmony of interests. We are constrained to believe that Vergennes could have had his war with England if he had been willing to draw up at once the necessary detailed military and naval arrangements with his ally and to guarantee Portugal and Minorca to Spain. The Spanish conquest of Portugal and the consequent uneven rise of Spain in the European balance of power was a big price to pay

[4] Yela, *op. cit.*, pp. 76–79. For text of note of Oct. 8, 1776, Grimaldi to Aranda, see Doniol, I, 603–613.

for the abasement of Great Britain, but worth it if the proposed war against England should mean sure victory. As Vergennes received Grimaldi's answer, he heard of the rout of Washington's army at the battle of Long Island (August 27, 1776) by Howe's newly transported forces. On this news Vergennes immediately reversed his rôle and began to talk as insistently for peace as a few weeks before he had argued for war. He immediately got out of his proposal to Spain by affecting to consider the Spanish reply as too indefinite and based on a policy of delay. With curious but altogether characteristic logic he argued to the King that as a result of this victory over the Americans England was no more immediately dangerous. "The English with an establishment in America for their winter quarters," he wrote, "seem less to be feared than wandering around on the sea and not knowing where to find a refuge." [5] The King agreed. After Long Island and in view of the reservations of the Spanish reply, Maurepas, the principal minister, also quickly became pacifist and humanitarian. That battle put a temporary quietus on hostile action by the family allies. Vergennes sent a non-committal reply to Spain and fell back to a patient "watchful waiting," with continued secret assistance and verbal encouragement to the Americans.

The Declaration of Independence was accompanied by the appointment, in the United States Congress, of a committee to draw up a plan of treaties to be negotiated with foreign powers, particularly with France, the nation first "pitched on," as Franklin put it. This committee, consisting of John Adams, Benjamin Franklin, John Dickinson, Benjamin Harrison, and Robert Morris, deliberated for some weeks, and finally brought in a report, July 18, which was adopted with some modifications, September 17, 1776.[6] The report included a model set of articles for treaties of commerce and amity, and in addition some par-

[5] Doniol, I, 619.
[6] The text of the plan is printed in *Journals* under date of September 17, 1776, and in Savage, *loc. cit.*, pp. 132–134. For highly valuable commentary thereon see E. C. Burnett, "Notes on American Negotiations for Commercial Treaties, 1776–1786," *A.H.R.*, XVI, 579–587. Its part in the subsequent treaties of the United States may be traced in Carlton Savage, *Policy of the United States toward Maritime Commerce in War* (Washington, G.P.O., 1934).

ticular articles for insertion in a treaty with France. The general
principles of the model "Plan of 1776" were picked by the committee out of eighteenth-century European practice, as reflected
in the treaty of Utrecht and generally in the treaties of the small-
navy powers: free ships free goods, freedom of neutrals to trade
between port and port of a belligerent (a repudiation of the new
British Rule of 1756), restricted and carefully defined lists of
contraband not including foodstuffs or naval stores, and, generally, considerate treatment of neutral shipping. These were the
principles of maritime practice which were coming increasingly
into usage in Europe and which Great Britain, with her surpassing
sea power, would not admit as international law, because the
greater the liberty left to neutral carriers in the time of war, the
greater the help to Britain's small-navy enemies who had to rely
on neutral shipping. We shall have occasion to revert to these
features of the "Plan of 1776" in this and another chapter.[7]
It furnished the model for all, except one, of the eighteenth-
century treaties of the United States, and may be regarded as a
charter document of early American maritime practice. At this
time the committee discussed the policy of contracting any foreign
alliance. Although the possibility had been repeatedly debated in
Congress, these very first instructions to accredited envoys of the
United States did not permit such a connection. As we have seen,
the plans of Vergennes himself did not yet call for an alliance
with the United States, even though at this moment he was proposing to Spain a war against England. The plan of Congress was
for a treaty of commerce and friendship, perpetual in character;
protection by France to American citizens and vessels from the
Barbary corsairs, with a reciprocal right of nationals and vessels
of each party to sail in the other's naval convoys; and the adoption
of the maritime principles recently selected. In case war with
Great Britain should result from France's thus recognizing independence, the United States would agree merely not to assist
France's enemy with men, money, ships, or contraband. It would
not bind itself to make common cause with France nor to make
a common peace with a common enemy. France was expected to

[7] See below, pp. 61, 170.

agree to make no conquests of British dominions on the continent of North America or adjacent islands, all of which was to be left as a field for further American expansion. It was fortunate that France no longer had any territorial ambitions in North America.

Congress drew up instructions, September 24, 1776, to accompany the plan. These allowed the agents of the United States to make certain minor concessions in the anticipated negotiations— if necessary it might be stipulated that the United States agree not to acknowledge British allegiance under any conditions, and to give no special trade privilege to Great Britain not enjoyed by France. An important stipulation provided against any precipitate peace with Great Britain by either the United States or France: in case France should become involved in war with Great Britain as a result of the present treaty, neither party should make a separate peace with the common enemy until after six months' notice that negotiations had commenced. The diplomatic commissioners of the United States were to solicit the Court of France for arms and ammunition to be sent to America under French convoy and to get, if they could, a few good foreign military engineers for the service of Congress. Then follow two significant paragraphs:

"It is highly probable that France means not to let the United States sink in the present Contest. But as the Difficulty of obtaining true Accounts of our Condition may cause an Opinion to be entertained that we are able to support the War on our own Strength and Resources longer than, in fact, we can do, it will be proper for you to press for the immediate and explicit declaration of France in our Favour, upon a Suggestion that a Re-union with Great Britain may be the Consequence of a delay."

This was the trump card which the commissioners later played with perfect success.

"Should Spain be disinclined to your Cause, from an Apprehension of Danger to his Dominions in South America, you are empowered to give the strongest Assurances, that that Crown will receive no Molestation from the United States, in the Possession of those Territories." [8]

[8] *Journals*, V, 813–816.

Additional instructions (October 16, 1776) directed the Commissioners to try to obtain from other European states, through their diplomatic agents at Paris, recognition of the independence of the United States and treaties of amity and commerce, provided that the same be "not inconsistent" with that to be made with France, and "that they do not oblige us to become a party in any war which may happen in consequence thereof, and that the immunities, exemptions, privileges, protection, defense and advantages, or the contrary, thereby stipulated, be equal and reciprocal." A few days later Congress further ordered the Commissioners to procure from France, by purchase or loan, eight battleships, well manned and fitted for service.[9]

Everybody knew that French recognition of the independence of the United States would be the signal for war between France and Great Britain, to say nothing of what would follow France's furnishing the United States with eight fully equipped and manned battleships. But so averse was the United States Congress to involvement in any European war that in these, the first instructions ever penned to accredited American diplomatic representatives, it shrank from committing itself to an alliance against a common enemy, with whom it was desperately contending for its very independence and sovereignty.

Our first plenipotentiaries to be sent to a foreign court consisted of Benjamin Franklin, who as a member of the Committee had helped to write the instructions; Silas Deane, already in France as a purchasing agent and observer; and Arthur Lee, who up to this time had been serving as the correspondent of Congress in London. He took the place of Thomas Jefferson, author of the text of the Declaration of Independence, who had originally been chosen to serve on the joint commission with Franklin and Deane, but who declined the mission.[10]

Franklin landed in France December 4, 1776. It was he, rather than the Commission, who personified the American cause during the decisive year 1777. His arrival in France was interpreted as

[9] *Journals,* VI, 884.
[10] The illness and death of his wife and other family misfortunes compelled him to refuse the post at this time.

an indication that the United States would not soon negotiate for
a reconciliation with England.[11] France soon forgot the interesting "merchant" and able agent, Silas Deane, now overshadowed
by the reputation and picturesque personality of his greater colleague. The unstable temperament and choleric disposition of the
equally patriotic Lee made him a man with whom neither friend
nor foe cared to deal. Franklin, venerable printer, philosopher,
philanthropist, and patriot, had by no means passed the peak of
life, with all his seventy years. The most important work of this
public servant lay still ahead of him. The American virtuoso was
the greatest man whom the New World had yet produced, and
he was, with the possible exception of Voltaire, the best-known
person in the whole world. His name, on every lip as soon as his
arrival in France was announced, and his face, which soon appeared on every lady's snuff-box, served to retrieve the prestige
which the American cause had lost in French public estimation
by the defeat of Long Island.

Franklin had a flair for feeling public opinion, and for approaching it. The policy of Vergennes rested on the cold-blooded
calculations of eighteenth-century diplomacy, weighed in the chill
balance of European power. Back of these calculations and a part
of them, ready to support them, was the warm-hearted sympathy
of the French people, in so far as they were articulate, for the
struggling American Colonies. In reality, except for the approaching identity of interests in the world of international politics, the
people of France and of America had had little in common except
rather vague moral pulsations. But the immortal generation of
eighteenth-century French philosophers did not deal wholly with
realities. They lived in a world of divine discontent and yeasty
speculation. They speculated about the laws of the physical uni-
verse. They speculated concerning the laws of the social world.
Groping for a solution for France's profound political problems,
they eagerly searched the horizon for what they yearned to be-
hold. Wistfully they gazed across the Atlantic. There they saw a
great mirage, reflecting what they looked for. The French intel-
ligentsia found in the American Colonies a spectacle that appeared

[11] Wharton, II, 224.

to them, in the uneasy intellectual conditions of the *ancien régime*, a kind of moral and social ideal, an Utopia almost too real and too good to be true: a nation of tillers of the soil, philosophers all, tolerant, pious, reasonable, happy beings without the curse of great cities, enervating luxuries, crimes, and other infirmities of civilization. The typical personal representative of this ideal was Franklin.[12]

It was indeed too good to be true. Granting that the American Revolution did offer a spectacle more notable and less materialistic than any other great event which had yet occurred in the eighteenth century, the people of the Colonies did not possess the perfect measure of Utopian qualities which French writers like Voltaire and the Abbé Raynal attributed to them. Frontier influences and the touch of virgin acres on European immigrants had fixed in the fiber of American social character a strain of that radical philosophy which imbued the revolutionary spirit in both France and America toward the end of the century. Both led by different channels to the hypothesis of the social compact and the world-shaking theory of popular sovereignty, but neither has led to social perfection either in France or in America.

Vergennes was aware of the force of this public opinion. He stimulated it, and Franklin worked upon it too. The Philadelphian with his fur cap was careful to appear in French society as a simple philosopher and patriot, a virtuous eighteenth-century Cincinnatus.[13] Behind this outward simplicity lay a profound and crafty mind. A newspaper man by profession, he was constantly alive to the value of a "good press" for the United States in Europe, and he assisted agents of the French Foreign Office in

[12] For most scholarly and thoughtful studies of the psychological affinity of French public opinion for the American Colonies, see Bernard Faÿ, *L'esprit révolutionnaire en France et aux Etats-Unis à la fin du XVIIIᵉ siècle* (Paris, 1925), particularly pp. 1–112; and the several works of Professor Gilbert Chinard, notably *Les refugiés huguenots en Amérique* (Paris, 1925), introduction; *Les amitiés américaines de Mme. d'Houdetot* (Paris, 1924).

[13] For one of the best appreciations of Franklin's immense popularity in France, see A. Aulard, *La Révolution Française,* années 37 et 38, Nos. 51–52 (Sept.–Oct., 1918), pp. 385–416. The E. E. Hales' *Franklin in France,* 2 vols. (Boston, 1887), was first to print many documents relating to this phase of his career.

preparing propaganda for the French journals [14] and for other Continental gazettes. Into frequent products of his own pen, sometimes anonymous or under pseudonym, he poured his inimitable homely qualities of example and persuasion, in those words, understandable to everybody, which already had made "Poor Richard" famous.[15] He even stooped to a low place [16] on at least one occasion later in the war and printed, on his own little press at Passy, false accounts of British Indian atrocities,[17] doubtless under the conviction that they could easily be matched with reality, and that this was no more than a reply in kind to such British propaganda as the falsified letters of Washington.

Never was a people more stirred with sympathy for a foreign cause than were the French in 1777. This was the year when the chivalrous Lafayette [18] embarked, with the connivance of Vergennes, to join the American cause as an officer in Washington's army; when the Comte de Broglie, seeking for himself a stadt-holderate in America, sent de Kalb over to prepare the way for it,[19] when the Prussian officer Steuben left France to drill the

[14] For Vergennes and the press, see Faÿ, *op. cit.*, pp. 61–64.

[15] For example, see his "Comparison of Great Britain and the United States in regard to the Basis of Credit in the two Countries" (1777), "The Sale of the Hessians" (1777), "A Dialogue between Britain, France, Spain, Holland, Saxony, and America" (1777), "A Catechism relating to the English National Debt" (1777), all in Vol. VII of Smyth's *Writings of Benjamin Franklin,* 10 vols. (New York, 1905–1907).

[16] "When you come to a low place, stoop." *Poor Richard's Almanack.*

[17] Franklin got out a "Supplement" of his own to the *Boston Independent Chronicle,* No. 1705 (1782), a sheet generally resembling the original in typography and advertising matter, but having inserted into it some horrible accounts of buying scalps of women and children, and of bloody massacres by the Indian allies of Great Britain. There is a rare original copy of the spurious edition of the *Independent Chronicle* in the Division of MSS. of the Library of Congress. See also Smyth, *op. cit.,* VIII, 437–447.

[18] Professor Louis Gottschalk, in a paper on Lafayette read at the International Historical Congress at Warsaw in 1933, established the connivance of Vergennes. His contribution is to appear in a biographical study. Lafayette's career in America is summed up in attractive form, from many sources, including Doniol and the French archives, in Charlemagne Tower, *The Marquis de LaFayette in the American Revolution,* 2 vols. (Philadelphia, 1901).

[19] The Comte de Broglie, a French diplomat and courtier, brother of the Marshal Broglie, devised a scheme to get himself made an American dictator under terms which might pave the way for the creation of something like a stadtholderate in America, comparable to the title of Prince Ferdinand of Nassau, or as some commentators have seen it, to that of William of Orange. See Doniol, II, 50–97; Wharton, I, 392.

American army, when scores of French officers besieged the American Commissioners with offers of military service under Washington—most of them not without expectations of high rank and pay.[20] All this was to the inner satisfaction of the French Court, despite outward gestures of disapproval, for the benefit of England. Lafayette's adventure won the plaudits of the kingdom. The American cause was now on every tongue. Vergennes and his master had behind them, in their policy of intervention in the American Revolution, the sympathetic politico-religiosity of the leaders and articulators of French thought.

The activities of the American commission during the year 1777 were directed toward securing from France open recognition of independence and alliance, as well as a continuance of the stream of secret assistance. Congress soon departed from its first cautious opposition to alliances and authorized its agents to make such tenders as might be necessary [21] to secure the immediate military assistance of France and Spain and their recognition of American independence. Before the arrival of Franklin, Deane, without word from Congress, had gone so far as to draw up articles of a treaty with Spain and France, guaranteeing the territories of those powers in the New World, sharing the Newfoundland fisheries, and excluding British ships from any American waters.[22] The Commissioners, after hearing of Burgoyne's ominous invasion of New York, already ventured on their own authority to offer not to make a separate peace in case France or Spain became involved in a war with Great Britain as a result of making a treaty of amity and commerce with the United States.[23] With official sanction they now renewed their offers, presenting the project of Congress for a triple alliance, including Spain as well as France, peace not to be made until Portugal should be conquered and British authority expelled from the continent of North America and the West India Islands—a peace based on the joint consent of the three allies.[24] In February of 1777 his

[20] Corwin, *French Policy and the American Alliance, op. cit.,* pp. 90–91.
[21] Wharton, II, 240.
[22] Wharton, II, 216.
[23] Wharton, II, 260; *Writings of Franklin* (Smyth ed.), VII, 19.
[24] Corwin, *op. cit.,* pp. 96–97. The object of the war was outlined in proposals

fellow commissioners delegated Lee to go to Spain to seek the recognition and alliance of that country. Lee was turned back at Vittoria by Grimaldi [25] personally, not without being given promises of secret aid from Spain, promises which were subsequently carried out.[26] Vergennes unofficially received Franklin and his colleagues and allowed them to ship out cargoes of munitions in French and American bottoms. The ports of France—and of Spain—remained open to ships of commerce flying the American flag. To help on the activity of the American commission in France, Louis XVI granted in January, 1777, a clandestine loan of 2,000,000 *livres*, without defined terms of payment.[27]

France was bound by her treaties with Great Britain since 1713 not to receive into her harbors the prizes or privateers of Britain's enemies, except in stress of weather, shipwreck, or other real emergencies, nor to allow private ships of war to be fitted out there.[28] Notwithstanding this, American privateers entered

addressed separately, by Deane to Vergennes, and by Franklin to Aranda: the independence of the United States and the enfeeblement of Great Britain. In case of a French alliance only, there should be a joint conquest of British possessions in America: those on the mainland and the islands adjacent to it, including Newfoundland and the Bermudas, to go to the United States, and the sugar islands and one half the Newfoundland fisheries to go to France. For the French conquest of the sugar islands the United States would agree to furnish up to $2,000,000 of provisions, and six frigates, as well as all other possible assistance. In case Spain should come in, the United States would assist that monarchy in the conquest of the town and harbor of Pensacola "provided the inhabitants of the United States shall have the free navigation of the Mississippi and the use of the harbor of Pensacola"; and should France and Spain desire it, the United States would declare war on Portugal because of that power's refusal to receive American vessels in its harbors, and would continue in the war until Portugal should be conquered and made a part of Spain. Peace was to be made only by mutual consent of the allies. See Silas Deane to Vergennes, March 18, 1777, Doniol, II, 319, and Franklin to Aranda, April 7, 1777, Wharton, II, 304, and *Journals of the Continental Congress* for Dec. 30, 1776.

[25] Grimaldi had just been succeeded as principal minister by Floridablanca. For best description of this incident, see Yela, *op. cit.*, I, 161–180.

[26] Wharton, II, 250; Yela, pp. 161–180.

[27] For French and Spanish loans and subsidies, see below, p. 92.

[28] See articles XV, XVII, XIX, XX, XXVI, XXVII of treaty of Utrecht, for obligations of neutrality between the two parties. This treaty was specifically renewed by the treaty of Paris of 1763. The treaty of 1763 also renewed the old Anglo-Spanish treaties of commerce, notably that of Madrid of 1750; but a study of these later documents does not reveal any of the inhibitions as to privateers and prizes, or the provision, free ships free goods, which character-

French harbors, under various excuses, fitted out there with war gear, brought back prizes and turned them into gold *livres* by collusion with French buyers without the formality of admiralty condemnation. Vergennes's efforts to stop this were apathetic and dilatory, though he constantly assured the well-informed British Ambassador that France was taking every step to cause her treaties to be observed in good faith. At least three public cruisers were fitted out clandestinely by the American Commissioners in French ports in 1777 and set forth on the Atlantic. Spanish policy in regard to American privateers and their prizes was similar to that of France, even in Spanish-American harbors, which were nominally closed to all foreign flags.[29] Vergennes caused the neutrality of France to be enforced on these points only when Lord Stormont, the British Ambassador, presented him with evidence so formidable and conclusive as to leave open no avenue for cavil or evasion, or when he wanted to make some gesture of deception to the British Ministry. On one such occasion all shipments of munitions on French ships for American account were stopped in French ports, and orders were sent out recalling leaves of absence to French officers departing for service with the United States. But it was hinted to the American envoys that this was only a temporary expedient, France not being ready for war; at any rate soon afterward the supply ships were allowed to depart.[30] Actually France was under no obligations to stop "private" shipment of munitions from her ports.

As a result of the activity of the American privateers, British commerce in the Channel and elsewhere was so harassed in 1777

ized the Anglo-French treaty at Utrecht; there is, however, a list of contraband, and non-contraband, the latter not excluding naval stores.

[29] In September, 1776, secret orders were sent to all Spanish ports, both in the peninsula and in America, to admit American privateers and their prizes. In the case of the colonial ports of Spain, it was stated that privateers flying the flag of the United States, and their prizes, should be received, in cases of emergency, similarly to those of England or France, without permission to trade. Yela, *op. cit.*, I, 71.

[30] Franklin and Deane to the Committee of Secret Correspondence, Paris, March 12, 1777, Wharton, II, 283. For official French note to the British Ambassador recognizing France's obligation not to receive privateers and prizes, nor to allow outfitting of ships of war, see Flassan, *Histoire générale et raisonnée de la diplomatie française*, 6 vols. (Paris, 1809), VI, 146.

that insurance rates rose to over 20 per cent. In these violations of neutrality Great Britain had abundant cause for a declaration of war against France, had it been desired.[31]

The activities of American privateers became so embarrassing to England by the middle of 1777 that Vergennes had to make up his mind to expect a possible ultimatum on the subject from Great Britain. On July 23 he indited another memoir to the King saying that the time had come for France "either to abandon America or to aid her courageously and effectively." Secret assistance was no longer sufficient to keep up the war in America through all crises.[32] What had now come to be necessary was an offensive and defensive alliance with the United States, by which each party to the treaty—Spain was considered in all these thoughts of Vergennes as going hand in hand with French policy—would agree not to make peace without the consent of the others. The Americans should be informed right away of the King's intention, and any step to be taken must be made before the reassembly of the British Parliament set for January 20, 1778, when a change in ministry might occur and upset all calculations. The French navy, Vergennes pointed out, had by now been restored to a strength equal to the demands of a joint war of the Family Allies against England.

Again the King consented to a war proposal, conditional upon the agreement of Spain. Again Vergennes dispatched to Spain a memoir making the proposition. This time it found the Spanish Court much less receptive. The "foreigner," Grimaldi, had been replaced at Madrid by the proud Murcian, Floridablanca; a Spanish expeditionary force had chastised the Portuguese on the La Plata; the subtle Pombal had fallen from power in Lisbon; an armistice had intervened in June, 1777, between Portugal and Spain to bring to an end their conflict in South America. The new Spanish Foreign Minister had embarked upon a new Portuguese policy: conciliation with that neighboring kingdom and absorption of it by a projected dynastic marriage instead of by

[31] For cruisers, privateers, and prizes, see documents in Wharton, II, 287, 322, 364, 377, 379, 387, 433–436.
[32] Doniol, II, 460–469.

conquest. Floridablanca also had a clean-cut program for the Anglo-American situation. He continued Grimaldi's policy of opposition to American independence and also adopted that of secret assistance to the colonial forces to keep the war going, but he was for avoiding any profitless war with England for the advantage of French policy. He contemplated at this time a mediation by France and Spain between Great Britain and her revolted Colonies, on the basis of a truce which would bring something short of actual independence for the Colonies and leave them and the mother country still hostile to each other—something like the twelve years' truce between Spain and the revolted Netherlands in the early seventeenth century, which had been guaranteed by France and England. The proposed American truce would be guaranteed by Spain and France.[33] But Floridablanca was also fearful of French patronage and anxious to take a stiffer attitude than that attributed to the Genoese Grimaldi.[34]

The new orientation of Spanish plans forced Vergennes to cling to his policy of marking time. American privateers in French harbors were suddenly and summarily ordered out, without allowing further delay or pretext; their prizes, brought too openly in, were restored to their British owners; a few persons engaged in fitting out armed vessels were imprisoned; and renewed orders against the exportation of warlike stores were issued[35]; but the

---

[33] Yela, *op. cit.*, I, 183–187. Much of the French correspondence with Spain is printed in Doniol, II, 432–609.

[34] Aranda, writing from Paris, told his new chief that Grimaldi's despatches had been marked frequently by "superficiality and lightness and by the lack of attachment to which is susceptible one who could not pronounce properly the words *cuerno, cebolla,* and *ajo* [ham, onion, and garlic]. Thank God we are now all one, and your Excellency is in charge of affairs." This private letter of June 22, 1777, is to be found in the Library of Congress collection of transcripts of the correspondence of the Spanish Foreign Office with its ambassador at Paris. The original is in the Archives of Simancas, *Sección de Estado, Libro 179, moderno.* Floridablanca's private letters to Aranda show his determination to get something for Spain out of the situation, without war, and that he and Aranda agreed on a policy of "dissimulation and serenity" as to France (*del disimulo y la frescura*). Floridablanca to Aranda, July 19, 1777.

[35] "To us it [the French Court] privately professes a real friendship, wishes success to our cause, winks at the supplies we obtain here as much as it can without giving open grounds of complaint to England, privately affords us very essential aids, and goes on preparing for war. How long these two parts will continue to be acted at the same time, and which will finally predominate, may

French Government refused to comply with the suggestion of the British Ministry that public proclamation be made of its orders to admiralty and port authorities on the subject of American privateers and prizes. When it was decided not to go as far as this, secret orders went out to hold up, for fear of eventualities, the departure of all French vessels, and to send a note of warning, against possible war, to the French fishing fleet on the Grand Banks, as well as to shipping in the Levant. But the British did not care to press the issue further at that moment. The Ministry at London chose to regard the banishment of the privateers as a disavowal of French connivance with American violations of neutrality.[36] The American Commissioners later ordered their naval officers to dispose of prizes in French and Spanish waters.[37] Nobody rebuked them.

Even had Spain acceded to Vergennes's proposition, it is not certain that France would have gone to war, because for a second time discouraging news of British victories arrived inopportunely from America,—the successful and rapid operations of Burgoyne's army around Ticonderoga. That discouragement evaporated a few months later when Burgoyne's campaign became involved in difficulties in the upper Hudson River valley which led to the dramatic surrender at Saratoga (October 17, 1777).

be a question." Franklin, Deane, and Lee to the Committee of Foreign Affairs, Passy, Sept. 8, 1777, Wharton, II, 388–389.

[36] Doniol, II, 525–539.

[37] Franklin and Deane to Capt. John Paul Jones, Jan. 16, 1778, instructs him to be careful of offending the neutrality of any power whose ports he frequents, but to send in prizes to Goularde and Moylan, L'Orient; S. and J. H. Delaps, Bordeaux; Gardoqui and Son, Bilbao, and Leogane and Co., Courogne. Franklin Papers, *Miscellaneous,* II, 398, Library of Congress.

CHAPTER V

The Franco-American Alliance

All watchful waiting on the part of France came to a close when the news arrived on December 3, 1777, of Burgoyne's surrender to the American army at Saratoga. That great stroke on the Hudson disposed the North Ministry to a "material change of system," [1] to a policy of conciliation with America based on the colonial demands of 1775, which George III had once rejected so imperturbably. Lord North proposed a reconciliation, in short, which should repeal the obnoxious legislation passed since 1763 and leave the Colonies within the Empire, possibly in the shape of several dominions autonomous in all matters of internal government. While the bills to this effect were being formulated for presentation to Parliament when it should convene, in January, 1778, following the recess, the Ministry used its capable intelligence service, as well as some complaisant private individuals, to get in touch with the American commissioners at Paris before they should have attached themselves by any formal connection to France. Agents hurried across the Channel to interview Deane and Franklin, whom British spies had reported, before the news of Saratoga, to be favorable to a peace without victory and averse to an alliance with France. Paul Wentworth, one of the old colonial agents—for the Colony of New Hampshire—in London before 1775, was the emissary chosen for this purpose by William Eden, then an undersecretary in the North Ministry, whose argus-eyed secret service covertly patrolled the continent of Europe. Wentworth had no powers. His function was to feel out the American commissioners.[2] He had

[1] Lord North to the King, Dec. 4 [1777], *Correspondence of King George the Third*, 6 vols. (London, 1928), III, 504.

[2] "This expedition of Mr. Wentworth may, very possibly, end in nothing, but, (as he speaks entirely from himself, having never had a word of conversation upon his present errand either with Lord North or anybody else

an interview with Deane on December 15, 1777, and another one on the following day; and later, on January 6, 1778, he saw Franklin, in Deane's presence, in a memorable meeting. In these supposedly secret conferences Wentworth sketched out vaguely the terms of peace which the North Ministry was willing to offer. Franklin and Deane [3] prudently refused to commit themselves except to a regularly accredited envoy, or to talk of any terms of peace except those based on absolute independence. Wentworth in the first interviews tempted Deane with offers of high political place in the new régime which was hoped for in America, if he, and his colleagues, would use their power and influence for such a settlement short of independence. It was not effective. Franklin's loyalty was unshakable; and such offers as were made to Deane during these weeks of temptation did not produce the intended results.[4] Franklin agreed to see Wentworth

except Mr. Eden) Lord North hopes and believes that no mischief can arise from it, especially as he has the greatest confidence in the discretion and ability of Mr. Wentworth. The least good consequence that can be expected from this journey is that Dr. Franklin and Mr. Deane's sentiments will be better known than they are at present." Lord North to the King, Dec. 23, 1777, *Correspondence of King George the Third,* III, 519.

[3] Arthur Lee had been reported by his secretary, who was a British spy, not to favor any peace by compromise. Hence he was avoided by the British, who attributed, without sufficient reason, a different sentiment to Deane and Franklin. Lee at this time did not enjoy the confidence of his colleagues nor anybody else, though his patriotism cannot be questioned.

[4] That efforts were made to do so, in 1778 and thereafter, seems certain. See an enigmatic letter of North to the King, January 30, 1778. *Correspondence of King George the Third,* IV, 29. Cf. phraseology of this letter with the King's to North of March 3, 1781, *ibid.,* V, 200. Silas Deane's later career was tragic. Recalled by Congress in 1778, after the consummation of the alliance, he returned to France in 1780 to adjust his official accounts, which had been questioned. He now deserted the cause of American independence and of the French alliance. Suspected by Franklin and others of treasonable contact with the British, he fled to the Netherlands. There he corresponded with Paul Wentworth in January, February, and March, 1782; and with Andrew Allen, one of Shelburne's Tory informers (Shelburne Papers, Vol. 87 [Library of Congress photostat]). George III wrote to Lord North, March 3, 1781, of Deane as of one whose services had been offered, and a series of Deane's letters, stretching over several weeks, was conveniently "intercepted" in a group by the British secret service and published in New York. They advocated a peace with Great Britain without independence. Deane lived in England from 1783 to 1789, where he did not refuse to shake the hand of Benedict Arnold, whom he thought a misunderstood man, though he tried later to avoid him. He died in 1789 just after embarking for America. Congress in 1842 recognized the justice of Deane's financial claims against the United States by paying his heirs $37,000 for expenses in-

only on condition that there should be no allusion to such things. Wentworth returned to London in January, without results.

The fear that the British Ministry, staggering under the blow of Saratoga, was about to offer to the Colonies peace terms generous but short of independence had an immediate effect in France. Anxious lest such terms might be accepted by the war-weary Americans if recognition of the United States and more decisive aid were withheld any longer, Vergennes hastily promised (December 17, 1777)—without waiting to consult on that step fully with Spain—such recognition and a treaty. The French Ministry felt that if something were not done quickly, the long-awaited chance, at last at hand, for sundering the British Empire might pass and be gone forever. It was further evident that, once France brought on a war with Great Britain by making a treaty of friendship and commerce with the United States, there must be some guaranty that in the future the United States would not accept alluring peace terms from Great Britain and thus leave France confronting her traditional enemy alone. That dreaded contingency made an alliance the necessary accompaniment of any treaty.

Vergennes anxiously waited a fortnight for Spain's answer to his pressing proposal to join France in such an alliance. But Floridablanca was set against recognizing American independence and resented the promises which had just been made by France without Spain's sanction. Realizing that France must go in alone if at all, and anxious lest further delay should lose the golden opportunity forever, Vergennes informed the American Commissioners (January 8, 1778) that the King was disposed to grant their request for a treaty and an alliance.[5]

curred by him, 1776–1778. The correspondence of Deane was brought together by Charles Isham, and published in 1890 in *N.-Y. Hist. Soc. Collections.* The Connecticut Hist. Soc. published a supplementary volume in 1930 in its *Collections,* Vol. XXX.

[5] The above three paragraphs are based on a wealth of documentary material contained in the Stevens *Facsimiles,* much of which is summarized in my article on "British Secret Service and the French-American Alliance," in *A.H.R.,* XXIX, 474–495; on the correspondence in Doniol, II, 611–793; on Yela, using the Spanish despatches, I, 247–269; on the correspondence of the American Commissioners, printed in Wharton, II; and on *The Correspondence of King*

Well might Saratoga be ranked among the "fifteen decisive battles of the world"!

A month more of delay followed before France definitively committed herself to the American alliance—delay protracted with the hope of being somehow able to bring Spain to the same proposition. A vain hope it was, even though Montmorin, the French Ambassador at Madrid, had prophesied that when confronted with the necessity of deciding immediately, Spain would come in.[6]

The plenipotentiaries of the United States and of France signed two treaties on February 6, 1778. The treaty of amity and commerce, with the exceptions about to be mentioned, conformed almost identically with the articles of the "Plan of 1776" laid down by the Continental Congress in the original instructions to the Commissioners to France. All the principles of neutral rights in time of war, and the ordinary articles for mutual protection of shipping, extending to that of convoy; for shipwrecked mariners, rescues from pirates, and so forth, were inserted into the treaty almost word for word out of the plan. The political articles of the original plan, providing that the United States would not assist Great Britain in case the treaty should bring on a war between France and that power, were superseded by the articles in the treaty of alliance between France and the United States of the same date. Instead of the commerce of each state receiving in the ports of the other the same privileges as given to nationals, the conventional most-favored-nation privileges were stipulated, but with this interesting innovation, of recent French origin [7]: that when a concession to another nation had not been made freely but in return for compensation, such a concession would not extend to the most-favored party except

George the Third. See also Valentín Urtasún, Historia diplomática de América, 2 vols. (Pamplona, 1920 and 1924), I, 494–527; and Corwin, pp. 158–172.

[6] Doniol, II, 701, 747.

[7] Vernon G. Setser, "Did Americans Originate the Conditional Most-favored-nation Clause?" Jour. Mod. Hist., V (1933), 319–323.

in return for similar compensation.[8] This novelty became the basis of American policy thereafter. In addition France promised certain free ports for American vessels in the West Indies and in France proper; and an article was added for the mutual residence of consuls, under terms of a consular agreement to be worked out later. The article of the original plan calling for the protection of American shipping against the depredations of the Barbary States—the British protection naturally had ceased with the Revolution—became simply a stipulation for the good offices of the King of France.[9]

The treaty of "conditional and defensive alliance" (*alliance éventuelle et défensive*) was so entitled because it was to come into effect in the eventuality of war resulting between France and Great Britain, a war to begin "either by direct hostilities" or by Great Britain's hindering the commerce and navigation of France in a way "contrary to the Rights of Nations, and the peace subsisting between the Two Crowns." The articles which follow are of such capital importance in early American diplomacy that every sentence is of significance.

Article I bound the alliance: in case war should break out between France and Great Britain, the two allies "shall make it a common cause, and aid each other with their good Offices, their

[8] In 1783 Vergennes proposed a supplementary article deleting this exception. By a resolution of May 11, 1784, Congress gave the assurance "that it will be our constant care to place no people on more advantageous ground than the subjects of his Majesty [the King of France]." When Franklin communicated this resolution to him, Vergennes in a formal reply assumed that this was a declaration in the name of the United States that it would "be careful not to treat any other nation, in matters of commerce, more advantageously than the French nation," and in return gave assurance of a "perfect reciprocity" on the part of France. See Hunter Miller's edition of *Treaties and Other International Acts of the United States of America* (Washington, 1931), II, 158–161.

[9] The treaty of commerce as signed contained two articles: Article XI, which made French West Indian molasses exported to the United States by American citizens free from any French export tax; and Article XII, which in turn exempted from American export tax goods exported from the United States, by French subjects, for the French West Indian molasses islands. The Congress ratified the treaty without reservation, unanimously, May 4, 1778; but in a resolution of May 5 instructed its representatives at the Court of France to seek to expunge Articles XI and XII. This was subsequently done in September at Versailles, by separate negotiation, consisting of an exchange of declarations between Vergennes and the American Commissioners, each party being equipped with full powers therefor.

Counsels and their forces, according to the exigence of Conjunctures as becomes good & faithful allies." Article II stated: "The essential and direct End of the present defensive alliance is to maintain effectually the liberty, Sovereignty, and independence absolute and unlimited of the said united States, as well in Matters of Gouvernement as of commerce." Article III left each ally free to judge of the efforts it should deem proper to employ against the common enemy. Article IV, to a certain extent supererogatory, stated that the two allies might draw up particular military conventions for particular enterprises in common. Article V read: "If the united States should think fit to attempt the Reduction of the British Power remaining in the Northern Parts of America, or the Islands of Bermudas, those Contries or Islands in case of Success, shall be confederated with or dependant upon the said united States." Article VI was a renunciation by the King of France of all future possession of the Bermuda Islands "as well as of any part of the Continent of North america which before the treaty of Paris in 1763. or in virtue of that Treaty, were acknowledged to belong to the Crown of Great Britain, or to the united States heretofore called British Colonies, or which are at this Time, or have lately been under the Power of the King and Crown of Great Britain." It is noteworthy that this did not exclude France from future possession of territory on the North American continent which had not before or after 1763 belonged to Great Britain, for instance, Louisiana west of the Mississippi or the "Island" of New Orleans. Nor did it forbid France from other islands than the Bermudas,—Newfoundland, Cape Breton, for example,—as had been stipulated in the original plan of Congress; nor from a conquest of inshore fishery rights, an objective which Vergennes never lost sight of.[10]

Article VII reserved for France a free hand in the conquest and future possession of British West India islands. Article VIII, highly important: "Neither of the two Parties shall conclude either Truce or Peace with Great Britain, without the formal consent of the other first obtain'd; and they mutually engage not to lay down their arms,

[10] Dallas D. Irvine, "The Newfoundland Fishery; a French Objective in the War of American Independence," *Can. Hist. Rev.,* XIII (Sept., 1932), 268–285.

until the Independence of the united states shall have been formally or tacitly assured by the Treaty or Treaties that shall terminate the War." Article IX renounced for either party any compensations or after-claims on one side or the other, whatever the event of the war. Article X provided that other powers which had received injuries from England might be admitted to the alliance, "under such conditions as shall be freely agreed to and settled between all the Parties." Article XI was the famous perpetual mutual guaranty of territory: "The two Parties guarantee mutually from the present time and forever, against all other powers, to wit, the united states to his most Christian Majesty, the present Possessions of the Crown of france in America as well as those which it may acquire by the future Treaty of peace; and his most Christian Majesty guarantees on his part to the united states, their liberty, Sovereignty, and Independence absolute, and unlimited, as well in Matters of Government as commerce and also thair Possessions, and the additions or conquests that their Confédération may obtain during the war, from any of the Dominions now or heretofore possessed by Great Britain in North America, conformable to the 5th and 6th articles above written, the whole as their Possessions shall be fixed and assured to the said States at the moment of the cessation of their present War with England." Article XII provided that the reciprocal guaranty of the preceding article should come into force "the moment such War shall break out." But the alliance was to be an alliance, even though war should not occur between Great Britain and France during the American Revolution, for the same sentence continued: "and if such rupture shall not take place, the mutual obligations of the said guarantee shall not commence, until the moment of the cessation of the present War between the united states and England shall have ascertained their Possessions." Article XIII provided for ratification in six months by both parties; and in the concluding paragraph of the treaties it was stipulated that the articles had been signed by the plenipotentiaries "both in the French and English Languages declaring Nevertheless that the present Treaty was originally composed and concluded in the French Language." A separate and secret article reserved the right of the King of Spain to agree to both treaties.[11]

A second separate and secret article, providing for an annual subsidy during the war from the King of France, was drafted during the negotiations and proposed, but not adopted.[12]

Considering the circumstances and the position of the French monarchy and the United States, the treaties exhibit terms of a most magnanimous character on the part of France, and students of the documents have marveled that the struggling United States could have secured in them such a large part of its original desires, or that France should have reserved for herself no more privileged position. The answer is that France did not want to appear before the world as contending for special privileges for herself in America. France wanted the sympathy of the neutral maritime powers in Europe, for the purpose of preventing the war from extending further on the Continent, and for the service of neutral carriage of naval stores, foodstuffs, and non-contraband colonial products as defined by the American treaty of commerce and amity. The prime purpose of France was the achievement of the independence of the United States. That also was the principal aim of the United States. There was a complete coincidence of vital interests surrounded by an atmosphere of revolutionary affinity and the fervor of French public opinion. Both treaties suited exactly the immediate purposes of each party to them, though not through the unlimited, unseen future.

Following the negotiation of the treaties, preparations were made for official recognition of the representatives of Congress; on March 20, 1778, they were received ceremoniously by Louis XVI in his court at Versailles.

All the diplomatic maneuvers of the American agents in France had been known to the British Foreign Office. The interviews of Deane with Vergennes, his arrangements with Beaumarchais, the

[11] The French and English versions of the treaties are quoted in parallel columns in Hunt and Ford's scholarly edition of the *Journals of the Continental Congress*, XI, 419–453. The above quotations, however, are taken from Hunter Miller's more authentic *Treaties and Other International Acts of the United States of America*, II (Washington, 1931), 35–40.

[12] There is a copy of it in Franklin Papers, *Miscellaneous*, IX, 2219, in the Library of Congress.

confidential conferences of the three American Commissioners, the shipment of nearly every cargo of munitions, the negotiation of the treaties—all these were speedily conveyed to London. Edward Bancroft, the confidential secretary of Silas Deane and later of the commission itself, was in the employ of the British Ministry, and so remained, undiscovered, throughout the war. Within forty-two hours after the signature of the treaties of February 6, 1778, Bancroft got copies of them to Whitehall, at least so he later stated—a remarkable feat, from the point of view of the cumbersome methods of transportation which then prevailed.[13] Though the British Government was at all times wide awake to the deception of French policies and discounted perfectly the fulsome and false assurances which Vergennes continually made to Lord Stormont, it at no time cared to make an issue of them. French neutrality and surreptitious assistance to the American revolutionists were preferable to the open warfare of France, which meant the employment of the French navy to convoy shipments of munitions to America, to capture British shipping, to occupy British naval forces in other than American theaters of war. This was particularly the case when the departure of the munition ships was so well known to the Admiralty, through the perfect intelligence system operating in neutral France. The open belligerency of France was a strategic blow of the first moment, and it signified the danger also of Spain's entrance into the war. It was a shock to British prestige in the neutral European countries; and the attitude of the neutral maritime states, as we shall soon see, was of paramount importance to the progress of British naval operations.

After the signature of the American alliance, both France and Great Britain were reluctant to strike the first blow; for the question of offense or defense was most important in view of the ancient alliance of the Netherlands with Great Britain; and France, with the Americans now safe from the arms of England, was utilizing all possible delay to perfect her naval forces.[14]

[13] *A.H.R.*, XXIX, 474–495, *op. cit.*, for Bancroft. For other spies see Wharton, I, 539–551.
[14] See Minutes of the French Council for March 18, 1778, Doniol, II, 847.

Great Britain at first professed not to know of the existence of the treaties, but Vergennes was studious to have his ambassador formally notify the British Government (March 13, 1778) of the treaty of amity and commerce. The fact thus became generally known in Europe, as the French Ministry desired it should, in order to offset, when conveyed to America through English gazettes, the impression which might be made by news of the announced British peace offer. This was followed by the recall of the ambassadors by both courts. Hostilities began in a very uncertain way—from the point of view of who struck the first blow—in a naval skirmish of French and British forces off Ushant, on the evening of June 17, 1778.[15]

Parliament enacted, March 9, 1778, the bills which Lord North had proposed, enabling the government to enter into a peace negotiation with the revolted Colonies on the basis of a repeal of the objectionable legislation since 1763—a peace of home rule for America within the Empire. Copies of the bills had been hurried across the Atlantic before their passage, in order if possible to prevent ratification of any French alliance. The articles of the French treaties reached America just after the arrival of the new bills of Parliament but before the English peace delegates themselves. The treaties arrived in the nick of time. Members of Congress were already considering the wisdom of opening parleys [16] with the commission when it should arrive; for thanks to the perfection of the British secret service and its coöperation with the fleet, nearly a year had passed without direct word from Franklin and his colleagues. Until three or four days before the arrival of the treaties on May 2, Congress had no inkling of the great diplomatic success.[17] Both treaties were ratified May 4, 1778, two days after their arrival. A French Minister Pleni-

[15] Doniol, III, 147.

[16] Burnett, op. cit., III, 179–215.

[17] "We have read a letter written by a friend, dated House of Commons, February 13, in which we are told that you had concluded a treaty with France and Spain, which was on the water towards us. Imagine how solicitous we are to know the truth of this before we receive any proposals from Britain, in consequence of the scheme in Lord North's speech, and the two drafts of bills now sent to you." Lovell, for Committee of Foreign Affairs, to the Commissioners at Paris, York [Pennsylvania] April 30, 1778, Wharton, II, 567. See also Burnett, op. cit., III, 198–200.

potentiary, Gérard, appeared with d'Estaing's fleet at Philadelphia, July 12. As he made his way up the Delaware, the plain people said to him: "You have come to our help. We shall go to yours when you wish it." Congress dined and wined King Louis's minister with the turtles and drinks which the British peace commissioners, by way of ingratiation, had recently caused to be sent to some of its members to prepare their digestions for Lord North's peace offers.[18] The not unpromising British peace maneuver of 1778 proved an utter failure.[19] Nor were the various approaches made informally by unaccredited agents of the North Ministry to Franklin, in France,[20] successful in breaking the United States from the new French connection, so ominous for England.[21] Such were the dramatic results of Vergennes's op-

[18] Gérard to Vergennes, Philadelphia, July 19, 1778, Doniol, III, 270.

[19] For papers relating to the history of this peace maneuver see Stevens, *Facsimiles*, Vols. IV, V, XI, XII, which contain the papers of the Carlisle Commission, the correspondence between William Eden, who prepared the bills, and who was a member of the commission, with the government, and many other valuable sources as yet little utilized by historians. See also *Carlisle Papers*, in 15th Rept. Royal MSS. Commission.

[20] Franklin, when starting out for France in 1776, had desired to be empowered to treat with England on the basis of independence and, if possible, the cession of Canada; and both before and after the signature of the French treaties he ventured, without powers, to indicate to these officious persons from London the willingness of the American Commission to make peace on that basis, but without any particular commercial privileges to Great Britain. Such a peace would have fulfilled perfectly the purpose of the new Franco-American treaties, without the necessity of a war between France and Great Britain. The North Government was unwilling thus to present uncontested such a victory to French diplomacy. Realizing this, Franklin flirted with the English parliamentary opposition and even sent an agent of his own to London, in February, 1778, without success. Stiffer blows than those at Saratoga were necessary to bring about a change of ministry in London.

See Franklin's letters: to James Hutton, Feb. 1, 1778; to David Hartley, Feb. 12, Feb. 26, 1778; to William Pulteney, Mar. 30, 1778; Wharton, II, 483, 492, 504, 527. The agent sent by Franklin to London was Jonathan Loring Austin, the courier by whom Congress had sent to the Commission the news of Saratoga. He kept a journal which was used by the E. E. Hales when preparing their *Franklin in France;* and a highly imaginative memoir, based on his statements to his family, was published shortly after his death, in the *Boston Monthly Magazine,* for July, 1826. David Hartley's mission to Paris is described in G. H. Guttridge's *David Hartley, M. P., an Advocate of Conciliation, 1774–1783* (Berkeley, California, 1926), pp. 280–287.

[21] After the passage of the North bills, William Eden, mainspring of the new peace commission to America, made a last vain attempt to detach Franklin from the dreaded new alliance. Some new proposals, the exact nature of which remains unknown, for Franklin had them burned, were again brought to Paris

portune decision for an American alliance. Had he delayed his negotiations with the American deputies a few weeks longer, the Colonies might conceivably have remained within the British Empire as a self-governing dominion, and in that case how different would have been—for better or worse—the international history of the nineteenth and twentieth centuries.

The American war had spread to Europe. France had restored the balance of power by recognizing the existence of a sovereign state in the New World. What would be the attitude of the other powers of the Old World?

by a British "negotiator"—presumably Wentworth—with hopes that the Carlisle Commission might enhance its chance of success by carrying across the Atlantic Franklin's own approval of the new conciliatory measures. See that portion of Silas Deane's Memorial which was first printed in 1928 (together with a hitherto unprinted letter of Franklin of April 7, 1778, relating to the proposals) by C. M. Andrews, in Yale University Library *Gazette*, II, 53–68.

CHAPTER VI

Austria and Spain in 1778

When France decided, in December, 1777, to intervene in the American war without the concurrence of Spain, if need be, the horizon of Europe to the east seemed clear and quiet. The American policy of Vergennes and his increasingly adventurous attitude in the face of England had been possible because the lull in European affairs gave him some assurance against Continental disasters, like those suffered during the Seven Years' War. Spain and Austria were defensive allies of France. Russia, a possible factor in any combination against France's Austrian ally, was occupied in disputes with the Turks over the treaty of Kutschuck-Kanairdji of 1774. The powers of central Europe were digesting tranquilly the stolen fruits of the first Polish partition. The King of Prussia, enjoying a quiet and secure old age after the addition of Austrian and Polish territory, was not ready to make war on his ancient enemy, especially for the sake of relieving England, which had deserted him in the negotiations of 1763. But any involvement of Austria with Frederick the Great, her old-time foe, would be certain to test the resolution of Vergennes's new American policy.

A test was at hand, on the eve of the signature of the American alliance. The European calm was suddenly broken by an aggressive move on the part of Austria, which caused Frederick the Great to stir from his peaceful repose. One day, or perhaps two [1]

---

[1] La Luzerne, French Minister at München, wrote to Vergennes of Maximilian's death by a special messenger who left at 7 P. M., December 30, 1777. The date of the receipt of his despatch is not endorsed, but it could hardly have taken more time in transit than La Luzerne's despatch of January 4, 1778, received January 10. Archives Affaires Etrangères, *Correspondance Politique, Bavière,* CLX, 440, and CLXI, 9. Vergennes was also apprised of Maximilian's death by a letter from the Comtesse de Bavière dated January 5, 1778. *Ibid.,* CLXI, 23. Aranda's No. 1209 to Floridablanca, dated Paris, January 5, 1778, mentions Maximilian's death and speculates on it. Yela, *op. cit.,* I, 271. It would seem

days, before the French King and Ministry finally decided, in the meeting of the Royal Council of January 7, 1778, to promise to the United States an alliance as well as the already promised recognition of independence, news reached Paris of the death (December 30, 1777), of Maximilian Joseph, Elector of Bavaria, without an immediate heir. The event threatened to upset the balance of power by adding arbitrarily one of the largest states in central Europe to the hereditary possessions of the Austrian Hapsburgs. This happening, opening vistas of aggrandizement, already calculated in Vienna and nervously measured by the rest of Europe, offered to Vergennes a last warning to pause before he actually signed the American alliance. Would he prefer the opportunity of crippling Great Britain to the traditional Bourbon policy of profiting by central European disturbances to secure territorial additions for France in Belgium? Would he hesitate to throw down the gauge to England when certain that France's ally, Austria, would be speedily involved in another war with Prussia and might call for assistance?

With France and Great Britain apparently on the verge of war, and Russia somewhat anxious over the Eastern Question, Emperor Joseph II felt that Frederick the Great was helpless to prevent Austria from seizing the possessions of the late Maximilian Joseph, even as Frederick once seized Silesia from Joseph's mother. The Imperial armies had been reformed since 1763 and brought to a nominal parity with those of Prussia. Despite the peaceful predilections and anxiety of his mother, Maria-Theresa, the young Hapsburg ruler felt himself ready to confront the greatest military genius of Europe. He quickly resolved to take Bavaria to compensate Austria for the loss of Silesia. With his troops approaching the Bavarian frontier, Joseph II, four days after the Elector's death, prevailed on the Elector Palatine, Karl

that Vergennes had time to meditate on the significance of this news before taking the final decisive step on January 8, 1778. "The Elector of Bavaria died, at the end of December, 1777, at the very moment when the Count de Vergennes was working to establish the basis of his new system, which the independence of America was about to introduce into Europe." Biographical Memoir on Vergennes, 1788, in Archives Affaires Etrangères, *Mémoires et Documents, France,* Vol. 584. This is a review of Vergennes's diplomacy as Foreign Minister, of no value for the biographer, but has a few accurate generalizations, such as this one.

Theodor, the legal heir of Maximilian Joseph, to sign a partition treaty which recognized Karl's succession at the price of ceding to Joseph II the greater part of Bavaria. Austrian troops immediately occupied the newly ceded parts and more. To undo this Frederick the Great promptly mobilized his armies. The ravisher of Silesia assumed the novel rôle of guarantor of the rights of the small German states and of the Law of the Empire, and Joseph II, ruler of a ravished state, became himself ravisher. Austria promptly appealed to France for 20,000 troops, under the terms of the alliance of 1756, in case war with Prussia should occur. There was some hope in England that the outbreak of a Continental war might paralyze France.[2] Such were Chatham's last thoughts.[3]

Had Vergennes preferred Flanders to the abasement of Britain, we may presume that he still had hours enough to hold France back from an American alliance, after he received news of the Elector's death. In the Royal Council of January 7, 1778, he did not hesitate. After the American treaties were signed on February 6, Prussia and Austria each made tempting offers to France of territorial compensation in the Austrian Netherlands, if she would take part on one side or the other in the Bavarian Succession War. Only ten months previously [4] Vergennes had seriously considered seeking such compensation, when Austria had opened overtures for a prearrangement of the Bavarian Succession. Now it was too late. The unhesitating decision with which this statesman and his court rejected both Continental overtures shows the deadly earnestness with which he had decided on a war of revenge against Great Britain. There was to be no repetition of the blunders of the Seven Years' War,[5] not

[2] "Perhaps the Elector of Bavaria's death may be of use to us by setting the gentlemen upon the Continent at variance." Duke of Marlborough to Wm. Eden, January 8, 1778 (Stevens, *Facsimiles*, No. 350).

[3] L. von Ranke, *Die deutschen Mächte und der Fürstenbund* (Leipzig, 1871), I, 28.

[4] "On the continuation of overtures made by the Court of Vienna relative to the Bavarian Succession Question," Archives Affaires Etrangères, *Correspondance Politique, Autriche*, Vol. 331, fol. 278–295.

[5] Without space to elaborate upon the combination of circumstances from

even for the sake of that Flanders for which Louis XIV had fought four bloody wars in vain.

After some weeks of diplomatic sparring between the two states, accompanied by feverish military preparations, a bloodless war of maneuver and stalemate took place in Bohemia during the summer of 1778, while France and Great Britain were drifting into hostilities on the seas. When the armies went into winter quarters military activities ceased. While the two belligerents, Austria and Prussia, were appealing to France for support against each other, Vergennes was ardently negotiating with Spain to join the maritime war against Great Britain.

It was for France's interest to keep the Continent as quiet as possible while the decisive struggle with England was being finished on the sea. Furthermore, the main object of her diplomacy now lay at Madrid, and it was against traditional French policy

December 30, 1777, to the end of March, 1778, it may be sufficiently instructive to note the following dates:

December 30, 1777, death of Maximilian Joseph.

January 5 (at latest), 1778, Maximilian's death known at Paris.

January 7, 1778, Royal Council decides for alliance with United States.

February 6, 1778, Franco-American treaties signed.

March 6, 1778, Prussian Ambassador at Paris reads to Vergennes a letter just received from Frederick the Great setting forth offer of Prussian alliance (see Archives Affaires Etrangères, *Correspondance Politique, Autriche*, 334, fol. 320).

March 10, 1778, Vergennes sends word to Austria that France will remain neutral in any Austro-Prussian war resulting from the occupation of Bavaria (though, for the sake of France's ally Austria, Vergennes refused to give to Frederick the Great assurances of neutrality).

March 13, 1778, Vergennes instructs French Ambassador at London to hand to the British Court a copy of the Franco-American treaty of commerce and amity.

March 23, 1778, Austrian Ambassador at Versailles delivers project of territorial exchange to Vergennes (see *ibid.*, fol. 379). Though this did not offer outright any compensation to France, it was easy enough for any one intimate with previous Franco-Austrian conversations to read between the lines, as did the French Ambassador at Vienna (Breteuil to Vergennes, March 18, 1778, *ibid.*, fol. 379).

March 27, 1778, Vergennes informs Montmorin that secret orders are being issued to Admiral d'Estaing to take the Toulon fleet to America with Conrad Alexandre Gérard on board as Minister to the United States (Doniol, III, 6).

March 29, 1778, instructions for first French Minister to the United States approved by the Royal Council (*ibid.*, p. 157).

to tolerate a Hapsburg preponderance in central Europe, particularly through acquisition of a large state close to France's northeastern frontier. Vergennes therefore replied to the Austrian demands by a proposal of mediation. Before the proposal was answered, Frederick's ally, Catherine the Great of Russia, who had been able to arrange a settlement with the Turks, thanks to the relief of active French diplomacy at Constantinople, stepped in and demanded that Austria accept a mediation based on the evacuation of most of the occupied Bavarian territory, retaining a small contiguous part. To support this, Catherine mobilized 30,000 men in Galicia and made their commander, Prince Repnin, her representative in the mediation. Joseph II capitulated. The terms of the ensuing peace of Teschen (May 13, 1779, a month after the Franco-Spanish treaty of Aranjuez of April 12), under Franco-Russian mediation, were written by Vergennes but pushed home by the threat of Russian bayonets.

The mediation at Teschen restored the traditional position of France as the arbiter of European affairs. It was the first yield of Vergennes's diplomacy. It removed the Austrian menace. It gave to Catherine the Great the satisfaction of appearing as the protector of Germany and laid the foundations of that historical rapprochement between France and Russia, and between France and Prussia,[6] which was soon to be such a valuable adjunct to Vergennes's contemporary project of encouraging a combination of armed neutrals against British sea power. It also quickened the feeling of Joseph II against his French ally and presently stimulated him "to return the favor," that is, to retaliate by participating with Russia in an attempt at mediation in the war between England and the Bourbon monarchies. The connection

---

[6] Frederick II's concern at the possible attitude of France as Austria's ally, in case of the Bavarian succession question being precipitated, made him welcome the American Revolution as a means of occupying France with England on the seas. This was the real reason for his expressions of sympathy for the American revolutionists. For Franco-Prussian conversations before the Elector's death, see Doniol, III, 88–104. There are three excellent monographs on the Bavarian succession: Adolf Unzer, *Der Friede von Teschen* (Kiel, 1903); Harold W. V. Temperley, *Frederick the Great and Kaiser Joseph* (London, 1915); P. Oursel, *La diplomatie de la France sous Louis XVI; succession de Bavière et paix de Teschen* (Paris, 1921). See also E. F. S. Hanfstaengel, *Amerika und Europa von Marlborough bis Mirabeau* (Munich, 1930).

of the question of the Bavarian Succession with the diplomatic history of the United States will appear when we observe the course of French diplomacy with other states of Europe, especially Spain and the Armed Neutrals, and when we consider the peace settlement of 1782–1783.

The primary purpose of French policy after the American alliance was to get Spain into that alliance, or at least into the war against Great Britain, and to line up the neutrals of Europe in opposition to British maritime principles. It was achieved only with much difficulty by a combination of fortuitous circumstances and matchless skill on the part of the French Foreign Minister, but it was achieved, and the diplomatic isolation of Great Britain was one of the factors which helped to win the war, much as one may minimize the eventual military efforts of the Spanish and finally of the Dutch.

The policy of Spain, under the guidance of the astute Floridablanca, was not to be set by the necessities of her ally. France had rushed into the American treaties without waiting for Spain's concurrence. This precipitate action wounded Spanish pride and prestige and created actual distrust. Much less was Spain to be moved by the exigencies of the cause of American independence, to which the rulers of that monarchy were averse for obvious reasons.[7] Nor was Spain willing to go to war merely to cripple Great Britain by ensuring the independence of the United States.

As Floridablanca saw the situation in January, 1778, when notified of the French decision, the interests of Spain and of France in any war with Great Britain were very different. Spain, with her vast overseas possessions, had far more to risk than a few small sugar islands. At that moment, in addition to the great colonial empire, Spain incidentally had exposed on the seas such hostages to fate as the expedition of General Cevallos, returning home after having chastised the Portuguese on the Rio Plata, and the annual treasure fleet on its way to the Peninsula

---

[7] Montmorin's reports to Vergennes show sufficiently the hostility of Floridablanca and the Spanish King and Ministry to any consummation of American independence, particularly to Spanish recognition of it before British acknowledgment. See Doniol, *passim*, for example, III, 20, 575–576, 753; and Corwin, *French Policy and the American Alliance, op. cit.*, pp. 176–198.

from Vera Cruz. France might enrich herself by such American commerce as could be snatched from England and by valuable prizes of merchant shipping, but Spain had no desire to expand her commerce nor augment her widespread colonial possessions. According to French arguments, what Spain might get from a successful war was the protection of her American colonies in case of Anglo-American reconciliation, and the abasement of British sea power. This failed to impress Floridablanca. He never seriously believed in any such danger. As for the abasement of British sea power, he pointed out that the Colonies themselves had been able to bring Britain to such prostration as to ask for peace and (as he believed at that moment) to offer independence —why then did the insurgents need Spain's alliance? He wrote to Aranda, his plenipotentiary at Paris, who was pleading ardently for Spain's entrance in order to be in at the killing: "Our Court has to think how to fend off insults on its vast possessions in the Indies by destining adequate defensive forces for those places, and it has to be very circumspect until the return of the *flota* and of General Cevallos's expedition, and until it has in those seas the forces referred to. . . ." After the headlong action of France in December, 1777, Floridablanca felt that Spain could not implicitly rely on French constancy; for example, French embarrassment in Europe over such a matter as the recent Bavarian Succession question might serve as an excuse to withdraw from the American venture, after Spain might be committed to it.[8] The Spanish Ministry unanimously decided against war with Great Britain, and that power was informed that Spain had had no share in France's recent decision.[9] Under the circumstances, Vergennes never quite dared to demand the entrance of Spain as an obligation under the defensive Family Compact. The significance of this was not lost on the Spanish Foreign Minister.

[8] Floridablanca to Aranda, January 13, 1778, Yela, *op. cit.*, II, 188–195. In arguing against war with Great Britain in 1776 when Spain was eager for it, for the conquest of Portugal, Vergennes had, at his own convenience, cited such a thing as the possible precipitation of the Bavarian question, as a reason for French abstinence. See *ibid.*

[9] *Ibid.*, I, 269–304.

As weeks and months went on, as France became ever a more eager suppliant for Spain's help, as Vergennes grew more and more ready to make specific offers—Minorca, Florida, a share in the fisheries of Newfoundland, ejection of the English from Honduras, even the reconquest of Jamaica—Floridablanca calmly fixed in his own mind Spain's price: the recovery of Gibraltar. He would get this from one belligerent or the other. That tremendous citadel thus became a vital factor in the diplomacy of the American Revolution.

Floridablanca wanted Gibraltar from England as the price of neutrality. If he could get the results of war without war, so much the greater would be the measure of his statesmanship; but Gibraltar Spain wanted, and if her Minister could not get it peaceably, he was willing to go to war as France's ally if there were a reasonable chance of placing the Spanish flag again upon that giant guardian rock. This explains Spain's part in the diplomacy and in the military operations of the American Revolution; Florida and the smaller temptations beyond the seas, so quickly and eagerly offered by Vergennes, were not enough. Gibraltar must be recovered, by diplomacy or by war, and without recognition of American independence unless that were first acknowledged by Great Britain. In Spain the cause of the insurrectionists across the seas stirred no sympathy.[10]

Spain guardedly sounded the British Ministry, during the year 1778, as to rewards for neutrality. England, quite content with Spain's quiescence and only glad to keep her at peace, refused to make definite offers, and Floridablanca, foreseeing that whichever way the war ended he was unlikely to get the desired prize if he did not intervene, urged with increasing emphasis the mediation of Spain. If Great Britain could not be frightened into paying Gibraltar for continuing Spanish neutrality, Floridablanca could not get the fortress unless his nation went to war for it. But Spain could scarcely fall on the English for refusing to cede the place when asked. There must be a decent pretext. The entry of Spain into the war must appear to be in the interests of peace

[10] "The war against England had in France almost the atmosphere of popularity, something which did not exist in Spain." *Ibid.*, I, 342.

and of self-defense; therefore let a mediation be offered in terms calculated to be surely unacceptable. Spain could meanwhile arrange her terms with France, and after refusal of the mediation by Great Britain she could enter the war and get what she wanted : that Gibraltar which had been wrested from her at the beginning of the century.

Hardly were the terms of the Franco-American treaties known in Madrid than the Spanish project for mediation was formulated—as early as April, 1778, before hostilities had broken out between France and Great Britain. Escarano, chargé d'affaires at the Spanish embassy in London, suggested to Lord Stormont, May 9, that the cession of Gibraltar might be worth while to avoid a disastrous war. Mansfield replied that Gibraltar was of great importance to England, and that he was not sure that anybody could prevent a war now that things had gone so far. A few weeks later open hostilities commenced with France. Floridablanca now transferred from Lisbon to London the Count of Almodóvar as a new ambassador to press the project of mediation, to suggest that Great Britain ought to be willing to pay and pay well for Spain's neutrality, and to listen to "specific positive offers and the means of guaranteeing them." Without making a formal proposal, Almodóvar hinted to the British Ministry that Great Britain might make an offer, Gibraltar for instance. The correspondence of Floridablanca with his ambassador, as laid open by the Spanish historian Dánvila, leaves no doubt as to what this servant of Charles III was trying to get.

"The illusion of that [British] Ministry is great if it thinks to involve France in the affairs of Germany," wrote Floridablanca to Almodóvar, August 25, 1778. "I repeat that they should not lose time if they wish us to be friends." The ambassador was instructed to intimate to the British Government that if a peace settlement were not made soon, Spain feared she might be obliged to fulfil her obligations to France; and to say that Spain, while glad to be of service in promoting peace, if requested by the British Government and nation, was not herself asking nor proposing to do so. "They must know," stated Floridablanca in

a covering confidential note, "that what we do not get by negotiation we know how to get with a club. Neutrality is a noose
which they hold out to Your Excellency, and only when it is
accompanied by specific positive offers and means of guaranteeing
them, can we begin to think about it." After having offered mediation, September 29, an offer which met with no satisfactory
response, he instructed Almodóvar to sound the Court of London
as to Spain's interests. Almodóvar reported confidentially, December 29, 1778, on interviews with Weymouth, the Secretary of
State for Foreign Affairs. The Spaniard had suggested the cession of Gibraltar and Minorca. Weymouth replied that, for such,
Spain's friendship must be fixed in *very solid terms*. Almodóvar
did not feel empowered to respond further to this suggestion.[11]
"The King does not sell his favor or mediation," the ascetic
Murcian then instructed Almodóvar, "and he might say drily
that all the grievances which we have to claim and all our rights
and interests are reduced to safeguarding the treaties and fulfilling that of Paris. If that Court thinks we might be entitled to
some favor, you already know the points on which this can be
explained; that Your Excellency has signified them, the principal
being *that pile of stones of Gibraltar,* which is only a matter of
expense and care to them, disturbing to us, and an impediment
to permanent friendship." [12]

England would not offer Gibraltar nor anything else for Spanish neutrality. Aranda, the ambassador at Paris, reported in
February, 1779, that the principal points of dispute between
Prussia and Austria had been settled, and that peace seemed
certain in Germany. Cevallos's transports were long since home,
and the treasure fleet was safe in Spanish peninsular ports.[13] On
April 3, 1779, Floridablanca dispatched to Great Britain an ultimatum in the form of terms of mediation. Before it could be
answered, the Convention of Aranjuez had been signed between

[11] See Manuel Dánvila y Collado, *Reinado de Carlos III,* 6 vols. (Madrid,
1893–1896), V, 10, 17, 19–23, 33–34.
[12] *Ibid.,* V, 39. Italics mine.
[13] They began to arrive in July and August, 1778. Doniol, III, 492–493.

Spain and France, April 12, and ratified at Versailles, April 28, providing for Spain's entrance into the war in case England should refuse the terms of Charles III's final offer, so studiously composed as to be unacceptable.

CHAPTER VII

THE FRANCO-SPANISH ALLIANCE

The Spanish ultimatum to Great Britain marks the culmination of a train of diplomatic conversations and notes during the year 1778 and the early months of 1779. Great Britain had refused to listen to peace, as long as France retained in America an expeditionary force and as long as any power by mediation tried to adjust the colonial and purely domestic affairs of the British Empire. It was therefore evident that, should Spain make this last point a condition of mediation, England would not accept. France, on her part being bound by the alliance with the United States, was loath to discuss peace except on the terms of American independence, secured through an actual recognition by a treaty of peace or, more imperfectly, through a long-time truce suggested by Spain (a possibility in which, according to Vergennes,[1] Franklin acquiesced) on the model of the truce that ended the wars of the Dutch Rebellion.[2] Vergennes, however, was willing to allow the Americans to negotiate a separate treaty with Great Britain, so long as it went hand in hand with the main negotiations and was contingent upon them; this might have overcome British scruples at the presence of a third party.[3]

The Spanish ultimatum was in the form of a note, dated April 3, 1779, to the British Ambassador at Madrid, Lord Grantham, for delivery to his Court, in reply to a previous note of his, answering Spanish requests for British peace terms. In London,

[1] Vergennes to Gérard, Dec. 25, 1778, Doniol, III, 613. Doniol states (*ibid.*, III, 616, note 1) that Wharton assured him that nothing in Franklin's printed works nor his papers refers to this proposed truce of 1778.

[2] Article VIII of the Franco-American Alliance: "Neither of the two Parties shall conclude either Truce or Peace with Great Brittain, without the formal consent of the other first obtain'd; and they mutually engage not to lay down their arms, until the Independence of the united states shall have been formally or tacitly assured by the Treaty or Treaties that shall terminate the War."

[3] Vergennes to Gérard, Dec. 25, 1778, *op. cit.*

Almodóvar was instructed to wait a few days, even eight or ten, for a satisfactory answer, following the arrival of the note at the British capital.[4] These were the terms: a suspension of arms indefinitely between Great Britain and France, not to be ruptured without one year's notice by either party; mutual disarmament, within one month in Europe, within four months in America, within eight or twelve months in Africa and Asia. Plenipotentiaries of both belligerent courts were to meet at a peace conference, under the mediation of Spain, with Madrid suggested for the seat of conference. The King of Great Britain, *at the intervention and mediation of the King of Spain,* was to grant a separate suspension of arms to the "American Colonies," engaging *to the King of Spain* to observe the terms of the suspension, and promising not to break it without a year's notice in advance to the King of Spain, that this monarch might inform the same "American Provinces" about it. A mutual disarmament similar to that between France and Great Britain should take place. The boundaries of the "parties" were to be fixed on the basis of territory occupied by each at the suspension of arms. "To settle the different objects and others relating to the solidity of the said suspension and the effects it is to produce while it lasts, one or more commissioners from the Colonies shall repair to Madrid, and His Britannic Majesty will send his own, under the mediation of the King (if it is necessary) to settle the above articles, and during this time the Colonies are to be treated as independent in fact."

In proposing that the American "Colonies" be recognized as independent *de facto,* during the time of the negotiations, Spain was by no means inconsistently encouraging the recognition of the independence of the *United States.* Floridablanca was merely taking a leaf from the text of the English instructions to the Carlisle Peace Commission of the previous year. Under authority

----

[4] "In a word, they want to make a good negotiation and they are insulting the mediator, without showing the least gratitude to the one who can save them something. If they want to make war and wish His Majesty to withdraw his mediation, let them say so clearly and not treat us like children." Confidential note of Floridablanca to Almodóvar, Madrid, April 3, 1779, covering a copy of the ultimatum; cited by Dánvila, *op. cit.,* V, 49.

of an act of Parliament those instructions had enabled British commissioners to treat with representatives of the Colonies as independent *de facto* during the negotiations;—but the instrument with which it was proposed to seal the negotiations was carefully calculated to extinguish effectively any semblance of independence.[5]

The Spanish mediation ultimatum, which was an ultimatum only to Great Britain though the text was sent also to France, was the result of British refusal to make to Spain the desired "specific positive offers and means of guaranteeing them." Carefully couched to avoid any recognition of American independence even by implication, with the stipulation of the duration of *de facto* independence most ambiguously written, it circumvented Spanish aversion to actual independence and offered to Great Britain the possibility of peace by compromise, which at that moment would have left George III in possession of New York and Long Island, Rhode Island, a large part of Georgia, and an indeterminate area of the Northwest. If accepted and enforced, it would have left the American question uncertain and unsettled under a vague truce guaranteed by a power unfriendly to American independence and willing to barter about it with Great Britain for non-American equivalents. It would have left British troops in the most strategic parts of the United States. In short, it would have knifed the liberty of the newborn nation. More than that, the Spanish ultimatum was so written that it gave George III, had he so chosen, the opportunity of pushing France into an ugly dilemma: if the British King had accepted the mediation—and by accepting it, he would have found a solution of the war infinitely better for the Empire than the final settlement—France would then have been required either to accept also, or to reject. If she accepted—and there is no indication that Vergennes would then have accepted a truce which left British troops

[5] The relevant part of the ultimatum is printed by Doniol, III, 850–851, and the complete text in pamphlet form by the *Imprenta Real de la Gazeta,* in Madrid, 1779, a copy of which is in the British Record Office, *State Papers, Foreign,* 94/254. The instructions to the Carlisle Peace Commission are printed in S. E. Morison's documentary publication, *Sources and Documents Illustrating the American Revolution, 1764–1788* (Oxford, 1923), pp. 186–203.

in occupation of indubitable portions of several of the American States [6]—the Franco-American alliance would have broken down, a desirable consummation for British diplomacy. If France had rejected the Spanish ultimatum after Great Britain had accepted its terms, the Family Compact would have been pried apart. "Very fortunately" (the words are Vergennes's) the stony obstinacy of the British monarch spared the United States this real danger. George III's Ministry refused to participate in any peace conference which allowed even a *de facto* independent status to the "Colonies" while negotiating. Lord Weymouth, the Foreign Secretary, told Almodóvar that "Spain had worked too ambitiously, claiming Gibraltar and Minorca as rewards for the negotiation of peace." [7]

The terms of the secret Franco-Spanish Convention of Aranjuez, which had meanwhile been ratified, provided that in case Great Britain should refuse the Spanish peace terms, Spain should enter into the war against England and make common cause, at a time and in such manner as should be agreed upon (by diplomatic exchanges this had already been fixed for the second week in May). Professing to put in execution Article XVI of the Family Compact,[8] they agreed to concert military and naval operations, already being worked out, for the joint prosecution of the war, particularly contemplating a descent on the island of England. They agreed that neither ally should entertain peace overtures from the enemy without communicating them to the other; any treaty or agreement with the enemy must be by common consent, and no peace nor suspension of hostilities should occur until Gibraltar should have been restored to Spain and the

[6] He bitterly protested to Floridablanca [i.e., by Montmorin] against the terms. See Corwin, *French Policy and the American Alliance, op. cit.,* p. 215, who gives reference to Doniol; and V. Urtasún, *História diplomática de América,* II, 276.

[7] Dánvila, *op. cit.,* V, 55–56. He professed, however, to be willing to discuss other mediation terms.

[8] This article stipulated that when the two powers should find themselves at war with the same enemy or enemies (instead of only one power first being attacked and its family ally coming to its aid with stipulated forces), the obligation of stipulated amounts of naval and military forces should cease and both allies should make war jointly, agreeing by special conventions on the degree of mutual assistance.

old treaty provisions relative to the French port of Dunkerque should have been removed; or in default of that objective, something else which the King of France might desire. In addition to these *sine qua non* of peace, the allies agreed to use all their efforts to secure from the enemy: for Spain (in addition to Gibraltar) the possession of the river and fort of Mobile, Florida; expulsion of the English from the Bay of Honduras and execution of the prohibitions relative thereto stipulated by the treaty of Paris of 1763 to prevent any establishment in that Bay or in other Spanish territories[9]; revocation of the privilege to British subjects to cut wood on the Campeche coast; and finally the restitution of Minorca; for France (in addition to the restoration of Dunkerque) the expulsion of the English from Newfoundland; absolute and unlimited liberty to trade with the East Indies and to acquire and fortify factories there; recovery of Senegal, with full liberty to trade on the coasts of Africa, outside of the English factories; irrevocable possession of the Island of Dominica; and the abolition or the full execution of the treaty of commerce between Great Britain and France at Utrecht, in 1713. In case France should gain possession of Newfoundland, Spanish subjects were to be admitted to the fisheries there; and in case the British should be ejected from the Campeche coast, French subjects were to be allowed a share in the woodcutting at that place.

Since France was already pledged to another ally not to make peace until the absolute and unlimited independence of the United States should be established, either formally or tacitly, it is enlightening to note the article of the Convention of Aranjuez which referred to the United States. Vergennes had tried in vain to insert the following from his own draft: "The independence

[9] Article XVII of the treaty of Paris of 1763 provided for the demolition of fortifications erected by British subjects "in the Bay of Honduras and other places of the territory of Spain in that part of the world" and for undisturbed continuance by British subjects "cutting, loading and carrying away logwood," who might for that purpose unrestrictedly occupy the "houses and magazines which are necessary for them, for their families, and for their effects" with "the full enjoyment of those advantages and powers, on the Spanish Coast and territories, as above stipulated." The loose phraseology of this article opened up possibilities of endless dispute and friction.

of the United States of North America being the essential basis of the engagements which His Most Christian Majesty has contracted with them, the two contracting parties mutually engage not to lay down their arms until that independence shall have been recognized by the crown of England." Floridablanca refused it, and a banal formula, a meaningless pious wish, was finally adopted.[10] Vergennes's failure to insert his own article is highly significant. In his anxiety to get Spain into the war, he had been obliged to make concessions which were certainly not violations of the Franco-American treaty, but which constituted what Professor Corwin calls a "flat incompatibility, technically, at least" with that earlier alliance. "Thus was the purpose of the war, in which the United States were already bound to remain to the end, altered and enlarged, not only without their consent, but without their knowledge." [11] This discerning authority, noting the concessions which Vergennes successively made to get Spain into the war, sees the French alliance, that indispensable instrument of American diplomacy, that life-saving alliance which procured American independence itself, as an example of the way in which even the most useful of alliances entangled the nation in purely European questions.

Vergennes had been hard pressed. Faced with Spanish requirements, he had finally instructed his ambassador at Madrid, Montmorin, to make any alterations which might be necessary in the French draft of the Convention. In effect this presented a blank check. Floridablanca quickly wrote in the word *Gibraltar*. Montmorin's despatch to Vergennes, announcing the Spanish decision to make war on Great Britain, contained this prophetic observation: "We ought however not to conceal from ourselves, Monsieur, how little interest Spain takes in the United States of America; we shall certainly have evidence of this in the course of the war, and especially when it comes to negotiating peace." [12]

[10] The French text of the Convention of Aranjuez, is printed, in parallel columns with the original French draft, by Doniol, III, 803–810. An English translation is printed in the appendix to Vol. I of *American Secretaries of State and Their Diplomacy*.

[11] Corwin, *op. cit.*, p. 205.

[12] Doniol, III, 771.

At the beginning Montmorin had warned Vergennes that it might be easier to get Spain in, for the sake of Gibraltar, Florida, and so forth, than to get her out of the war.[13]

Spain declared war on Great Britain, June 21, 1779,[14] after the French and Spanish fleets had already been operating together for several weeks.

Spain's entrance into the war, so desired by the United States and by France, now brought into the general diplomatic field her particular interests. Gibraltar was a purely European interest which nevertheless was to become a great factor in the diplomacy of the peace; there soon cropped up other interests of Spain in North America, more directly affecting the new republic. With these questions France could not help being concerned. She had now separate allies on either hand pulling in opposite directions, and was anxious to keep both effectively at work against Great Britain.

When the insurrection in America commenced in 1775 both France and Spain, independently, sent observers and emissaries to the scene. The mission of Bonvouloir, sent out by Vergennes, has already been noted. In February, 1776, Josef de Gálvez, Minister of the Indies, sent orders from Madrid to the Governor of Havana to dispatch secret agents to Pensacola, Florida, Jamaica, and other British colonies to report on the course of events, particularly the possibility of any accommodations between the Colonies and the mother country. The first agent destined to the revolted Colonies never reached them, because the packet on which he embarked from Havana was taken by a British frigate. There are traces of other emissaries having been sent from New Orleans and Havana with the purpose of giving the Spanish Ministry its own independent information about what was happening.[15]

It was next agreed between the two courts that each should send an agent to the Colonies, unaccredited officially. The French

[13] Doniol, III, 20.
[14] Dánvila, *op. cit.*, V, 66.
[15] For these agents see Yela, I, 67–70; and Kathryn Abbey, "Efforts of Spain to Maintain Sources of Information in the British Colonies before 1779," in *Miss. Vall. Hist. Rev.*, XV (1929), 56–68.

observer, Holker,[16] departed in November, 1777, but his activities were soon supplanted by French recognition of American independence and the appearance at Philadelphia of an accredited French Minister. The Spanish Minister of the Indies, Josef de Gálvez, on August 26, 1777, instructed the Governor of Havana to send two observers to the North American Colonies of England, one to remain at the principal seat of military operations, near some British or American general, the other to place himself at the seat of Congress.[17]

For the latter mission Don Juan de Miralles was appointed, a Cuban merchant and slave-trader of upwards of sixty years of age, who left Havana, December 31, 1777, and put in at Charleston, South Carolina, on January 9, 1778, under appearance of having been forced in by stress of weather.[18] He remained in the United States as an "observer" without diplomatic functions, but treated with all the ceremonious respect of a minister, until he died at General Washington's camp on April 28, 1780. He was

[16] Doniol, II, 615, 616; III, 172, 182. Holker became the first French consul in the United States. His original papers are now in the possession of the Library of Congress.

[17] Royal Order, Josef de Gálvez to the Governor of Havana (Navarro), San Ildefonso, Aug. 26, 1777, Archivo de las Indias, *Audiencia de Santo Domingo,* 81-4-36, No. 121.

[18] The above cited order of Aug. 26, 1777, of J. de Gálvez to Navarro, declared that the principal object of the Commission was that of furnishing information as to the state and progress of the war, particularly of any design against the American possessions of Spain or France; and to watch for any sign of accommodation between the two hostile parties "suggesting to the insurgents that whatever adjustment they might make without the protection or guaranty of the great powers, like France or Spain, would remain exposed to rupture, producing fatal consequences for the said Colonies."

Navarro's instructions to Miralles are dated Havana, Dec. 17, 1777, repeating the above, and laying down details for his accidental appearance, mode of transmission of despatches, etc. The despatches of Miralles to Navarro, with summaries of these to J. de Gálvez, and correspondence between Gálvez and Navarro in regard to Miralles's mission are to be found in Archivo de las Indias, *Papeles de Cuba, leg.* 1281, 1283, 1290 and 1301. (See R. R. Hill's *Descriptive Catalog . . . Papeles Procedentes de Cuba;* and *Indiferente General,* 146-3-11.) Other correspondence, including duplicates, may be found in Archivo Histórico Nacional at Madrid. Typed transcripts of most of this Sevilla material exist in the Library of Congress. I am indebted to Mr. Ramón Iglesia Parga of Madrid for information regarding Miralles. For papers of the other observer, de la Puente, who was sent at the same time from Cuba to St. Augustine, see *Papeles de Cuba* (Hill, *ibid.*) *leg.* 1290, 1301. See also Abbey, *op. cit.*

succeeded by his youthful secretary, Francisco Rendón, whose functions continued until the end of the war.[19] Thus, side by side with the regularly accredited French diplomatic representative, there was in Philadelphia during the Revolution a Spanish representative who, though he personally desired appointment as minister and was personally treated with all the deference shown to a minister, was obliged to refrain from any official function or any implication of recognition of the independence of the United States. It was from the reports to Gálvez of Miralles and Rendón, and other lesser agents, that Floridablanca's information about American affairs was gathered. This activity of these men, and the vital subjects concerned, namely, the western boundary to the United States and the question of the navigation of the river Mississippi, will presently occupy our attention, but we may first notice certain other indirect contacts between Spain and the United States, which developed out of the Spanish program of assisting the American insurrectionists with money and material in order to weaken both Great Britain and the United States.

The gift of a million *livres* by Charles III to Louis XVI in 1776 which was used, with an additional French million, for the purpose of financing Beaumarchais, was all that was given in joint clandestine operations with France. At that time Grimaldi had agreed with Vergennes that the Spanish Court would share all expenses which this sort of secret succor might entail. News of these ministrations was soon discovered by the British, and Floridablanca changed the channel of Spanish assistance. An opportune occasion for so doing was presented by the appearance at New Orleans early in September, 1776, of one George Gibson, with a commission from Major-General Charles Lee who styled himself as "second in command" of the American army. Gibson solicited a direct commercial intercourse with Spanish possessions, together with the assistance of Spain in securing the independence of the United States. He put two questions to the Governor of Louisiana: whether the acquisition of the city and port of Pensacola would be an agreeable object to the King of Spain, and

[19] For Rendón's papers see *Papeles de Cuba, leg.*, 1281, 1282, 1283, 1291, 1319, 1354 (Hill, *ibid.*), transcripts of most of which exist in the Library of Congress.

if so, would His Majesty deign to accept them from the United States? Gibson wanted answers to these in order that the United States might take the next step: to send their most eminent citizen to seek the protection of the King.

The answer of the Spanish Court was to indicate to the "Colonists," "with the greatest caution and secrecy that the King would like to see them have what they sought—the capture of Pensacola—and that *when their independence should be assured* he will treat with them for the delivery, as they promised, of Pensacola to Spain." [20] This was followed in January and February, 1777, by the shipment of military supplies from Spain to New Orleans and the transfer of a surplus of powder from the factory in Mexico. The following August, Bernardo de Gálvez, then Governor of Louisiana and nephew of the minister, sent word to the American Congress that he had in his possession the supplies which had been requested. Congress responded by sending a small force under Major Willing, supported by Oliver Pollock, who had become American agent at New Orleans and at Havana, to secure the supplies and capture the British settlements on the lower left bank of the Mississippi and to occupy Pensacola. Willing's abortive expedition, like George Rogers Clark's capture of the British posts in the Illinois country, was in part outfitted secretly by Gálvez, and more supplies and some money were subsequently issued to Pollock at New Orleans and Havana,[21] most of it before Spain's actual entrance into the war. In October, 1778, Spain otherwise violated neutrality in Louisiana by giving permission to Willing's men to go home through Spanish territory.[22] These American projects to take West Florida came to naught, notwithstanding the covert Spanish assistance. All Florida was thus left open for eventual Spanish conquest.

[20] Josef de Gálvez to the Governor of Louisiana, Madrid, December 24, 1776, quoted by Yela, *op. cit.*, I, 109. Italics mine.

[21] *Ibid.*, I, 107-112, 372-379; Kathryn T. Abbey, "Spanish Projects for the Reoccupation of the Floridas during the American Revolution," *Hispanic Am. Hist. Rev.*, IX (Aug., 1929), 265-279; James A. James, "Oliver Pollock, Financier of the Revolution in the West," *Miss. Vall. Hist. Rev.*, XVI (1929), 67-80.

[22] John Walton Caughey, *Bernardo de Gálvez in Louisiana* (Univ. Calif. Press, 1934).

During 1777 and 1778, Spanish financial assistance continued to be extended secretly in small sums to the American agents in Europe, notably Arthur Lee, without the mediation of France. The Spaniard who handled the money for this purpose was Don Diego de Gardoqui, of the firm of Gardoqui and Sons of Bilbao, through whose house some of the money reached the United States in the shape of military supplies.[23] After Spain's entrance into the war, $174,011 was advanced to the United States through John Jay, then diplomatic agent in Spain, to cover in part bills which Congress, reduced to desperate financial straits, had drawn without warning upon its representative in Madrid, in the hope that somehow he would raise the money to pay them. It is very difficult to ascertain exactly how much money and munitions Spain furnished to the United States during the American Revolution, because of the meagerness of records in the archives of either country. Very cautiously the Spanish authorities refused to commit themselves to any financial contracts with the Colonies, whose independence was not recognized. No American promises to pay were taken, nor apparently desired, and no evidence has been found to show that Spain regarded these expenditures as other than a secret subsidy to keep the insurrection going in America.[24] From such papers as exist in Spanish archives, particularly from summaries later made by Gardoqui, it appears that the total amount furnished to the Americans in supplies and in money, including the 1,000,000 *livres* given secretly through France in 1776, was approximately $400,-000. No payment was ever made for this. There is nothing to show that any was ever intended, or promised—except possibly in the case of cash secured by Jay in Madrid, and Pollock in Havana.[25] Floridablanca was very cautious not to accept any

[23] Yela, *op. cit.*, I, 379–383; II, 308, 315, 319, 321, 323, 375, 378.

[24] "Surely it suits us that the revolt of these people be kept up and we ought to desire that they and the English exhaust themselves reciprocally." Grimaldi to Vergennes, March 14, 1776, *ibid.*, II, 7.

[25] In his conversation on Sept. 3, 1780, with Gardoqui, about the possibility of loans—as an equivalent for which Gardoqui had hinted at specific considerations, such as recognition of the Spanish monopoly of the navigation of the Mississippi, ship-timber, vessels, tobacco, etc.—Jay replied that "the only consideration that Congress could offer was that which all nations at war, who

obligations for repayment of this financial aid or of other assistance.[26] In addition to this subsidy—compared with the French subsidy of $1,996,500—there was the money delivered to Pollock and to Jay: $74,087 to Pollock, and $174,011 to Jay,[27] sums the United States eventually chose to regard as loans, to be paid back with interest. They compare with the French loans, also subsequently paid back with interest, $6,352,500. We cannot say that this financial assistance was extended by Spain for the purpose of securing American independence, as was the case with France.

A summary of loans and subsidies appears on the opposite page.

borrow money, viz., to repay the principal with a reasonable interest after the war." Wharton, IV, 64.

[26] "For your private governance I will tell your Excellency that it is the King's intention in whatever assistance he renders to the Americans not to bind himself with promises and contracts, as much out of consideration of honor as of policy, combining all the present circumstances of Europe with our interests and the situation of our affairs." Floridablanca to Aranda, December 6, 1777, Yela, *op. cit.*, II, 161. Writing of aids in kind furnished through Gardoqui and Company, and via New Orleans, and of his (Lee's) understanding of them from his conversation with Grimaldi, Arthur Lee informed Floridablanca March 17, 1777, from Vittoria: "The marquis added, that his majesty would do these things out of the graciousness of his royal disposition, without stipulating any return, and that if upon inquiry any able veteran officers could be spared from his Irish brigade, the States should have them." Wharton, II, 290. I have found no record of Floridablanca disputing this. March 27, 1778, J. de Gálvez ordered the Governor of Havana to allow (*franquear*) 50,000 *pesos* secretly to the Americans, should they ask it, with hopes for more. *Papeles de Cuba, leg.* 1290.

[27] This represents the money paid back to Spain on this score after the Revolution, by Alexander Hamilton, Secretary of the Treasury of the United States. It is not possible to say whether it represents the principal alone, or the principal plus interest. The Spanish government accepted this as acquittal of that item. See my *Pinckney's Treaty, a Study of America's Advantage from Europe's Distress, 1783–1800* (Baltimore, 1926), pp. 369–381.

Summary of French and Spanish Loans and Subsidies [28]

FRANCE

Subsidies		Loans	
Date	Amount	Date	Amount
1776	1,000,000 *livres*	1777 (Farmers General)	1,000,000 *livres*
1777	2,000,000 "	1778 (in 21 instalments,	
1781	6,000,000 "	1778–1782)	18,000,000 "
Interest canceled		1781 (through States Gen-	
to Jan. 1, 1784	1,500,000 "	eral of Netherlands)	10,000,000 "
	10,500,000 "	1783	6,000,000 "
			35,000,000 "
or (at 18.15)		or (at 18.15)	
	$1,996,500		$6,352,500

SPAIN

Subsidies		Loans	
Date	Amount	Date	Amount
1776–1779	$397,230	1778 (to Pollock and to Wil-	
(including the 1,000,000		ling)	$74,087
livres via Beaumarchais		1781–1782 (to Jay)	174,011
in 1776, and later war			$248,098
material)			

[28] For French loans and subsidies (except the 1,000,000 *livres* from the Farmers General [guaranteed by the King]) see the funding agreements of July 16, 1782, and February 25, 1783, in Miller's *Treaties,* and repayment of the loans with interest from January 1, 1784, see A. Aulard, "La dette Américaine envers la France," *Revue de Paris,* 15 mai, 1 juin, 1925.

For analysis of the Spanish loans and subsidies, see my *Pinckney's Treaty, op. cit.* There is in the library of the George Washington University a MS. dissertation by Robert L. Lafolette, Ph.D. on "The Revolutionary Foreign Debt of the United States and Its Liquidation."

CHAPTER VIII

Spain's American Policy

While this secret assistance to the United States was being furnished from 1776 to 1779 and while Spain's diplomacy was being directed by Floridablanca toward the recovery of Gibraltar, the restitution of Minorca, and the achievement of other Spanish objects in the Gulf of Mexico and the Caribbean, two questions were taking shape which were to become major issues between Spain and the United States: the navigation of the Mississippi River; and the pendant question of the western and southern boundaries of those States which were contiguous with British or Spanish colonial possessions.

Spain had inherited from France a servitude fixed by Article VII of the treaty of Paris of 1763 on the navigation of the Mississippi,[1] and the vessels of British subjects continued to enjoy that navigation down to the eve of the American Revolution. But Spanish officials began in 1769 occasionally to hamper the right by not allowing British subjects to set foot on Spanish soil, nor to moor their ships to Spanish banks.[2] It was necessary, for any real use of the navigation, to be able to transfer goods from river boats to ocean-going ships, mooring the latter within Spanish territory. After hostilities began between the United States and Great Britain, the Spanish Government obstructed the navigation further and captured British ships sailing up the river.[3]

Governor Bernardo de Gálvez had assisted the unsuccessful Willing expedition, which descended the Mississippi in 1778 to capture Pensacola, expecting that later arrangements would be made for the delivery of Florida to Spain, as Congress had shown

---

[1] Above, p. 8.

[2] Vera Lee Brown, "Anglo-Spanish Relations in America in the Closing Years of the Colonial Era," *Hispanic Am. Hist. Review*, V, 370.

[3] Abbey, *op. cit.*, p. 269; J. Caughey, "Bernardo de Gálvez and the English Smugglers on the Mississippi," *Hispanic Am. Hist. Review*, XII, 46–59.

itself willing to promise. But Spanish colonial officials soon became apprehensive of the danger of future American aggression against Spain's adjacent territory.[4] This same fear appeared in Miralles's reports from Philadelphia, where he was able to measure the zeal for the settlement of the Ohio and Mississippi valleys, for which the navigation of the Mississippi was regarded as a necessary outlet. There was no further thought of assistance to any American military operations on the river. After the close of the year 1778, Spain was consistently opposed to any approach of the settlements or territory of the United States to the Mississippi, and the efforts of Spanish diplomacy, and incidentally some measure of military dispositions, were directed toward keeping the United States away from the river. If the American boundary should never be brought up to the river, the question of the navigation of the Mississippi, with all its implications and all its dangers, need not arise again.

The boundary question was more involved. Because this question becomes henceforth so important to the diplomacy of American independence, particularly during the peace settlement of 1782,[5] a statement is necessary here as to the colonial origin of the western and southern boundaries of the United States.

The boundary question, which became inextricably woven with the Mississippi question, goes back to the settlement of the English Colonies and is full of theoretical, political, and juridical argument. The colonies of Massachusetts Bay, Connecticut, Virginia, the Carolinas by royal grants during the seventeenth century— Georgia not until 1732—had received charters which granted them, under the prodigal prerogative of the English kings, strips of land across the continent from sea to sea. New York had acquired, through her treaty with the Five Nations in 1684, a protectorate over that confederation and its dependents which gave rise to sovereign claims to territory beyond the Ohio. These charter claims were fortified in their title by the effectual conquest in the Seven Years' War of all territory to the east of the Missis-

---

[4] Yela, op. cit., I, 373; Montmorin to Vergennes, November 12, 1778, Doniol, III, 576.
[5] See Chap. XVI.

sippi (with the exception of the "island" of New Orleans), recognized as British by the treaty of Paris of 1763. From then until the American Revolution there was no doubt that this territory to the east of the Mississippi was British, like Canada, nor was there any question that the colonial charter claims ceased thenceforth to extend across the river: that same treaty of Paris had amputated those claims definitively and indisputably at the Mississippi and the Iberville. After 1763 the respective claims of the several Colonies were in conflict among themselves, and their overlapping areas gave rise to the later intercolonial and interstate controversies.

In an effort to solve the administrative problems suddenly created by the expulsion of France from the continent, the King of Great Britain, by the famous proclamation of October 7, 1763, marked off the West as a vast Indian reservation, practically at the eastern watershed of the Mississippi basin, and enjoined the governors of the provinces to forbid further settlement there without special license from the Crown. At this time there existed a few settlements along the lower Mobile and the lower Mississippi; these were taken care of by creating for their governance the new province of West Florida. This was divided at the Chattahoochee–Apalachicola from the rest of Florida, henceforth called East Florida, and the line of 31° north latitude fixed as its northern boundary. On the west the boundary of West Florida was the Mississippi and the Iberville, thus bringing it up to the Spanish "island" of New Orleans, the only Spanish territory left east of the Mississippi after the peace of 1763. There remained on the east bank above 31°, and cut off from any effective government, some sparse British settlements in the Natchez district. Pressure of English land speculators caused the Crown to extend the northern boundary of West Florida to the latitude of the mouth of the Yazoo River. The proclamation (1764) effecting this extension of West Florida may be considered as finally removing this strip from any jurisdiction of the colony of Georgia. After that date, there still remained above West Florida the Indian reservation created by the Proclamation of 1763.

It would serve no useful purpose here to enter the legal labyrinths of conflicting State claims to western territory and the question of State versus Federal sovereignty over the hinterlands after July 4, 1776. One thing is certain: the American people, organized not only by the political entities of States but also by the larger union of the United States, possessed a sound claim to territory as far west as the Mississippi and as far south as the latitude of the Yazoo (south of this latitude the uncontested western boundary was the Chattahoochee), the boundary since 1764 of the loyal British colony of West Florida. At the line of the Yazoo the justice of the American claim ceased,[6] though after independence Georgia, and back of Georgia the United States, began to claim the line of 31° from the Chattahoochee to the Mississippi, the old southern boundary of Georgia before 1763.

Such were the issues between the United States and Spain which came before the attention of the first minister of France to the new American republic.[7]

Conrad-Alexandre Gérard, whom Congress received with grave and carefully studied ceremony [8] as the first accredited representative of a foreign power in the United States, was a professional diplomat who had served an apprenticeship in the courts of central Europe and who had been since 1766 chief clerk at the French Foreign Office—in 1778 he was chief of one of the four divisional bureaux into which the Minister Vergennes had reorganized his department. It was through him that most of the personal contacts had been maintained with the American envoys, before their recognition, and it was his name which had been signed to the treaties of February 6, 1778. A master of the English language, intimately associated with every detail of the American business, it became his duty to serve as the eyes, ears, and tongue of Vergennes in the United States, as he had done in France. The

[6] The same logic does not apply to the arbitrary boundaries of Quebec under the Quebec Act of 1774. The Proclamation of 1764 extending the boundaries of West Florida to the line of the Yazoo was universally accepted; the Quebec Act was never accepted in the revolting Colonies, and because it was itself one of the causes of the successful Revolution its validity cannot be invoked.

[7] *Pinckney's Treaty*, pp. 76, 93.

[8] For the ceremonial, carefully devised as appropriate for the reception by Congress of a diplomatic envoy of the rank of minister, see Wharton, II, 653–656, and Doniol, III, 269–271.

fact that he could no longer confer directly and immediately with his superior, now that a reply to every despatch from Versailles required at least three months, gave him an added measure of responsibility and a greater latitude of initiative in the purpose of his mission, which was to watch the new ally and to prevent the English from engaging it in any defection.[9] His instructions [10] may be summarized as follows: to see to it that neither party to the alliance make any peace or truce without the consent of the other; to resist all British peace maneuvers; to promise Congress that France would not lay down her arms until the independence of the United States should be assured; to manage the situation in the United States in favor of Spain, yet without appearing to speak for Spain, by leaving a free hand for that power ultimately to acquire the Floridas, a share in the Newfoundland fisheries, and the island of Jamaica; not to encourage, though in the last resort he might acquiesce in, the conquest of Canada by the United States, for continuing that country under British possession would serve to make the United States feel the need of French friendship "and thus bind it more closely to us." [11] Vergennes wrote his ambassador in Madrid to inform the Spanish Court that Gérard was instructed to show the same zeal for Spanish interests as for French in America; he presently bade Gérard, characteristically, to state to Congress that it was only for the sake of the United States that France had entered the war.[12]

We may note that though the Floridas and the fisheries are mentioned here when speaking of Spanish interests, Vergennes at this time gave Gérard no instructions about the navigation of the Mississippi or the western boundary of the United States. That

[9] Thus in so many words did Vergennes describe it in a despatch to Montmorin, March 27, 1778. Doniol, III, 8. This was before the American treaties had been ratified by Congress and while it was still uncertain whether the North peace proposals of the Carlisle peace commission of 1778 would be accepted in America. See also "Memoir of Instructions to Gérard," March 29, 1778, *ibid.*, III, 153–157.

[10] For the text see Doniol, III, 153–157.

[11] He was also to explain why more subsidies could not be granted, should they be requested. Nevertheless France continued to grant subsidies, in Paris, to the United States. For tabulation of subsidies and loans made by France to the United States during the war, see above, Ch. VII, note 28.

[12] Doniol, III, 281. See above, Ch. II, note 6.

nation should be discouraged from any conquest of Canada, but no anxiety is shown about conquests elsewhere on the continent, except Florida, not even in the neighborhood of the Mississippi,— if we should grant, for the sake of later discussion, that the western country was to be regarded as still British and thus open to conquest.

It would appear from such investigations as have been made in the Spanish and French archives that Floridablanca's anxiety about the western boundary of the United States did not antedate the signature of the Franco-American alliance;[13] nor did he appreciate the significance of the Mississippi question until it was called to his attention during the year 1778 by colonial officials of Spain in Florida and Cuba and by despatches from Miralles, the observer who had been sent to the revolted American Colonies. The year 1778 was a crucial one in Franco-Spanish relations, when the American leaders were anxious to draw the naval power of Spain into their alliance with France and Vergennes was gradually increasing his offers to Spain. It was during these very months that Floridablanca became conscious of the American issues. He who in March, 1778, had professed to be content with the Mississippi as an obvious boundary, now at the end of that year[14] refused to commit himself to any such line, realizing that it would bring the Americans to the bank of a river which they would seek to navigate to the Gulf of Mexico, a waterway which might become an avenue of penetration into Louisiana, the rampart of Mexico itself. This stand of Floridablanca was soon made known to Vergennes, who, increasingly eager to get Spain into the war, found himself attached to an overseas ally already at variance with Spain's interests in the Mississippi Valley and tainted with the dreadful vices of insurrection and republicanism. In vain he had tried to persuade Floridablanca that republican neighbors, divided into different autonomous States without any great unity among themselves, could never be dangerous.

That the original instructions to Gérard did not mention spe-

---

[13] On this see Corwin, *op. cit.*, 240-242; Yela, *op. cit.*, I, 254; Doniol, *op. cit.*, III, 22.
[14] Doniol, III, 578, 585.

cifically the Mississippi, nor the boundary question, is sufficient testimony that they had not become live issues when the envoy left Toulon on April 13, 1778. Gérard, on the spot and in contact with the Spanish observer, Miralles, later took it upon himself as consonant with the general character of his instructions to urge Miralles that Spain herself might solve the Mississippi question by an independent conquest of the "British" territory on the east bank, and to urge Congress to set its western boundaries in accordance with Spain's interests, so as to avoid antagonizing a power which both the United States and France would fain see come into the war on their side. He followed this with the argument that Article XI of the alliance did not guarantee to the United States their territory west of the mountains, which was still British, nor their possessions at all, until they should have been fixed at the cessation of the war with Great Britain.[15]

The attempted Spanish mediation of 1778–1779 prompted Vergennes to request Congress to define its terms and to send a plenipotentiary to Europe empowered to sign a peace. When it came to laying down the terms, a five months' debate (March–

[15] Corwin, Ch. XI, with references to Gérard's despatches in Doniol.
Article XI reads as follows: "The two Parties guarantee mutually from the present time and forever, against all other powers, to wit, the united states to his most Christian Majesty the present Possessions of the Crown of france in America as well as those which it may acquire by the future Treaty of peace: and his most Christian Majesty guarantees on his part to the united states, their liberty, Sovereignty, and Independence, absolute, and unlimited, as well in Matters of Government as commerce, and also thair Possessions, and the additions or conquests that their Confederation may obtain during the war, from any of the Dominions now or heretofore possessed by Great Britain in North America, conformable to the 5th and 6th articles above written, the whole as their Possessions shall be fixed and assured to the said States at the moment of the cessation of their present War with England." This must be read in conjunction with Article XII which immediately follows: "In order to fix more precisely the sense and application of the preceding article, the Contracting Parties declare, that in case of a rupture between france and England, the reciprocal Guarantee, declared in the said article shall have its full force and effect the moment such War shall break out; and if such rupture shall not take place, the mutual obligations of the said guarantee shall not commence, until the moment of the cessation of the present War between the united states and England shall have ascertained their Possessions."
At best this language of the two articles is ambiguous, but Corwin argues perspicaciously that by implication Vergennes had previously unquestionably accepted the Mississippi as the boundary of the United States, and more explicitly the right of its citizens to the full navigation of that river.

August, 1779) took place on the question whether the United States should claim as a right its ancient colonial common share in the British Newfoundland fisheries, a demand which no interpretation of the French alliance could sanction as a *sine qua non*. During these months Gérard did his best to persuade Congress to moderate the western boundary claim, but that body gradually became more emphatic about the Mississippi, while the French Minister transferred his attention to the more dangerous tendency to insist on the fisheries also, to secure which he plainly told Congress that France would not prolong a war otherwise acceptably ended. So far as we are at present concerned with the Spanish-American issue, the peace terms defined on August 14, 1779, to guide the American plenipotentiary—John Adams, of Massachusetts, was presently elected for that commission—demanded as *sine qua non:* (1) independence, (2) the Mississippi as the western boundary of the United States and the line of 31° north latitude as the southern boundary on the West Florida frontier. Soon afterward John Jay of New York was sent as American diplomatic representative to Madrid, to seek from that proud court the recognition of American independence, an alliance with the United States and France, confirmation of the boundary above mentioned, recognition of the American right to navigate the Mississippi to the sea, with a port of entry in Spanish territory below 31°, and a subsidy, or at least a loan, of $5,000,000.[16]

For all this the United States, feared by the Spanish King and Ministry for its potentialities of aggressive expansion, contemned for its unholy spirit of insurrection, regarded only as a cat's-paw in the great game against Great Britain, had nothing to offer. It was already at war, and France was by now secretly committed by the Convention of Aranjuez to continue the war until Gibraltar was restored to Spain. The United States was bound to France not to make a separate peace with Great Britain. What more could Spain ask? Where did there exist any reason, from Floridablanca's point of view, for recognizing the independence of the United States or for yielding to any of its presumptuous demands?

Once in the war, Spain speedily captured West Florida for

[16] *Journals of the Continental Congress,* September 27, 1779, XV, 1118.

herself, and from her posts on the west bank of the Mississippi at Arkansas and St. Louis sent expeditions across the river which resulted in the establishment of Spanish claims to the other side, below and above the Ohio.[17] This ended Spanish military action on the North American continent. Spanish naval coöperation was bungling and disappointing to the French, and mostly busied with the blockade of Gibraltar.

When the Spanish ally joined hostilities with Great Britain, Vergennes, apparently without being asked, took some steps to further Spanish diplomacy in America. Acting upon the initiative already assumed by Gérard in Philadelphia, Vergennes, in despatches dated July 18 and September 25, 1779, instructed Gérard's successor, the accomplished La Luzerne, to support Spanish claims to territory east of the Mississippi and to continue to deny (as Gérard had denied) that the guaranty of Article XI of the Franco-American treaty of alliance extended to the lands claimed by the several States to the west of the Alleghenies; these remained British, subject to capture by Britain's enemies, and as for Florida, that must be set aside as Spain's prize.[18] La Luzerne exercised a more complete ascendancy over the Government of the United

[17] On November 22, 1780, a Spanish officer, Captain Baltazar de Villiers, led a detachment of troops from the post of Arkansas to the opposite, east side of the Mississippi, and formally took possession in the name of the King of Spain (see my *Pinckney's Treaty*, p. 93) of lands on that side of the river. In January, 1781, a small expedition of Spanish troops and allied Indians marched overland from St. Louis and captured the British post of St. Joseph, near the present Niles, Michigan, close to the southern end of Lake Michigan (but inland), and returned straightway to St. Louis (See F. J. Teggart, "The Capture of St. Joseph" in *Mo. Hist. Rev.*, V, 214–228). This expedition had no diplomatic purpose, and can be called little more than a raid (see Lawrence Kinnaird, "The Spanish Expedition against Fort St. Joseph in 1781, A New Interpretation," *Miss. Vall. Hist. Rev.*, XIX [1932], pp. 173–191), but, before retreating, its leader, the militia captain Eugenio Pourré, formally proclaimed Spanish possession over the whole Illinois River country, above the Ohio, on the east bank of the Mississippi. A signed and attested copy (in French) of Pourré's proclamation is in the Bancroft Library of the University of California. A description of the expedition was prominently published in the *Gazeta de Madrid* on March 17, 1782 (Wharton, V, 363) as the North Government was approaching its fall in England and the end of the war and a probable peace settlement were looming ahead. By these several military actions, Spanish troops had actually conquered the British province of West Florida and had made gestures of possession of the whole east bank of the Mississippi, both above and below the Ohio.

[18] Text of instructions printed in Doniol, IV, 224, 357.

States than any foreign envoy since his time, but even he was not able to persuade Congress to yield specifically its western boundary claims to Spain. The eventual contingent modification of Jay's instructions on the point of the Mississippi was due to his reports from Spain. Vergennes had assumed that Miralles would have received instructions to coöperate with France on these points; but La Luzerne found that Miralles had none—except on the point of urging Congress to make a military advance on East Florida to contain British troops while Spain captured West Florida and the lower Mississippi settlements.[19] It was therefore decided between the French Minister and the Spanish observer not to press Congress on the subject of the western boundaries and the Mississippi, but to allow those questions to be treated with Jay, whom Congress had sent to Madrid.[20]

Stimulated by the delegates from Virginia and other southern States, Congress, itself containing members who owned title to western lands, became increasingly conscious of the importance of the western boundary. Spain was already a belligerent and there was not so much reason to compromise as otherwise there might have been. French advice on this point became irritating.

[19] Immediately upon the declaration of war the Governor of Havana was instructed to propose to Congress, through Miralles, the sending of 4,000 American troops for a campaign against Saint Augustine, with possible expeditions against British settlements on the Mississippi banks and in the hinterlands (espaldas) of Louisiana, probably meaning the Illinois country. This was the subject of negotiation between Miralles (supported by the French Minister) and Congress, and of discussions between him and General Washington. The British possession of Savannah was a strategic block to any American attack on East Florida. In 1779, troops were sent south for a campaign against British forces in the southern States; and an American officer, Colonel Ternant, was sent to Havana to discuss ways and means of a concert of land and sea forces between Spanish and American forces to expel the British from Georgia and Florida. Meanwhile Bernardo de Gálvez had captured West Florida. Navarro, the Governor at Havana, answered the mission of the American officers by stating that he had no instructions to coöperate. See Real Orden, confidential, Josef de Gálvez to Navarro, San Ildefonso, Aug. 29, 1779, Archivo de las Indias, Papeles de Cuba, leg. 1290; Miralles to Congress, Philadelphia, November 24, 1779; Miralles to La Luzerne, Philadelphia, November 29, 1779; Miralles to Washington, Feb. 18, 1780, Archivo de las Indias; Navarro to Miralles, Havana, March 10, 1780, and April 25, 1780, ibid. leg. 1281. See also on this point Doniol, IV, Ch. VI.

[20] Miralles to J. Gálvez, Philadelphia, February 1, March 12, 1780, Archivo de las Indias, Audiencia de Santo Domingo, 87-1-8; for account based on La Luzerne's despatches, see Doniol, IV, 224, 335-361.

Vergennes, already aroused by the brusque statements of John Adams, who had arrived in Paris early in 1780 as peace plenipotentiary and who suggested opening direct negotiations with Great Britain,[21] thought it best to adopt a neutral attitude as between the conflicting interests of his two allies in the valley of the Mississippi.[22] At no time, really, had the French Minister's policy proceeded to actual demands on the United States in favor of Spain. The question of who was to possess the West, where American troops had occupied British posts in the Illinois country, which was later raided and claimed by Spain; where Spanish troops had taken possession up as far as the Yazoo, with an American post planted above at the mouth of the Ohio;—this vital question, on which the destiny of the United States as a future world power depended from the start, was thus postponed to the peace negotiations.

The mission of John Jay to Spain failed completely. He was there from January, 1780, to May, 1782. Floridablanca and his subordinates received him informally, paid such attention to him as diplomatic circumstances advised, and talked with him enough to draw out any offers which the United States was willing to make. They even encouraged him to believe that Miralles would be replaced by a more regularly accredited Spanish representative,[23] but there was never at any time really serious intention to recognize the independence of the United States or to do anything more favorable than to supply the American envoy with limited sums of money, enough to keep him from becoming too discouraged. Jay's presence in Spain was opportune for Floridablanca. The rebel agent served as an apparition to display to the English during peace parleys which the Spanish Minister had

---

[21] He was dissuaded from this by Vergennes, who later refused to discuss business with any one but Franklin, the regularly accredited Minister to France. Adams later went to the Netherlands (see below, p. 168), to which country he had a commission as United States Minister. For Adams and Vergennes, see Doniol, IV, 409–424; Wharton, III, *passim;* Sparks, *Revolutionary Diplomatic Correspondence,* V, *passim.*

[22] See instructions of June 3 and August 7, 1780, quoted by Doniol, IV, 428–429.

[23] Diego de Gardoqui of Bilbao was frequently mentioned in this connection. Miralles's correspondence with Navarro shows that he himself hoped to be appointed as a regular minister to the United States.

started with an enemy emissary who had been permitted to come from England.

With the sanction of the Spanish Council of State, Floridablanca had commenced this peace conversation secretly, in violation of the positive stipulations of the convention of Aranjuez against any such separate discussions. At the outset of the war Spain had expected an impressive victory as soon as the French and Spanish fleets should join in the Channel, in the summer of 1779, to convoy a French army to invade England. The flat failure of this spectacular plan, together with Rodney's defeat of Lángara's squadron off Cape St. Vincent, January 8, 1780, and the relief of Gibraltar, made Spain willing to discuss peace at least on her own terms. These discussions were initiated by an Irish priest, Thomas Hussey, who had been educated in Spain, had been chaplain of the Spanish embassy in London, and had remained in England, protected by his cloth, after the outbreak of war as head of the Spanish intelligence service there. Hussey's real profession was not unknown to the British Government, but he was allowed to accompany to Spain an English agent, Richard Cumberland, for the purpose of opening up a negotiation under the express conditions that neither Gibraltar nor the American Colonies should even be mentioned. Hussey succeeded in making the British Ministry believe that peace was not impossible on that basis; at the same time he successfully suggested to Floridablanca that in the last analysis England could be induced to cede Gibraltar. When these agents appeared publicly in Spain in June, 1780, Floridablanca was obliged to inform the French, since he could no longer conceal the negotiations. Vergennes was forced by circumstances to put the best face possible on a situation which alarmed him greatly and which soon caused him to turn to a Russian mediation and a proposed compromise peace as preferable to any peace-without-victory forced on him by Floridablanca's diplomacy.

In these negotiations with Cumberland, Floridablanca did propose the cession of Gibraltar to Spain and intimated that the remaining peace terms, so far as England and Spain were concerned, could then be arranged on the basis of the Peace of Paris of 1763, with a few minor diplomatic exchanges. To satisfy

Spain's obligations to France he professed that he wished the signature of the Anglo-Spanish definitive treaty to be dependent upon a simultaneous Anglo-French peace. To provide for France's obligations to the United States, he devised a "middle-of-the-road" formula intended at the same time to be acceptable to England: a long-time truce between England and the Colonies on the basis of the military *uti possidetis,* without any specific recognition of American independence. This truce would be reached by direct negotiations between Colonies and mother country, undertaken at the same time as the negotiations with Spain and France and to depend on them. The effect of such a peace would have been to withdraw French troops and navy from America and to leave the British in possession of the northern frontier, Maine, New York, Long Island, and in the South the ports of Wilmington, Charleston, and Savannah.

These conversations lasted throughout the year 1780, but, fortunately for the United States, George III would not accept the Spanish terms, and Cumberland was recalled in the spring of 1781. Before the negotiations finally had broken down, Vergennes had been frightened into welcoming a Russian mediation and into considering peace by a long-term truce *uti possidetis* in America, at the hands of mediators, providing he could induce the latter to bring this forward as their own proposal.[24]

Jay's presence was useful to Floridablanca as a means of attempting to hasten Cumberland's arrival in Spain and the acceptance of the Spanish peace program, under fear that otherwise Spain would conclude an alliance with the United States. This trick did not work, but it made Jay's sojourn at the Spanish Court so convenient for the purposes of Spanish diplomacy that Floridablanca seems to have been willing to furnish him with the $174,011 to keep him supported there for two years and pay a large measure of the drafts which Congress so recklessly drew on him. On the other hand, Cumberland flattered himself with

[24] Vergennes's "Memoir on the ways and means of concluding a truce with Great Britain, minuted in part by Rayneval, February 1781 (French)," Archives Affaires Etrangères, *Correspondance Politique, Etats-Unis,* XV, 269–278, transcript in Library of Congress. We shall recur in a subsequent chapter to this mediation diplomacy.

the thought that at least his otherwise unsuccessful sojourn had had the effect of frustrating Jay's mission; nevertheless Jay was not recognized even after Cumberland's departure. Spain was determined never to recognize American independence until after Great Britain should have done so, and in the course of the Cumberland conversations Floridablanca said as much to the British agent.[25]

Jay attributed Spanish hesitation and apathy toward him to the stand which Congress had taken on the Mississippi question, a stand which he himself approved. No treaty, no alliance with Spain, appeared to be possible as long as the United States should demand so much. Jay at this time was not for bartering the Mississippi for a Spanish alliance, an idea which horrified Franklin.[26] But Congress, impressed by what seemed to be the exigencies of the unfavorable military situation, empowered him, by resolutions passed February 15, 1781, to recognize the exclusive right of Spain to the navigation of the Mississippi below the boundary of 31°, in return for a Spanish alliance. Jay therefore included this concession, worded with reserve and ambiguity by proposing to relinquish and forbear the use of that navigation, in the draft of a proposed treaty of alliance, which also contained a mutual guaranty of territory.[27]

[25] For these negotiations see my volume on *The Hussey-Cumberland Negotiation and American Independence* (Princeton, 1931).

[26] "Poor as we are, yet as I know we shall be rich, I would rather agree with them to buy at a great price the whole of their right on the Mississippi than sell a drop of its waters. A neighbor might as well ask me to sell my street door." Franklin to Jay, Passy, October 2, 1780, Wharton, IV, 75.

[27] The articles proposed by Jay were:

1. Inviolable and universal peace and friendship.

2. Most-favored-nation privileges in respect to commerce, navigation, and personal rights.

3. "That they mutually extend to the vessels, merchants, and inhabitants of each other all that protection which is usual and proper between friendly and allied nations."

4. "That the vessels, merchants, or other subjects of his Catholic majesty and the United States shall not resort to or be permitted (except in cases which humanity allows to distress) to enter into any of those ports or dominions of the other from which the most favored nation shall be excluded."

5. "That the following commerce be prohibited and declared contraband between the subjects of his Catholic majesty and the United States, viz: All such as his Catholic majesty may think proper to specify."

6. "The United States shall relinquish to his Catholic majesty, and in future

This presented Floridablanca with the chance to make a clean-cut decision. On the one hand he might do as his ambassador in Paris, the Count de Aranda, had constantly advocated; that is, recognize the independence of the United States and have as a frontier neighbor in North America a friendly ally who would [28] guarantee the integrity of Louisiana and Florida and even the exclusive navigation of the Mississippi between Spanish banks. Or he might refuse such an alliance, feed the insurrectionists irregular quantities of supplies and money for the purpose of keeping them in the war against Great Britain, not recognize their independence in order to keep alive the possibility of a secret peace with England for the prize of Gibraltar, and abide the future without the friendship of this new nation of rebels. Acting for the interests of his country as he saw them, he chose the latter course. Jay prudently withdrew the offer to "forbear" American claims to navigate the Mississippi, an offer which had been made contingent upon an immediate Spanish alliance, and Congress formally approved his course.[29] In fact, with such vital issues between them, the interests of both Spain and the United States were best satisfied by their remaining co-belligerents rather than allies. The United States, as Jay perceived,[30] could have secured little additional advantage from having Spain as an ally, and for this would have paid the excessive price of the Mississippi and the guaranty of Spain's colonial territory in America.

To Floridablanca, Jay was little more than a disagreeably importunate though not inconvenient rebel, always begging for

forbear to use, or attempt to use, the navigation of the river Mississippi from the thirty-first degree of north latitude—that is, from the point where it leaves the United States—down to the ocean."

7. "That his Catholic majesty shall guaranty to the United States all their respective territories."

8. "That the United States shall guaranty to his Catholic majesty all his dominions in North America."

The propositions were submitted, September 22, 1781. Wharton, IV, 760–762.

[28] R. Konetzke, *Die Politik des Grafen Aranda,* pp. 141–145. "I think they are shortsighted and do not look very far into futurity, or they would seize with avidity so excellent an opportunity of securing a neighbor's friendship, which may hereafter be of great consequence to their American affairs." Franklin to Jay, Passy, Jan. 19, 1782, Wharton, V, 120.

[29] Wharton, V, 380.

[30] Wharton, IV, 743.

money.[31] On the other hand, Jay's mission to Spain produced certain ineffaceable impressions on his independent mind which were not to be without influence in the peace negotiations at Paris. On his outward voyage he had been accompanied by the returning French Minister, Gérard, who did his best to persuade him that the resolutions of Congress setting forth his instructions would ruin the Spanish negotiation, and that the guaranty of the French alliance did not include a guaranty of American territory up to the Mississippi, an old argument which Jay had heard before when President of Congress. The American landed at Cadiz with his suspicions of the good faith of France already germinating. "There are many reasons (hereafter to be explained)," he reported, "which induce me to suspect that France is determined to manage between us so as to make us debtors to their influence and good correspondence with Spain for every concession on her part, and to make Spain herself obligated to their influence and good correspondence with us for every concession on our part. Though this may puzzle the business, I think it also promotes it." [32] This not unjust appreciation of the brokerage of France between her two allies must have developed into a more bitter train when Jay learned of the existence of the article in the secret treaty of Aranjuez, which, as John Adams wrote to Jay's secretary, bound the United States to Spain without Spain's being bound to the United States.[33] Reflections of Vergennes's policy in

[31] "His two chief points were: Spain, recognize our independence; Spain, give us more money." Floridablanca to Aranda, September 29, 1782, Yela, *op. cit.*, II, 365.

[32] To the President of Congress, Cadiz, March 3, 1780, Wharton, III, 530.

On October 4, 1780, Congress had passed new instructions for Jay, at his advice, allowing him to make stipulations against abuse of the navigation of the Mississippi, but at the same time insisting on the right of navigation and on the boundary of 31°. Jay's increasing suspicion of France is seen in his letter to the President of Congress, April 25, 1781 : "I have had the honor of receiving your Excellency's letters of the 6th and 17th of October last, with the enclosures. They arrived the 30th day of January last. There is more than reason to suspect that the French Court were apprized of their contents before they arrived, and to believe that the construction of the treaty, by which the navigation of the Mississippi is supposed to be comprehended in the guarantee, does not correspond with their ideas on that subject." Wharton, IV, 384. See also *ibid.*, p. 738.

[33] Adams to Carmichael, Paris, April 8, 1780, Wharton, III, 603. William Carmichael was Jay's secretary. He remained in Spain after Jay's departure. In 1783 he was recognized as official representative of the United

trying to persuade the United States to yield to Spanish interests in the West also came to Jay through Montmorin, the French Ambassador in Madrid,[34] and increased his uneasiness as to the conduct of the French ally. The climax of his distrust came when he received his full powers as peace commissioner for the negotiations with England in 1782 and learned that Congress had agreed to place its plenipotentiaries in the hands of the French Foreign Minister on all details other than independence.[35]

Granting that Spain's principal purpose in the war was the recovery of Gibraltar, that her King and statesmen were opposed to any achievement of American independence, and bearing in mind the complicating factor which the Spanish demand for Gibraltar was to be at the final peace conference, there can be no doubt that her entrance into the war was a matter of alarm to Great Britain and of great cheer to the United States. It was a signal step in the isolation of Great Britain and it ranged against the British navy the largest naval force which had been left neutral. The value attached to Spain's entrance is seen by the price which Vergennes was willing to pay, Gibraltar, and by the price which the United States had ultimately offered, the Mississippi, for an actual Spanish alliance. Washington, who believed that sea power had the "casting vote" in the struggle, had written, October 4, 1778: "If the Spaniards would but join their fleets to France and commence hostilities, my doubts would all subside. Without it I fear the British navy has it too much in its power to counteract the schemes of France."[36] That both France and the United States overestimated the military significance of Spain, the events of the war tend to argue[37]; the advantages gained by

States. He held that post until 1790; from 1790-1794 he was chargé d'affaires; and from 1792-1794 he was joint commissioner with William Short. He died in Madrid in 1795. S. G. Coe's "The Mission of William Carmichael to Spain," in *Johns Hopkins University Studies in Historical and Political Science,* XLVI, No. 1, is an account of his diplomacy written entirely from American sources. See *Pinckney's Treaty, passim.*

[34] Wharton, IV, 738.
[35] Below, p. 190.
[36] Wharton, I, 360.
[37] "An alliance so sought for, so patiently pursued with such abnegation and so many repeated sacrifices, had rarely been so useless, so barren of results, or a better justification to powers who can put but little trust, and who believe in

diversion of units of the British fleet to the protection of Gibraltar are balanced by the involvement of French ships-of-the-line for the campaigns against that fortress, and by the disagreements in strategy and command that existed between French and Spanish naval authorities. The Spanish conquest of Florida was a positive advantage to the United States, simply because it replaced the British by a potentially weaker power on that frontier of future expansion. But we can point to little in the naval or military history of the war which shows operations helpful to the struggle which the United States and France were waging against England. The small flow of Spanish subsidies to America had little actual result; and, until further research into the effect of Spanish naval operations [38] on the general history of the war has shown the contrary, it is reasonable to assume that the Spanish participation was not a decisive military factor in the achievement of American independence. Certainly in a diplomatic sense Spain was not a benevolent influence for the success of the American cause. Spain preferred to win her own stakes without corresponding American successes.

The peculiar character of Spanish interests had its influence upon France's diplomatic relations with the United States. Dominated by his policy of reviving French power and prestige by seizing the rare opportunity to divide the mighty British Empire, Vergennes was impelled first to commit France to America without full consultation with Spain. Then, driven by the military necessities of the hour, he was obliged to make successive diplomatic concessions to Spain. During the mediation negotiations of 1779, with his Spanish diplomacy uppermost in his mind, he receded from a position of explicit independence for the United States to a tacit independence during an indefinite truce, a principle apparently accepted by Franklin as a basis for negotiations and one admissible under Article VIII of the Franco-American alliance. Then, to get Spain into the war, Vergennes accepted the Gibraltar article.

putting little trust in allies." Such is Doniol's judgment on the Convention of Aranjuez, III, 797.

[38] A. T. Mahan, *The Major Operations of the Navies in the War of American Independence* (Boston, 1913) does not analyze this problem.

But Vergennes was to travel even farther along the Spanish diplomatic boulevard. To give impetus to Spanish belligerency he and his agents at first were constrained to interpret with more and more limitations the guaranty of the Franco-American treaty and to seek to persuade the United States to give up the Mississippi. At no time, however, did he positively insist upon the acceptance of this sacrifice by his American ally for the sake of stiffening his Spanish ally; at no time, similarly, did he ever positively insist on his advice for western boundaries. Finally, as we shall see in a subsequent chapter, he was frightened, by Floridablanca's ominous discussions with the enemy, into considering a peace by mediation, which, had it taken place, would have been a violation of the Franco-American alliance. The effect on American diplomacy of the commitments which Vergennes had felt forced to make to Spain, in the convention of Aranjuez, was the natural result of the entanglement of the United States in European diplomacy by an alliance which was necessary to secure independence itself.

We must now turn from Spain to follow the ramifications of French policy elsewhere on the continent of Europe, and to observe the attempts of the new American republic to establish relations with other European powers during this, its struggle for independence.

CHAPTER IX

The Perilous Neutrality of the Netherlands

The entrance of France and Spain into the war against Great
Britain introduced new diplomatic problems, which would never
have arisen so long as the conflict remained restricted to the
British Empire. Of these the most serious and far-reaching concerned the questions of neutral rights, which ultimately involved
the Netherlands in the war and brought into being that brilliant
apparition, the Armed Neutrality of 1780, that lighted for the
moment the immediate field of diplomacy and left so luminous an
after-glow lingering over the whole domain of international juris-
prudence. These subjects we shall presently examine, but, before
turning to them, we must briefly note the attitude of the several
other principal European powers toward the United States.

Outside of France there was little general sympathetic interest
for the cause of the American Revolution, and this little was
of a passive, academic kind. The governments of all the nations,
other than France, were opposed to any recognition of American
independence and remained so, except in the case of the Netherlands, until after Great Britain in the summer of 1782 had opened
negotiations for peace with the plenipotentiaries of the United
States of America. In Denmark [1] and Sweden [2] and in the German
States [3] there was some sympathetic enthusiasm among liberals,

[1] S. J. M. P. Fogdall, *Danish-American Diplomacy, 1776-1920* (University
of Iowa, 1922), quotes a significant letter of the Foreign Minister, A. P. Bernstorff, October 26, 1776: "The public here is greatly taken by the (American)
rebels, not because of any knowledge of their cause, but because the independence
mania has really infected everybody, and because this poison spreads imper-
ceptibly from the works of philosophers even into the village schools."

[2] Harald Elovson, *Amerika i Svensk Litteratur, 1750-1820* (Lund, 1930),
portrays the reflection in Swedish literature of French exotic idealism about
America.

[3] H. P. Gallinger, *Die Haltung der deutschen Publizistik zu dem ameri-
kanischen Unabhängigkeitskriege, 1775-1783* (Leipzig, 1900), examines the contemporary German publicists and points out that public opinion among the
masses in Germany was quite dumb on the subject.

but it lacked force enough to influence the government's fixed policy. The kings of Portugal, Denmark-Norway, and Sweden, the Stadhouder of the Netherlands, the Emperor of the Holy Roman Empire (including its satellite Grand Duchy of Tuscany) all emphatically disapproved of revolt against the sovereignty of a legitimate monarch. Portugal was controlled by her powerful ally, Great Britain. None of them would think of recognizing a rebel American diplomatic agent.[4] Catherine II of Russia, remotest of all from the arena of conflict, neither disliked nor liked the Americans, cared nothing whatsoever about their theories of government, but felt that a separation from the mother country was the only solution for their difficulties with England. She looked at the question from the point of view of her own European interests and was determined not to interfere in the quarrel.[5] Frederick the Great of Prussia entertained a lively hatred for George III and the British Government which had deserted him in 1763 [6] and was consequently glad to see Great Britain involved

[4] For Denmark-Norway, Fogdall, *op. cit.;* Bancroft, *Hist. U. S.* 10 vols. (Boston, 1834–1874), X, 57; P. Fauchille, *La diplomatie française et la ligue des neutres de 1780 (1776–1783)* (Paris, 1893), pp. 53–55. For Sweden, Fauchille, *ibid.* For the Netherlands, F. W. van Wijk, *De Republiek en Amerika* (Leiden, 1921), p. 3. For the Empire (and Tuscany), Hanns Schlitter, *Die Beziehungen Österreichs zu den Vereinigten Staaten von Amerika* (Innsbruck, 1885), pp. 3, 144. Ralph Izard of South Carolina, who had departed to Paris with his family from a London sojourn at the beginning of the war, succeeded in getting an appointment as commissioner to the Grand Duchy of Tuscany, July, 1777. The Tuscan resident at Paris made it evident that Izard would not be received at that court, and the envoy was prudent enough not to go to Florence. His commission was revoked June 8, 1779. Schlitter (*op. cit.,* p. 144) prints a document showing that the Court of Florence, with the sanction of the Imperial Government, decided against receiving an American agent. Izard's mission, like the one of Arthur Lee to Spain earlier in 1777, and the later missions of William Lee to Vienna, and of Francis Dana to St. Petersburg, were examples of "militia diplomacy," which under the persuasion of the Adamses and Lees at times captured the fancy of Congress; namely, that militiamen of diplomacy should be mobilized and sent out to all corners of the earth to seek recognition, without knowing in advance whether there was any likelihood of their being recognized. Franklin disapproved of this policy: "A virgin state should preserve its virgin character, and not go about suitoring for alliances, but wait with decent dignity for the application of others." To A. Lee, March 21, 1777, Wharton, II, 298. For interesting reflections on militia diplomacy, see *ibid.,* pp. 289–294.

[5] F. A. Golder, "Catherine II and the American Revolution," *A.H.R.,* XXI, 92–96.

[6] Above, p. 70–71.

in difficulties, but this was for reasons of state, as was the case with Charles III of Spain, and not because of any admiration for republican states fighting for independence. The King of Prussia politely refused to receive an American agent, Arthur Lee, sent to him from Paris in 1777, and refrained from insisting on a recall of the British Minister, Hugh Elliott, when this person unblushingly superintended the theft and rifling of Lee's despatch box.[7] Frederick's own position in Europe on the eve of the Bavarian succession question made it impossible for him to think of incurring England's active enmity; but in the diplomacy that revolved about the American war he threw his influence on the side of France, both because he was glad to see England humiliated, without being destroyed, and because he wished to wean France away from any active support of his great rival Austria.[8]

Portugal, Denmark, the Netherlands, and Austria forbade their subjects to supply any contraband to the revolted Colonies[9]; but only Portugal, acting under pressure from her traditional ally, Great Britain, actually closed her harbors to American vessels engaged in innocent trade.

These European powers became more vitally concerned when the intervention of France in the American war spread that conflict to the continent of Europe and precipitated the ever-vexing questions of neutral rights. Whatever touched the great Atlantic sea powers, on the ocean and in their colonies, must of necessity affect their weight in the scheme of Continental alliances and potential combinations. With France, the ally of Austria, occupied in war with England, Frederick the Great could resist more easily

[7] This incident is described in several places, most interestingly in J. B. Moore's *Principles of American Diplomacy* (New York, 1923), pp. 21–23, but the reader may profitably consult the B. F. Stevens *Facsimiles*, Nos. 1454–1482, particularly 1460, 1468, 1482. Elliott received a gentle reprimand by his superiors for this theft, and also a reward of £1,000 cash. Wharton, II, *passim*. For A. Lee in Berlin, see R. H. Lee's *Life of Arthur Lee, LL.D.* (Boston, 1829).

[8] P. L. Haworth sums up the previous literature and analyzes the sources in his "Frederick the Great and the American Revolution," in *A.H.R.*, IX, 460–478.

[9] For Portugal in this respect see Wharton, II, 307; for Denmark, Bancroft, *op. cit.*, X, 57; for the Netherlands, below, p. 121; for Austria, Friedrich Edler, *The Dutch Republic and the American Revolution* (Baltimore, 1911), p. 36. The studies by K. E. Carlson, *Relations of the United States with Sweden* (Allentown, Pennsylvania, 1921), and A. B. Benson, *Sweden and the American Revolution* (New Haven, Connecticut, 1926), lack precision on this point.

Austrian designs on Bavaria. With the western powers involved in war, Russia could feel freer to continue her program of advance against the Turks. The possibility of prestige and advantage from the mediation of a powerful neutral was itself an inducement for the maintenance of neutrality. It was for the interest of all these powers to stand aloof as neutral spectators of the great maritime struggle and thus to protect and advance their own Continental interests. They succeeded in doing this, with one tragic exception, the Netherlands.

What a striking paradox it is that public opinion in the most absolute monarchy of western Europe flamed with enthusiasm for the American cause and supported heartily the cold-blooded designs of the royal ministers against Britain, while in a neighboring European republic the American principle of self-government, with its representative systems, evoked no popular interest or sympathy at all! The Dutch were interested in questions nearer home. The recent French occupation of Coisica loomed more significantly on their horizon than trans-Atlantic protests at the Stamp Act. The partition of Poland and the general struggle against the Jesuits were political events of more importance to the burghers of Amsterdam and Rotterdam than the assembling of the Continental Congress and the strife between Tories and Patriots in the provinces of British America. At home in the Low Countries men's minds labored with domestic issues now long since forgotten and even then little noticed by the world in general.[10] This absence of enthusiasm or even interest in the trend of events in North America existed notwithstanding the similarity of political institutions, religious backgrounds, revolts for independence.

Such apathy was not due to lack of information available to the reading public as to what was transpiring across the Atlantic, news that filtered through almost exclusively British sources. A few individuals, like Johan Derck van der Capellen tot den Poll, a member of the provincial assembly of Overyssel, and Jean Luzac of Leyden, editor of the *Gazette de Leyde,* were interested in the

[10] The so-called de Witten War, the Nijkerk religious dissension, and the dismissal of Professor van der Marck of Groeningen. Van Wijk, *op. cit.,* p. 2.

political principles of the Revolution, and Luzac sought to set forth American news abundantly and objectively; but the public did not respond. Nor did popular demand call forth those political pamphlets which later circulated in the Netherlands. They were rather in the nature of propaganda by English or French-American agents, calculated to interest the constituencies and thus the votes of the several provincial assemblies, and through them the States General or governing body of the United Provinces of the Netherlands.[11]

The constitutional structure of the Dutch state was responsible in part for the embarrassments and troubles which were to overwhelm that unfortunate republic. The seven provinces of Holland, Zealand, Utrecht, Guelderland, Overyssel, Groeningen, and Friesland had been united since their confederation at Utrecht in 1579. They varied in size, population, industry, to a less extent in religion. Each had its provincial assembly, composed of nobles and of deputies of the cities; and cities formed autonomous units with complicated representative conciliar governments for themselves. The principal sovereign and governing body of the Dutch Republic was the States General, which assumed in state parlance the title of Their High Mightinesses. We may ascribe their impotence to a species of constitutional infelicity akin to that which characterized the Confederation of the United States of North America: the necessity for unanimity of all provinces, whether large or small, on any important matter.[12] The States General declared war and made peace, and their resolutions, once adopted, were controlling and decisive on all matters. The executive was an hereditary prince, with the title of Stadhouder, descended by English royal marriages from George II of England. His principal functions were appointive and administrative. He had the federal executive officers largely under his

[11] Dr. van Wijk, *op. cit.*, has carefully analyzed this pamphlet material. A more general portrayal of it is to be found in F. P. Renaut's *La politique de propagande des Américains durant la guerre d'indépendance; C. W. F. Dumas et les Provinces-Unies, 1776–1780* (Paris, 1925).

[12] The American Confederation required unanimity for any amendment to the organic articles, but only a two-thirds majority of the States for important matters.

patronage, but the States General could always overrule him in matters of policy. He also had charge of military affairs, and nominally of naval affairs, which were really controlled by a College of Admiralty curiously made up of representatives from the maritime provinces. Nominally too, he had charge of foreign relations, with the assistance of a minister called the *Greffier,* but here again he was subject to the control of the States General, whose permanent secretary, the Grand Pensionary of Holland, more nearly approached the position of a minister of foreign affairs than did any other dignitary in the Republic.

The fact that the States General could override the executive caused the diplomatic corps to pay court to influential members of that body, to the provincial assemblies which elected the States General, even to the municipal councils which sent delegates to the provincial assemblies. The small area of the Low Countries and the proximity to each other of the principal cities made it possible for foreign diplomats to circulate among them with ease. The cities, particularly The Hague, Amsterdam, Rotterdam, Haarlem, Dordrecht, became hotbeds of intrigue by diplomatists who wanted to capture their influence in the States General for some favored measure of foreign policy. The Stadhouder retained a certain reserve of power in his ability to control some one or more of the rural provinces, like Guelderland, and so by obstructing unanimity to prevent change. Thus he could block the wishes of an overwhelming majority of the provinces, including that of Holland, which might itself be considered as representing more than half the nation, with the city of Amsterdam a preponderant factor in the maritime trade of the United Provinces. Against this *liberum veto* the province of Holland had one powerful if disruptive expedient. The revenue of the Republic, like that of the American Confederation, came in quotas from the individual provinces; if Holland, dominated by Amsterdam, should withhold its quota, which in 1778 amounted to 57.7 per cent of the total taxes for the support of the Government,[13] all the provinces must face a

---

[13] F. P. Renaut, *Les Provinces-Unies et la guerre d'Amérique* (1775–1784), 2 vols. (Paris, 1924, 1925), p. 419.

crisis of national disorder. Amsterdam was thus a focal point of politics, foreign as well as domestic.

Dutch domestic politics involved two parties: the Stadhouder and his dependents and supporters, and the Patriots. The Stadhouderians were monarchial in tendency and pro-English. The actual Prince, William V of Orange, the son of Princess Anne of England (eldest daughter of George II), possessed almost as strong a personal attachment for that country as had his mother. He looked to England for support against the republican tendencies of the opposition. He derived his local strength from the gentry of the inland agricultural provinces, where he had extensive hereditary possessions, and from the patronage of his appointive powers. A young man of weak and indecisive character and no resourcefulness, he leaned heavily on the able Duke of Brunswick, commander of the army and generally a British sympathizer. The Stadhouder's party always favored increase of land forces rather than of naval armament, and it had been English policy since Ryswick (1697) to support the Dutch against the aggressive ambitions, first of France and then of Austria, to command the Belgian coast of the Channel. Since March 3, 1678, there had been an alliance between England and the Netherlands. The treaty of Westminster laid down the obligation of mutual assistance and defense of all of each party's "rights, etc., both by land and sea," in case either should be attacked; pledged each against a separate peace, truce, or armistice; and allowed recruiting in each other's territories. For any attack on the Netherlands, Great Britain promised a defending corps of 10,000 men; reciprocally a Dutch corps of 6,000 men and twenty men-of-war were to come to the assistance of Great Britain.[14] In the negotiations following and confirming the peace settlement of Utrecht, this alliance was renewed, together with the maritime treaty of 1674, and a separate article in 1716 specified that the *casus foederis* was understood to apply "not only when either ally is

---

[14] *Collection of all the Treaties of Peace, Alliance, and Commerce, between Great-Britain and Other Powers, 1648 . . . 1783* (London, Debrett, 1785), I, 213.

attacked in open hostility, but also when one of its neighbors makes preparations of war against either party, or threatens either" in any way whatsoever.[15]

If the Stadhouderian succession was thus linked to a pro-British policy, the Patriots were anti-British and pro-French. They were divided into two groups (or rather they were animated by two diverging views) which were not clearly separated until the time of the French Revolution: the aristocrats, who were opposed to English patronage and consequently to the Stadhouder, and the liberals, who were opposed to the Stadhouder because he, and England behind him, stood in the way of the progress of liberal ideas. The latter were strongest in the trading and maritime centers, particularly Amsterdam. Looking sympathetically toward France and French intellectual radicalism, they had less fear of being swallowed by that monarchy than of being overwhelmed by the monarchial tendencies of the Orangeists assisted by English power. When England got into difficulties with America, and later with France and Spain, the Patriots naturally saw their opportunity to oppose more successfully the Stadhouder, though, we repeat, they manifested no particular interest in trans-Atlantic political principles.

The outbreak of hostilities in America in 1775 had produced trade questions which assumed increasing importance to Holland. The opening of American harbors to direct commerce with Europe, for such as wished to defy the British prohibitions, presaged to eager traders the possible breakdown of that colonial monopoly which had been so ruinous to Dutch navigation and greatness since the middle of the seventeenth century. Even though no direct commerce with the revolted Colonies was legal in the eyes of British law, it was legal to carry anything to neutral French harbors in Europe or in the West Indies, or to St. Eustatius or other Dutch harbors in the Caribbean, from whence cargoes ultimately found their way to American ports. A goodly portion of the powder and other supplies that reached Washington's army through French means in 1776 and 1777 was handled

[15] G. F. de Martens, *Supplément au recueil des principaux traités* . . . , 10 vols. (Gottingue, 1802–1828), I, 125.

by the Dutch somewhere along the ocean roads.[16] The Dutch Government itself, States General as well as Stadhouder, at the beginning of the revolt had no intention of assisting the Americans even secretly. The Stadhouder abhorred and contemned the Declaration of Independence and sympathized with efforts to extinguish the insurrection. The States General, acting at the behest of the British Ambassador, issued a proclamation, March 20, 1775, prohibiting, under heavy penalty, for six months the export from Dutch harbors, European or colonial, of munitions in English ships or vessels flying the English flag (that is, American vessels) or in ships of other nations, including the Netherlands, except by special license. The license required oaths that the exporter had no knowledge that the goods were being shipped directly or indirectly to the British Colonies. It should be noted that this prohibition did not refuse admission of American-owned ships to Dutch harbors. The regulation applied to exports from the Dutch West India Colonies—St. Eustatius and Curaçao—as well as home ports, and heavy penalties were prescribed for contravention. The British Government was satisfied with the letter of this proclamation, which was extended successively for one year, in August, 1775, October, 1776, and November, 1777.[17]

The execution of the prohibition gave cause for much complaint. A great clandestine traffic sprang up, by way of French harbors, and notably by way of the Dutch West Indian island of St. Eustatius. The Dutch Admiralty officers were traders themselves and did not hasten to carry out the edicts of the States General in Holland. It is therefore not surprising that efforts to do so in the colonial harbors were sometimes only perfunctory. St. Eustatius, an islet of seven square miles, one of the three

[16] The British Ambassador at The Hague in April, 1776, reported that 800 barrels or 85,000 pounds of gunpowder had been shipped from Amsterdam for France, and certainly was destined to the American Colonies. A British informant in Rotterdam reported that eighteen Dutch vessels, laden with powder for the American market, had sailed from Amsterdam for St. Eustatius between January 1 and May 15, 1776. American sources reveal huge shipments of powder from St. Eustatius to Charleston and Philadelphia. J. F. Jameson, "St. Eustatius in the American Revolution," *A.H.R.*, VIII, 688.

[17] Edler, *op. cit.*, p. 27. I have found no record of it having been extended again, after French recognition of American independence and the intervention of France in the war. Dutch and other historians are obscure on this point.

minute Dutch possessions in the Leeward group, was a free port open to all flags coming and going with non-contraband. The local population had come to depend on American provisions for their existence. Such imports were an allowed trade and American agents and supercargoes were there to look after it; but these people had their eyes principally fixed on munitions of war, for which they were willing to pay abnormally high prices.[18] Despite the vigilance of British naval officers and their carelessness about respecting the precise boundaries of Dutch territorial waters, a part of these prohibited goods reached their ultimate destination.[19] Even English ships came to participate in this trade with the enemy.[20] In vain the British Ambassador requested more effective enforcement of the munitions embargo, and proposed to the States General a rationing system of certain imports to the Dutch Colonies. This Their High Mightinesses would not accept, nor the more drastic request for the cessation of all commerce between the Dutch West Indies and the revolted Colonies. Any active move required unanimity, and the Amsterdammers would not be expected to sacrifice their prodigious war profits. The States General did go so far as to remove the Governor of St. Eustatius in 1776, after British complaints, and to appoint Johannes de Graaff, who soon proved more objectionable than his predecessor. In November, 1776, a rebel brigantine, the *Andrew Doria,* flying the novel Stars and Stripes, came into the roadstead of St. Eustatius. She saluted the local fort with thirteen guns. The commander of the fortress, mistaking the ship for a merchant vessel, returned a salute of eleven guns, as was customary. At least such was the explanation given by de Graaff in a tardy official inquiry many months later.[21]

[18] Edler cites sources to show that gunpowder sold at St. Eustatius brought a profit of 120 to 400 per cent; that a trader could lose two out of three cargoes and still profit handsomely.

[19] For the rôle of the Dutch West Indies in the commerce of the American Revolution, see van Wijk, *op. cit.,* pp. 25–31; Edler, *op. cit.,* pp. 37–61; F. P. Renaut, *op. cit. (Provinces-Unies),* I, 189–216; and particularly J. F. Jameson, *op. cit.,* pp. 683–708.

[20] Van Wijk, *op. cit.,* p. 124.

[21] Jameson, *op. cit.,* p. 691, has pointed out that this was not, as it was long supposed to be, the first foreign salute to the American flag. The Danish fort at St. Croix returned the salute of an American schooner flying the new flag

The British Government made an issue of this incident, coupling the obnoxious salute with the violations of the Dutch munitions embargo. It demanded, February 21, 1777: (1) disavowal of the salute, (2) dismissal of de Graaff and his appropriate punishment, and (3) more efficient enforcement in the West Indies of the munitions embargo. If within three weeks the Ambassador should not receive a satisfactory answer to this ultimatum, couched in a very high and peremptory tone, he was instructed to leave the country. At the same time (February 15, 1777) orders went out to British naval commanders to search all Dutch ships going in or out of St. Eustatius and to send in to British ports all of them found to be carrying munitions or material for clothing. The States General called Governor de Graaff home to answer personally the charges made against him but did not dismiss him nor punish him; and they reaffirmed the earlier instructions to West Indian officials against the export of military stores to the American Colonies. They further explicitly stated that they would not hesitate to disavow acts of their officials which might in the least be construed to constitute a recognition of American independence. With this the British Government professed satisfaction, and immediately revoked the naval orders of February 15, though of course the revocation could not be notified before captures had already been commenced.[22] De Graaff returned to The Hague, some eighteen months later, submitted a voluminous printed volume of defense, was completely exonerated, not without an expression of confidence in his character, and sailed back in triumph to his island, late in 1779.[23] By that time many things had come to

over a cargo of gunpowder in October, 1776, several weeks before the *Andrew Doria* incident of November 16, 1776.

[22] Renaut, *Les Provinces-Unies et la guerre d'Amérique*, I, 208, states that by the autumn of 1777 about eighty Dutch ships had been detained in the West Indies; but we are uncertain whether they were all detained under this decree.

[23] Van Wijk, *op. cit.*, pp. 25–31; Renaut, *op. cit.*, I, 207. "De Graaff went out again as governor, and conducted himself so acceptably to the Americans that two of their privateers were named after him and his lady; and his portrait, presented sixty years afterward by an American citizen grateful for the 'first salute,' hangs in the New Hampshire state-house. Of his defense no more need now be said than that an observance of neutrality which gave to the one belligerent such absolute contentment and to the other such unqualified dissatisfaction can hardly have been perfect." Jameson, *op. cit.*, p. 695.

pass in Europe, including the entrance of France and Spain into the war.

Before French intervention in the American war, two other minor questions of "neutrality" arose in the Netherlands. Pressed for immediate, trained man-power to suppress the American revolt, and discouraged at the prospects of recruiting and drilling it soon enough in England, the British Ministry attempted to borrow or hire the services of foreign soldiers. In addition to the hiring of mercenaries from small German princes, dealers in cannon-fodder, there was another possibility: the employment of a Scottish Brigade of 6,000 men which for a long time had been incorporated in the Dutch army. Originally recruited in Scotland in 1570, it was one of the several foreign units which had been enrolled from time to time under the flag of the States General. Its men had served with William III in England during the years 1690–1700, thus constituting a remote precedent for such a loan. In 1775 the rank and file were no longer foreign, though the officers still were principally Scots. In August of that year while negotiations were proceeding with German princes for the hire of troops, the North Government approached the Stadhouder for the loan of these 6,000 men. The Prince, commander-in-chief of the army, favored the loan, but the Duke of Brunswick advised against it, and anyway it was the States General which controlled the matter. This fact necessitated debates *ad referendum* in the several provincial assemblies, a majority of which appeared to favor the proposal. In the Province of Overyssel, van der Capellen opposed lending the brigade, as a violation of neutrality, and thus introduced himself as a proponent of the American cause as well as of the political principles on which it rested.[24] When the matter eventually came up for resolution by the States General, that body (April, 1776) followed the lead of the province of Holland and, consenting, attached so many conditions to its consent—not the least of which was that the troops were not to be used outside of British possessions in Europe—that it was in fact

[24] Van Wijk, *op. cit.,* pp. 21–25.

a refusal, and the British Government did not press the subject further.[25]

The refusal of the Scottish Brigade may have had a decisive influence on British fortunes in Massachusetts and elsewhere, for if General Gage had received the reinforcements for which he appealed, it might not have been necessary for his successor to evacuate Boston in the spring of 1776. On the other hand the Dutch Government, in contradistinction to Frederick the Great, made no objection to the passage through its territory of unorganized bodies of mercenary German recruits for shipment on British transports; the larger problem presented by a British request for the passage of organized regiments coming down the Rhine was solved for the Netherlands by Frederick's refusal to let them go through his territory of Wesel.[26]

Thus indirectly in both the question of the Scottish Brigade and that of the military passage of Dutch territory, the States General was able to evade any definite pronouncement on neutrality in the conflict between Great Britain and the rebellious Colonies. The Netherlands was determined not to recognize the independence of the United States—that meant war with England and disaster for a nation with no adequate navy and no ally. We cannot say positively that the Netherlands even recognized the belligerency of the United States before 1778, though no such juridical distinction existed at that time.

No formally accredited diplomatic representative of the United States arrived in the Netherlands until 1780, but from the very beginning of the Revolution—before the Declaration of Independence—Charles William Frederick Dumas had served there as a paid observer and agent. We recall that the Committee of Secret Correspondence of the Continental Congress had retained this interesting friend of America,[27] to whom the United States

[25] Edler, *op. cit.*, p. 32; Renaut, *op. cit.*, I, 89–108; H. T. Colenbrander, *Patriottentijd*, 3 vols. (The Hague, 1897), I, 115–118; van Wijk, *op. cit.*, pp. 21–24.

[26] Van Wijk, *op. cit.*, p. 31; Renaut, *op. cit.*, pp. 107–108. Later in the war (during Frederick's Bavarian embarrassments) he did not refuse passage to British mercenaries.

[27] Franklin to C. W. F. Dumas, Philadelphia, Dec. 19, 1775, Wharton, II, 64.

owe a debt of gratitude never adequately recognized, to discover if possible the disposition of the several courts of Europe with respect to assistance for, or possible alliance with, the American Colonies. Dumas's services during these early years were those of collecting such international information as he could pick up at The Hague—which was then a sort of listening post for European politics in general—and relaying it to the Committee and, after 1776, to the American Commissioners at Paris. He also helped to disseminate American propaganda with good effect in a country where the British Ambassador had subsidized local pamphleteers.[28] He worked with great discretion but more or less under the eye and guidance of the French Ambassador. His activities, though they may have helped somewhat to neutralize public opinion, had no great effect on the apathy of the Dutch toward the American cause.

The involvement of the Netherlands in the war came not from any relation of that republic to the British Colonies in North America. It resulted from embarrassing problems that confronted the Dutch only after the intervention of France, and at a time when the naval forces of the United Provinces had sunk so low as to destroy respect for their pronouncements and to eliminate any expectation of a real defense of their rights.

For the neutrals of western Europe the outbreak of hostilities between France and England entirely changed the aspect of the

Dumas, 1721-1796, born of French parents in the German principality of Brandenburg-Anspach, was a naturalized Dutchman of Swiss education, an energetic *littérateur* who made a precarious living as tutor, translator, pamphleteer, and editor. He edited among other things an edition of Vattel which he sent to Franklin in 1775. Beginning with an inquiry about the intended emigration of himself and family to America, Dumas became one of the American philosopher's many friendly foreign correspondents on divers curious ideas and things. The alert penman, who was eager for some sort of regularly paid occupation, took up his duty of correspondent with great enthusiasm and even exaltation of soul, and continued with unquestionable loyalty. Early American diplomatists who met him were unanimous in praise of his able and loyal services. Dumas's letter-books and papers are now preserved in the Rijksarchief at The Hague. Facsimiles of those which deal with American affairs are in the Library of Congress. An inventory of the papers, together with the best biographical note, is published in the 1918 Report (*Verslag*) of the Rijksarchief.

[28] F. P. Renaut, *op. cit.*, I, 53, and same author's *La politique de propagande des Américains durant la guerre d'indépendance; C. W. F. Dumas et les Provinces-Unies, 1776–1780*, II.

war. In this purely maritime war sea power was the decisive factor. It was the policy of each great belligerent to increase its naval strength and to weaken that of its enemy. On such simple motives was based the attitude of France as well as of Great Britain toward neutral shipping. On the other hand, it was the policy of the neutral maritime powers—the Netherlands, Sweden, Denmark-Norway, the carriers of the world—to preserve intact their neutral position, based on their own interpretations of international law and treaty rights, and in addition to derive as much commercial profit as possible from the abnormal trade and navigation requirements of the belligerents. To the Netherlands particularly, the preservation of a neutral position and of capacious definitions of neutral rights was of such paramount importance that all parties and leaders were agreed on it. The great issues and difficulties came from the impossibility of defining neutral rights satisfactorily for both belligerent adversaries and from the anomalous treaties with Great Britain.

Economically the preservation of a liberal interpretation of neutral rights was important to the Netherlands because of the war profits of neutral carriage. The gradual subsidence of Dutch maritime activity and power since the naval wars with England, a decline which continued after the English alliance of 1678 and the struggle against Louis XIV, had been reflected in a drooping commerce and a deteriorating navy.[29] As maritime activity and strength decreased, Dutch business became transformed. The Dutch became the world's greatest international bankers,[30] instead of the world's greatest carriers. Amsterdam was Europe's money market, with loans placed directly or indirectly with the governments of England, Austria, Spain, Russia, and elsewhere. As compared with the swift, direct, and cheap movement of goods and money in the present day, the cumbersome system of credit exchange and purchase prevailing in the eighteenth century gave to the masters of credit facilities chances to extract a profit at

[29] For the melancholy condition of the Dutch navy at this time see Colenbrander, *Patriottentijd*, I, 154–157.
[30] P. J. van Winter, *Het Aandeel van den Amsterdamschen Handel aan den Opbouw van het Amerikaansche Gemeenebest* (The Hague, 1927), I, Ch. I.

every step, just as eighteenth-century transportation multiplied tolls and freight-handlers. These loans brought in the prevailing market rate of interest, as fixed by a European state's national credit, plus an important bonus or commission of 4 to 6 per cent, with various further annual charges for collection and handling of interest. Moreover the accumulations of previous years of Dutch profits and interests were invested in foreign countries, notably in English government bonds and in property everywhere beyond the republic's own boundaries.

In addition to this unmeasured amount of wealth invested outside of the country, there were the valuable Dutch colonies. Though deprived of New Netherland and of the old factories in Brazil, the United Provinces still possessed, through the medium of the quasi-governmental East India and West India companies, a scattered array of rich possessions all over the globe. The Dutch East India Company paid an average of 20 per cent annual dividends from 1750 to 1770, and 12½ per cent for longer stretches of years.[31] It had taxed the ingenuity of Dutch statesmen to keep clear of the several wars of the eighteenth century. A war with any enemy was bound to be disastrous, but a conflict with a great maritime power like Great Britain would be certain to open a series of calamities: the stoppage of interests, the possible confiscation of invested principals abroad, the cessation of profitable banking business, the cloture in part of agriculture exports, the collapse of carrying trade, the loss of colonies. Everything was liable to be lost, nothing likely to be gained, except with the assistance of a powerful and victorious ally. This prospect included the further loss of the chances of profitable loans to belligerent countries, and the substitution therefor of the burden of an increased national war debt.

Already the surreptitious commerce with North America had restored to prosperity the flagging navigation of Holland. The prospect of neutral carriage to British, French (particularly), and Spanish ports opened up new vistas of profit for the ship-

[31] F. P. Renaut, op. cit. (Provinces-Unies), I, 56.

owners of Amsterdam, Haarlem, and Dordrecht, profits which would vanish the minute the Provinces became a belligerent. From every point of view Dutch neutrality was desirable. From every point of view it was also vulnerable and perilous.

CHAPTER X

The Netherlands and Neutral Rights

The fundamental issues in the age-long controversy over neutral rights concerned principally four questions: (1) whether neutrals might enjoy a right to trade in innocent goods between port and port of an enemy power, including colonial ports, if the grant had not been made *bona fide* before the outbreak of war; (2) the degree of protection to be enjoyed by neutral property and ships on the high seas; (3) what constituted contraband; (4) what constituted legal blockade. Up to the time of the American war, the attitude of the naval powers of Europe on those questions had been determined by self-interest and expediency, but there was a distinct opposition of policy discernible between those powers possessing large navies and their smaller maritime neighbors. States passed by chapters of history from one of these opposing groups to the other, and changed attitudes accordingly.

(1) Take the question of neutral trade between enemy ports. In 1674 France, at war with the Netherlands, then a superior sea power, opened up to neutral English ships her coastwise carrying trade (*petit cabotage*), ordinarily in times of peace reserved exclusively for the French flag. The Netherlands protested and threatened to regard these English ships as enemy vessels. England defended the practice and appealed successfully to the letter of her treaty rights.[1] During the Seven Years' War, France, at war with Great Britain, went a step further and opened her colonial traffic (*grand cabotage*), normally reserved for French bottoms only, to Dutch carriage. The British immediately pro-

[1] By the treaty of peace between Great Britain and the States General of 9/21 February 1673/4 the maritime treaty of 7/17 February 1667/8 was renewed for nine months, and was soon superseded by the maritime treaty of Dec. 1, 1674. Both of these maritime treaties allowed neutral trade with enemy ports in noncontraband articles.

tested and constructed a new dictum, the Rule of 1756,[2] to stop this practice. This particular question did not arise during the earlier years of the American Revolution, because no belligerent opened to outsiders its coastwise or colonial traffic. International law on this point remained uncertain. This question came up during American neutrality in the wars of the French Revolution and Napoleon.

(2) The status of neutral property and ships at sea was a live issue in 1776–1783, as it had been since the beginning of the Atlantic Age of navigation. From the thirteenth century to the Age of Discovery, the crystallized law of the Mediterranean states had been the *consolato del mare:* namely, that neutral property (contraband always excepted) was safe from capture on enemy ships, but that enemy property was subject to capture on neutral ships.[3] It was a perfectly logical distinction which preserved to the stronger sea power the advantage which his larger navy gave him over his enemy. Deviations, unfavorable to neutrals, occurred from this rule when in the fourteenth century some states joined the fate of the neutral ship with the confiscated enemy cargo. Francis I of France exceeded the severity of the *consolato del mare* in 1533 and 1543, by declaring neutral property also forfeit if found on enemy ships; and went to the extreme limit not only of confiscating enemy property in neutral bottoms, but of presuming any fraction of enemy property to taint the remaining neutral cargo and the neutral vessel as well, making all subject to confiscation. This was repeated by French naval ordinances in 1584 and in 1681; and in 1744 France proclaimed again the dictum of confiscating enemy property in neutral ships and also neutral property in enemy ships. England generally followed the milder law of the *consolato del mare,* unextended.

The states with small navies when engaged in war with a stronger maritime power naturally desired to have recourse to neutral shipping to carry on their commerce and bring in their

---

[2] That a belligerent which in times of peace closes its colonial trade to foreign ships cannot, in times of war, open that trade to foreign neutrals, without making those neutrals liable to capture as enemy ships.

[3] This was sometimes known as unfree ships free goods, free ships unfree goods.

military supplies, because they could not protect their own ships with their own naval forces. The policy of the big-navy states impelled the small-navy powers, who were generally neutral carriers in time of war, to negotiate treaties, wherever and whenever possible, by which enemy property in neutral ships passed free; as a concession to the big-navy powers they agreed that neutral property on enemy ships should be subject to confiscation. Thus evolved the maxim of free ships free goods, unfree ships unfree goods, a principle distinctly favorable to neutral shipping,[4] particularly so when combined with the right to trade between port and port of an enemy state, as stipulated, for example, in the Anglo-Dutch maritime treaty of 1674. Various reasons of diplomatic expediency led the prominent naval powers, including France and England, occasionally to make such treaties as these, notably in the peace of Utrecht of 1713. But they were often arbitrarily interpreted or positively ignored; and unilateral pronouncements reverted to the principle of *consolato del mare*. England consistently maintained that special concessions for particular reasons in individual treaties did not alter the ancient law of nations, where it stood outside the range of such treaties.

(3) When considering the immunities of neutral property and navigation, every one agreed that they did not cover contraband of war. What was that? Originally definitions of contraband were limited to weapons of war. The above-mentioned French ordinances of 1543 and 1584 extended the category of contraband to "munitions of war," and numerous seventeenth-century treaties went further than that, bringing in soldiers, money, and provisions, as well as ships and naval stores; that is, they included some things which were more generally susceptible of peaceful use than of hostile employment. It was the practice of England, when not bound by treaty concessions to the contrary, to consider all naval stores, and sometimes provisions and grain, as

---

[4] Because it enables the neutral to take over belligerent carrying trade. The concession to belligerents in regard to confiscation of neutral property in enemy ships does not balance the great advantage to neutrals of free ships free goods, because neutral property is not so likely to be carried on belligerent ships as is enemy property on neutral ships.

contraband. But again, beginning with the later seventeenth century, nearly all the prominent sea powers had made, here and there, treaties restricting contraband to an enumerated list of implements and munitions of war, sometimes specifically excluding naval stores from the contraband articles, and sometimes carefully excluding all else. These novel regulations occurred principally in those treaties which called for free ships free goods and right of neutrals to trade between port and port of the enemy in non-contraband.

(4) The immunities of neutrals were not considered to permit carriage of goods of any kind to blockaded ports. Before 1780 there was no agreement as to what constituted a blockade. The Dutch in 1584 and 1636 and the Spanish in 1633 conceived the idea of simply declaring enemy harbors blockaded, without placing cruisers in front of them. When England and the Netherlands in 1689 *declared* the French coast under blockade and prohibited all commerce with it, Denmark and Sweden negotiated an alliance for the protection of their French trade against this "paper blockade" and forced the belligerents to relinquish it. Although there was a tendency for the treaties of the eighteenth century to stipulate that a blockade must be a real one, no general agreement had been reached on what constituted reality. The question of blockade did not come up, in the American war, until the siege of Gibraltar by Spain in 1779.

In short, international law then as now was in a state of uncertainty and evolution. It may be said, however, that of the four questions just examined the principle of the *consolato del mare* was still regarded as the prevailing international law in regard to the status of neutral property on the high sea, except when specifically set aside by particular treaties. Nevertheless in these newer treaties the old law was yielding to the new doctrine of free ships free goods: between 1650 and 1780, thirty-six treaties were concluded establishing free ships free goods, and only fifteen followed *consolato del mare.*[5] As to the other three issues the law was in a

[5] Matzen, in J. B. Scott, *Armed Neutralities of 1780 and 1800* (New York, 1918), p. 167.

much less certain status when the United States appeared as a sovereign nation to cope with these troublesome questions.[6]

The actual interests of each great maritime belligerent in 1778, as distinguished from any juridical concepts, were simple enough, and those interests served as axioms for the legal positions that were assumed in answer to the protests of neutrals. England had 122 fighting ships of one kind or another to France's sixty-three,[7] and despite the deployment of many of these vessels in American waters, she was still the stronger naval power. To maintain this superior maritime strength it was necessary to prevent France from replenishing and increasing her navy during the war. Both belligerents depended on outside sources for naval stores: masts and other ship's timbers, tar, pitch, hemp, cordage, canvas, wrought iron, etc. Most of these came across the North Sea from Scandinavia and the Baltic.[8] England's superior naval strength and geographical position enabled her to jeopardize any extensive French shipping in the Channel and North Sea, and thus to cut off the carriage in French bottoms of those vitally necessary navy-building commodities, or indeed of any other enemy goods. At the same time, she could protect the flow of Baltic naval stores in both British and neutral bottoms to her own arsenals. By denying the principle of free ships free goods and construing contraband to include naval stores of all kinds, she could further effectively deprive France of recruiting her weaker naval forces and merchant marine by the help of neutral shipping and could seriously injure French commerce in general. Conversely it was to

[6] The historical background of these several questions of neutral rights is adequately summarized, from a voluminous literature, by Carl Bergbohm, *Die bewaffnete Neutralität, 1780–1783* (Dorpat, 1883). Philip C. Jessup and Francis Deák deal carefully with historical aspects of belligerent right to seize enemy property in "The Early Development of the Law of Neutral Rights," *Political Science Quarterly*, XLVI (Dec., 1931), 481–508.

[7] Spain had sixty-two. These figures are taken from Colenbrander, *Patriot-tentijd, op. cit.*, I, 153.

[8] North America was another source, at least for all of these except iron and canvas, and the control of naval stores was one of the several principal bases of rivalry between France and Great Britain in the great wars of the eighteenth century. But the value of North America as a source of naval stores was mostly for accumulations in times of peace. The voyage was too long to cater to immediate requirements, and in 1778 the principal developed sources of naval stores were in the Colonies then in revolt.

the vital interest of France at this time to see that the Dutch and Danes and Swedes and other neutrals enjoyed, without challenge, these more liberal principles of free ships free goods and a specifically restricted list of contraband which would not include naval stores, on the ground that those commodities were equally susceptible to consumption for peaceful purposes. Under governance of these principles, naval stores could proceed without interruption into such French ports as the overtaxed British navy found it impossible really to blockade. The vital interests of France thus coincided with the interests of the neutrals. Those of Great Britain were opposed. French policy supported what the world has since called a more liberal and enlightened conception of neutral rights, which the Declaration of Paris (1856) may be said to have embodied in international law, but it supported them only because it was for the interest of France to espouse these principles.[9]

Great Britain would have been able to operate without challenge in 1778 against Dutch neutral commerce, on the principle of the *consolato del mare,* if the old Anglo-Dutch maritime treaty of 1674 had not stood in the way. This agreement stated that in case one of the parties were belligerent and the other neutral, the principle of free ships free goods should apply, excepting always contraband of war; and that contraband of war should include only a definitely enumerated list of warlike implements. The treaty further specified that naval stores and ship's timbers should not be accounted contraband. A separate explanatory article very expressly confirmed the freedom of neutral trade by these principles directly to enemy ports and between enemy ports.[10] Almost hand in hand with this ancient treaty went the Anglo-Dutch alliance

[9] "It was France's only way of assuring supplies to her ports and the maintenance of her navy, indispensable conditions for a naval war against England. France herself could not furnish the necessary shipping materials, and her fleet, particularly her merchant fleet, had been perceptibly reduced by the Seven Years' War; she herself would not have been able to import all necessities; for after the outbreak of hostilities with Great Britain they offered good prize." Fauchille, *Ligue des neutres, op. cit.,* pp. 16–17.

[10] Latin text in J. du Mont, *Corps universel diplomatique du droit des gens,* 8 vols. (Amsterdam, 1726–1731), VII, Pt. I, 282; English text in Chalmers, *Collection of Treaties between Great Britain and Other Powers,* 2 vols. (London, 1790), I, 172.

of 1678, by which each power bound itself to come to the active assistance of the other if attacked or threatened. It was because of this treaty of alliance, as well as the defensive clauses in the Family Compact with Spain, and in the Franco-Austrian alliance, that both France and Great Britain had evaded any formal declaration of war.

Great Britain had not felt constrained to invoke the *casus foederis* of the Dutch alliance as long as the conflict was restricted to a purely civil war, but after the beginning of hostilities with France she felt free to demand its fulfilment. If the United Provinces should insist upon the definitions of the maritime treaty of 1674 in regard to contraband and neutral cover, a procedure which the British Cabinet thought would ill become an ally, the British could reply by requesting active military assistance against France. *Ipso facto* Dutch belligerency as an ally of England would stop trading with the enemy. Should the Dutch repudiate the old alliance, King George III need have no compunctions in abrogating the embarrassing maritime treaty. Then the British navy could proceed unrestrained to enforce the traditional prize law against neutral Dutch shipping.

With the control of Dutch neutrality of such vital importance to each belligerent, the Low Countries, particularly the province of Holland and the maritime cities, became the scene of a diplomatic duel between the rival ambassadors, Sir Joseph Yorke and the Duke de la Vauguyon. In this contest Yorke relied on his acquired prestige and established connections with the Stadhouderian party and the title-holders of British funds. Vauguyon's task, following out a policy carefully outlined by Vergennes as early as July, 1776,[11] was to stir up the Patriot opposition and to exploit the eagerness of the Amsterdammers for the war profits already tasted in the forbidden trade with the American Colonies, profits which promised to multiply if France should enter the conflict. If the voice of the Province of Holland could be made to speak for the maintenance of neutral rights, as written into the

[11] See Vergennes's memoir of July 7, 1776, Doniol, I, 527–529; and his original instructions to Vauguyon, of Nov. 28, 1776, Fauchille, *op. cit.*, p. 28.

English treaty of 1674, and at the same time to reject the *casus foederis* of the treaty of 1678, half the diplomatic battle would be won; for Holland's vote could estop any operation of the alliance, whilst a demand for enforcement of the treaty principles, made by this most powerful and influential province, would be a far-advancing stride toward that goal.[12]

The French decrees of prize law were so phrased as to assist France's diplomacy with the neutrals, particularly the Netherlands. The first French pronouncement regarding prize law, made on June 24, 1778,[13] was quite inconsistent with the principles proclaimed in the Franco-American treaty of commerce and was soon modified. It suggests that Vergennes did not, at that first moment, have in mind the value of nursing the several neutrals toward a common armed defense of liberal principles against Great Britain. The royal proclamation of this date, with the avowed object of stimulating and rewarding the ardor of French privateers, reenacted the naval ordinance of August, 1681. This celebrated code had accepted the principle from the *consolato del mare*.[14] It said, as to contraband: "Arms, powder and bullets, and other munitions of war, even horses and equipment transported for the service of our enemies, will be confiscated, in whatever vessel they may be found, no matter to whom they may belong, even if to our subjects and allies." [15] It will be observed that this does not specifically include naval stores, nor does it pointedly specify that all goods not enumerated shall never be contraband. Immediately after the proclamation of this ordinance the French Government realized the unfortunate effect which it would have on any policy of stimulating neutral opposition to Great Britain and how, under existing

[12] The Dutch shrank away from a French proposal for a triple treaty for the definition and maintenance of neutral rights by France, Spain and the Netherlands. Fauchille, *op. cit.*, p. 89.

[13] June 16, 1778, when the French frigates *Pallas* and *Licorne* were seized by an English squadron, was proclaimed the date of beginning of the war, in a letter of Louis XVI to the Admiral of France, April 5, 1779. Piggott and Omond, *Documentary History of the Armed Neutralities, 1780 and 1800* (London, 1919), p. 82.

[14] See articles 6 and 7.

[15] Article 11.

unequal naval power, all French imports would be cut down if France so unreservedly followed these severe English principles.[16] The chief significance of this short-lived ordinance of June 24 is to demonstrate that when France presently adopted a different policy as to neutrals she did so not with the motive of introducing into international law a more enlightened theory as to neutral shipping, but for the purpose of exploiting dicta that supported her vital military and political interests. The fact that within a few weeks France could proclaim now one and now the opposite principle, now the rule of the *consolato del mare*, now free ships free goods, now the latter in European and the former in far eastern seas,[17] also shows conclusively that what seems to-day the more liberal doctrine was not international law at that time.

A new royal ordinance of July 26, 1778, speedily reversed French prize law in order to accomplish two purposes: first, to secure neutral carriage to French harbors, according to the principle of particular treaties incorporating free ships free goods, between the Netherlands and England (1674), and Russia and England (1766), and which France had guaranteed to Denmark (1742); second, to influence and to coerce neutral governments, particularly the States General, to *enforce* this doctrine against Great Britain, which was also the doctrine of the Anglo-Dutch treaty of 1674 and the Franco-American treaty of 1778, that naval stores could not be contraband. Otherwise put, the ordinance of July 26 aimed to make neutrals force Great Britain into letting them take to the enemy naval stores so that he might repair and build up his fleet in order to equal, surpass, and finally overpower the British navy. It forbade French armed vessels to detain neutral ships, even when proceeding from or destined to an enemy port not blockaded, except when carrying contraband. The definition of contraband of the preceding ordinance of June 24, which did not mention naval stores, was left unchanged. Further it sig-

[16] Fauchille, *op. cit.,* p. 68.

[17] Even after the reversal of the ordinance of June 24, 1778, by the new proclamation of July 26, 1778, the principle of June 24—that is, the code of 1681—was proclaimed in 1781 in special instructions to the governors of the East India colony of Ile de France and Bourbon. Piggott and Omond, *op. cit.,* p. 83.

nificantly reserved the right to revoke this "liberty" to neutral shipping, if England should not accord similar treatment within six months.[18]

Vergennes thus hastily put forth a new plan to undo the mistake of the earlier decree. Could the neutrals with their weak naval power prevail on the mistress of the seas to yield to the designs of her enemy? The Netherlands, most important carrier of all the neutrals, had the guaranty of the English treaty of 1674, but this was counterbalanced by the alliance which they had made to support England against any attack or even mobilization by an enemy.

It was on this century-old and now decrepit alliance that British diplomacy relied to bring the Dutch to terms in matters of prize law. Before the actual outbreak of war in Europe, Yorke felt out a leading member of the Amsterdam city government and promised that England would not ask for the help stipulated in the alliance of 1678 and would not interfere with Dutch shipping to the French West Indies, if the Republic would refrain from allowing the ships of its subjects to take naval stores to French ports. If the intimations were intended as a means of stirring the Assembly of Holland or members of the States General themselves, they had no effect.[19] The Amsterdam shippers and merchants already had their hands on the new war profits from the transport of naval stores. Following the failure of his overture, the ambassador received instructions from the British Foreign Office to the effect that Great Britain would never permit the citizens of the Netherlands to become carriers for her enemies, that the old claim of free ships free goods would never be admitted.[20] In July, British cruisers began detaining Dutch vessels in the Channel and elsewhere; by September, twenty-nine had been taken; in October, forty-two more. The formal instructions to British privateers, of August 5, 1778, were vaguely worded as to free ships free goods; they did not expressly allow the taking of enemy property from neutral ships, nor did they actually for-

[18] Fauchille, pp. 67–73; full French text in Piggott and Omond, *op. cit.*, p. 89.
[19] Colenbrander, *op. cit.*, I, 133.
[20] Suffolk to Yorke, April 14, 1778, cited by Edler, *Dutch Republic, op. cit.*, p. 99.

bid it.[21] Characteristically the Admiralty reserved the principle, and expediently refrained from asserting it for the time being. The numerous captures during the summer of 1778 gave Vauguyon a chance to stir up the trading elements of Holland to urge the States General to protest and to increase the naval forces of the Republic adequately to protect its commerce.[22] On September 28, 1778, the Dutch Ambassador in London delivered a memorial by the States General protesting several enumerated spoliations and in general the violation of Dutch neutral rights as fixed by the treaty of 1674, particularly the seizure of ship's timbers enroute to France.[23]

The British answer was not immoderate, if we consider the fact of the alliance of 1678. It did not contest the principle of free ships free goods, but it insisted on including naval stores and especially ship's timbers in the category of contraband. Great Britain stood ready to purchase at appraised value naval stores seized on Dutch vessels and to allow compensation for damages occasioned by detention of the ships.[24] Dutch bottoms with non-contraband cargoes (as defined by England) would be allowed free passage even to enemy ports. Except for the inclusion of naval stores within the list of contraband, this was in conformity with the maritime treaty of 1674, and Great Britain was offering to pay for the contraband instead of confiscating it. The British position is not surprising in view of the heavy obligations of the Netherlands under the alliance of 1678, as renewed in 1716. England now endeavored to couple the two treaties in the Anglo-

[21] "That the commanders of ships and vessels, so authorised, as aforesaid [*i.e.*, commanders or privateers], shall bring all ships, vessels and goods, which they shall seize and take, into such port of this our realm of England or some other port of our dominions not in rebellion, as shall be most convenient for them, in order to have the same legally adjudged on in our high court of admiralty of England, or before the judges of any other admiralty-court, lawfully authorized within our dominions." August Hennings, *Sammlung von Staatsschriften, die, während des Seekrieges von 1776 bis 1783 . . . öffentlich bekannt gemacht worden sind . . .* (Altona, 1785), II, 44.

[22] Fauchille, *op. cit.,* pp. 74–77.

[23] Edler, *op. cit.,* p. 104, cites text in Bancroft transcripts. See also Fauchille, *op. cit.,* p. 78.

[24] Suffolk to Welderen, Oct. 19, 1778, as cited by Edler, *op. cit.,* p. 107, from Bancroft transcripts. Piggott and Omond, *op. cit.,* p. 104, print an uncertain summary from the *Annual Register.*

Dutch conversations. Yorke suggested a joint commission to settle the relation of mutual obligations, proposing that, pending the outcome of the conference, the Netherlands were not to insist on the immunity of naval stores and Great Britain was not to demand fulfilment of the alliance.[25] In fine, the British Ministry offered to waive the right to military assistance by the old alliance of 1678 if the Dutch would give up only one article, but a very vital one, of the treaty of 1674, namely free passage for naval stores to France. It was a not unreasonable proposal to a nation whose people would not support the antiquated British alliance. To refuse this reasonable compromise was to do so in the face of the British navy and to throw the Republic at the feet of France, to which it was bound by no protecting alliance and which was unable to protect Dutch commerce against British prize law. Rejection of the English proposal might also mean the probable loss of the carriage to French ports of innocent enemy property; for Great Britain could hardly be expected to observe the other provisions of the treaty of 1674 if the Dutch refused to execute the articles of the alliance. To spurn the British propositions and really to insist on the freedom of naval stores meant, finally, war itself.

The Stadhouder naturally would have accepted them, and so would Brunswick; but the Amsterdammers saw their golden profits vanishing, and the Grand Pensionary of Holland, van Bleiswijk, had now superseded Brunswick in the counsels of the timorous Prince. The States General repelled the proffered conference and declared for the fulness of its rights under the treaty of 1674. From then on, the men who directed the destiny of the defenseless Netherlands at this trying period proceeded more and more precariously along the narrowing plank of neutrality.[26] Having refused the British offer, they declined in almost

[25] It was to be hoped, said Yorke, that the result of the conference would induce Their High Mightinesses "not to authorise their subjects to carry naval stores under convoy to France, as being the most dangerous object to the security of Great Britain." Piggott and Omond, *op. cit.*, p. 106 (from quotations in a summary printed in the *Annual Register* for 1779, p. 421, of Yorke's note of November 2, 1778, to the States General).

[26] Colenbrander, *op. cit.*, I, 135. It is the opinion of this eminent Dutch authority that the English offer should have been accepted.

the same breath to take the necessary steps to defend their treaty rights of 1674. On November 19, 1778, the States General voted to exclude ship's timbers from the rights of convoy, but not other naval stores. The trading interests were now demanding increased armaments and the actual sending-out of convoys.

The resolutions of November 19, favoring the principle of limited convoys, satisfied neither belligerent. Great Britain replied by Admiralty instructions to cruisers to seize all Dutch ships laden with naval stores,[27] but to let innocent cargo pass free. For the present, George III's Government refrained from presenting the formal demand for the *casus foederis*. Vauguyon, on his side, after a preliminary visit to Amsterdam, presented a note to the States General inquiring whether or not the United Provinces were determined to maintain a perfect neutrality, which meant of course whether they were determined to protect with their ships of war the carriage of naval stores to French arsenals. A failure to insist on "perfect neutrality" (as defined by France), said he, would be followed by a suspension of the particular privileges announced in the ordinance of July 26, 1778, upon the expiration of the conditional six months.[28] To this the States General returned only a vague and unsatisfactory answer. Immediately (January 16, 1779) Vauguyon communicated a copy of a French decree,[29] to take effect January 26, revoking as far as the Netherlands were concerned, the neutral privileges of July 26, 1778. On January 28, the States General, under the impulsion of Holland, declared for unlimited convoy, but only as soon as the maritime resources of the Republic would allow it, and at the same time summoned the College of the Admiralty to deliberate and advise upon ways and means, a meeting which resulted only in further postponement. The announcement of these deliberations had led the French Government to postpone until March 1, 1779, the execution of the revocatory measure. On that day it went into effect. It withdrew the neutral "liberties" existing during the previous provisional six months, and now ordered, for

[27] Hennings, *op. cit.*, II, 59.
[28] Colenbrander, *Patriottentijd*, I, 137; Fauchille, pp. 97-98; text in Wharton, II, 854.
[29] For text see Piggott and Omond, *op. cit.*, p. 108.

an indefinite provisional period, the capture and confiscation of enemy goods on neutral Dutch ships. It further laid a special tax on all Dutch vessels entering French ports.[30]

The most significant and indeed an invidious part of the revocatory decree was the exception from its operation of ships belonging to citizens of the cities of Amsterdam and Haarlem, on the grounds of their conscientious efforts to procure unlimited convoys.[31] The purpose of this exception was twofold. In the first place, these two cities carried a greater portion of Dutch trade in naval stores to France; by allowing their ships to come in tax-free, France could still assure a continuing supply of such cargoes of these indispensable materials as could get through the British navy. In the second place, by favoring the Amsterdammers so signally it was intended to prevail upon other excluded, and therefore jealous, maritime cities to make the same demands and thus to swing over the whole province of Holland to demand unlimited convoys. It was a suggestion to the whole nation that unlimited convoy would bring back the "liberal" privileges of the ordinance of July 26, 1778.

These postponements of enforcing the decree, whether so intended or not, afforded opportunity for a great fleet of about 300 merchant vessels to leave the Texel for French ports. Most of them carried ordinary innocent cargoes, but fifteen contained naval stores. A convoy of nine warships accompanied the fleet, with specific orders to exclude from its protection cargoes of ship's timbers but not other naval stores. The fifteen vessels, some with the unprotected timber and some with protected naval stores, mingled with the whole aggregation. It would have been necessary for the British Admiralty not only to contest by armed force the Dutch claim to protection of all naval stores except ship's timbers but to challenge and to search through the whole convoy to find even the unprotected *bois de construction*. The

[30] This particular discrimination was perfectly possible in view of the absence of any treaty between France and the Netherlands. Since the Dutch shrinking from Vergennes's proposals of January, 1778, the French Foreign Minister had followed studiously a policy of keeping his hands free, the better to be able to coerce the neighboring republic. Colenbrander, *op. cit.*, I, 169.

[31] Piggott and Omond, *op. cit.*, pp. 108–109.

British Government was not at this time prepared to cut the Gordian knot. The whole fleet passed unmolested through the Channel. A vast amount of supplies, including some naval stores, thus arrived in France before the revocatory decree took effect. Now that the last-mentioned decree was finally in operation, now that the French had repudiated, so far as the Dutch (except for the Amsterdammers) were concerned, the doctrine of free ships free goods—which even the British had not yet contested with the Netherlands—could the British navy be expected to let another such mixed convoy pass free again with naval stores hidden in it? The Dutch Minister at the Court of St. James answered this question in a despatch in April, 1779, stating that new naval orders had been issued to arrest and bring in all vessels bearing naval stores to the enemy, even if under convoy.[32]

The repeal of the privileges of July 26, 1778, with the studied and sinister discrimination in favor of the Amsterdammers, was the principal French thrust in this diplomatic duel at The Hague. The British still reserved their counter-stroke, the formal demand of the *casus foederis* of 1678. The year 1780 in Dutch diplomacy may be epitomized in the growing strength and success of the Patriot party, manipulated astutely by the clever young Vauguyon, in its campaign to overthrow the resistance to unlimited convoy marshaled by the veteran Yorke. The French discrimination had been singularly successful. Other cities of Holland, observing all the profitable French war trade monopolized by Amsterdam and Haarlem, broke away from the opposition. The provincial assembly of Holland voted on March 30, 1779, in favor of unlimited convoy, but France would not extend the Amsterdam exemptions to the whole province until it had taken more effective steps than a mere pronouncement to secure real action from the States General.[33] To coerce the other cities of Holland, France declared a special tariff of 15 per cent in addition to other discriminations of the revocatory decree, but leaving free entrance for naval stores.[34]

[32] Edler, *op. cit.*, p. 125.
[33] Colenbrander, *op. cit.*, I, 149–150.
[34] Decree of May 1, 1779, Fauchille, *op. cit.*, p. 137.

This pressure brought results. The Assembly of Holland within a few weeks resolved that the States General ought to put unlimited convoy into effect within four weeks.[35] In turn, France lifted the discriminations, in favor of the entire province, but for four weeks only, restoring them when the States General took no action. This time the exemption was extended to three other cities, Rotterdam, Schiedam, and Dordrecht, who had joined Amsterdam and Haarlem in threatening to withdraw their contributions to the general treasury if the unlimited convoy were not unconditionally granted.[36] It now became a matter of endless intrigue to prevail upon the other cities to come over to the threatening position of the five protestants. Vauguyon had a free hand from his government to grant special licenses to the citizens of approved cities, or even to approved individuals, and he dispensed these effectively through the French consuls. Delft, Leiden, Gouda, and Gorkum soon joined the five. They too received their reward from France.[37] Meanwhile, irritating incidents and measures increased the tension between Great Britain and the United Provinces and sharpened the feeling of the Dutch people at large, thus working into the hands of the Patriots and their whip, the French Ambassador.

When Spain declared war on England, June 21, 1779, the act was accompanied by a formal French manifesto of war until then unpronounced. This gave technically a double cause for England to call for the assistance of the Dutch. Observing the drift of affairs in Holland, Yorke advised, and was permitted to present, July 22, 1779, a formal demand on the States General for the *casus foederis* of the alliance. This demand was in the nature of a warning of what might happen if unlimited convoy were voted, rather than an ultimatum, and the States General delayed answer, even when the demand was repeated, Novem-

---

[35] Fauchille, *op. cit.,* p. 142; Colenbrander, *op. cit.,* I, 161.

[36] Colenbrander, *op. cit.,* I, 162–163. To discipline the agricultural towns of the northern part of the province, a French decree suddenly cut off the importation of Dutch cheeses, but indulgences and exceptions to French importers weakened the effect of this measure. For interesting documents bearing on the cheese embargo, see Colenbrander, I, 164, 384–388.

[37] *Ibid.*

ber 26. This neglect the British Ministry did not overlook; meanwhile, in September, de Graaff returned, exonerated, to his post at St. Eustatius, despite the British ultimatum of 1776 for his punishment. In October, the American commander, John Paul Jones, came into the Texel with the prizes he had made in his immortal battle with the *Serapis* and the *Countess of Scarborough*. He insisted on being treated as a belligerent naval officer, perhaps in a preconcerted attempt to maneuver the United Provinces into some kind of recognition of the belligerency, if not the independence, of the United States; but the Dutch Admiralty after much delay finally obliged him to depart, December 27, 1779, without having made any decision as to his status.[38]

Jones's visit, his popularity on shore, and Yorke's protests at the continued presence of the American flag in Dutch waters all helped further to quicken British resentment. As Jones lifted anchor in the Texel, another great Dutch limited convoy of merchant ships for French and Spanish ports, containing some vessels loaded with naval stores and convoyed by a few armed vessels under Admiral Bylandt, took advantage of the same fair wind. Several other vessels loaded with unprotected ship's timbers went out at the same time, but whether scattered among the convoy, as the British suspected, or sailing separately to get lower rates of insurance, no one knows certainly to this day. A British naval force, under Admiral Fielding, forcibly overpowered Bylandt's feeble convoy and took into port, in accordance with the recently announced British intentions, nine ships loaded with hemp and iron. The prize courts speedily confiscated both ships and cargoes. The cargoes of ship's timbers eluded capture and got safely to enemy port.

Though it is difficult to see how the British Ministry could have pursued any other course, this incident afforded a great success for French diplomacy. It swung Dutch opinion overwhelmingly to the Patriot party and its program. Van Bleiswijk himself went over to them completely. The unwilling Stadhouder was obliged to drift with the stream. A ringing protest to England against violation of treaty rights met only the shrugging re-

[38] Van Wijk, *op. cit.*, pp. 65–67.

ply that there was no longer any means of telling whether to regard the Dutch as allies, or as neutrals with no claim to special treatment. At the behest of the Patriots the States General, still playing for time and hoping for peace, referred two portentous measures to the provincial assemblies for discussion: proposed adoption of the principle of unlimited convoy, and a projected armament of fifty-two ships-of-the-line, to furnish the convoy and protect Dutch interests. The response of Great Britain to this was to present, March 21, 1780, for the third and last time, with a time limit of three weeks, the demand of the *casus foederis*.[39] One week earlier, the Province of Holland had already resolved against any treaty assistance to England, on the specious ground that the origin of the war was in America, while the treaty of 1678 was alleged to apply only when England became involved in a war in Europe.[40] The States General resolved nothing within the three weeks. A British order-in-council therefore finally declared (April 17, 1780) that the States General had deserted the alliance, and that thereafter the Dutch would be considered on the same footing with all other neutral states not privileged by treaty. The treaty of 1674 and all other treaties were annulled. Simultaneously an order to naval commanders required them to seize all Dutch vessels laden with enemy property or with "effects which are considered as contraband by the general law of nations."[41]

If the States General should accept unlimited convoy, vote for an armament on sea and deny any treaty help to England, wrote Vauguyon to Vergennes, the Republic would have done everything which France had desired in the beginning.[42] Events were now marching rapidly toward this perfect consummation of French diplomacy. One by one the provinces resolved for unlimited convoy and an adequate naval armament. The former measure passed the States General on April 24, 1780, and the armament provision shortly afterward. But too late, too late. It would

[39] Edler, *op. cit.,* pp. 131–132.
[40] Colenbrander, *op. cit.,* I, 168.
[41] Edler, *op. cit.,* p. 135.
[42] March 31, 1780, cited by Colenbrander, *op. cit.,* I, 169.

take months to complete the armament and man the ships, months to replenish the depleted dockyards. Meanwhile the new British orders delivered over Dutch navigation to a host of avaricious privateers. The French diplomatic victory meant the prostration of Dutch trade, navigation, and commerce, innocent as well as contraband. Louis XVI immediately restored the liberal maritime ordinance of July 26, 1778, and repealed the special tariffs and discriminations on Dutch ships in French harbors. But the French navy was unable to prevent the remorseless application of the British naval orders to Dutch shipping.

As these black clouds swept down from across the Channel and North Sea over the commerce and prosperity of the United Provinces, threatening perhaps the very independence of that country, a single bright ray of hope flashed suddenly forth from the northeastern horizon.

CHAPTER XI

The Armed Neutrality of 1780 and the Involvement of the Netherlands in the War

England's treaty relationships with the principal neutrals, other than the Netherlands, had not drifted very far from the *consolato del mare*. It is true that a comparatively recent treaty with Russia (1766) had allowed neutral trading to enemy ports with noncontraband and had narrowly restricted the contraband list so as not to include naval stores or any kind of provisions. As the Russian merchant marine was almost negligible these concessions had no real effect on the flow of naval stores to England's enemies; such articles were carried by Dutch, Danish, Swedish, and to a lesser degree before 1781 by Prussian ships. Old treaties with Sweden (1661) and Denmark (1670) followed the *consolato del mare,* and in both these treaties the contraband lists, while not specifically including naval stores, were extended (in the Danish treaty) to "all other instruments of war" and (in the Swedish treaty) to "all other things necessary for warlike use." With Prussia and with the Empire, Great Britain had no treaty stipulations covering these points; hence according to English theory the "ancient law" would govern. British cruisers and privateers proceeded to treat the shipping of these neutrals (excepting Russia) even more drastically than they had dealt with that of the Dutch. Protests came in to London from Denmark, Sweden, and Prussia as spoliation cases piled up in the prize courts. The Foreign Office declared to the protestants, on October 19, 1778, that, after November 10, neutral vessels and cargoes would be confiscated, if they carried enemy property or contraband, including naval stores.[1]

---

[1] Lord Suffolk to the Danish, Swedish, and Prussian Ministers, October 19, 1778. In the case of Swedish, Danish, and Prussian ships brought in before November 10, 1778, neutral cargo of an innocent nature and the ships them-

Thus did Great Britain take her stand firmly on the *consolato del mare* and the hostile character of naval stores. In doing so she was not violating her engagements, except to the extent of rather expansively interpreting the words "all other instruments of war" of the Danish treaty.[2] Denmark and Sweden therefore did not have any very solid grounds for protest except in the case of spoliations contrary to the accepted British practice. With Russia the English were more careful. Toward the end of 1778—after the answer to the Scandinavian protests—two Russian ships loaded with naval stores en route for Havre were brought into English ports and subjected to indefinite delay. After many months, in December, 1779, the English Ambassador assured the Russian Court that "the navigation of Russian subjects would never be detained or interrupted by British vessels." [3]

It was therefore not the violation of Great Britain's treaty obligations but the enticing offers of the French decree of July 26, 1778, which stirred the Scandinavians to action. After that decree had extended the principle of free ships free goods and called upon neutral states to secure from Great Britain an acknowledgment of the same "liberal" principle within six months, the Foreign Minister of Denmark, Count A. P. Bernstorff, sounded out the Swedish Court as to the practicability of an eventual diplomatic concert of the Netherlands, Sweden, and Denmark for the maintenance of neutral rights against England.[4] An event had occurred to bring Russian interests into play before such a pro-

selves would be released; contraband cargo of neutral ownership would be pre-empted at a fair price, with allowance for freight; court costs would be remitted; but all enemy property would be forfeit. These professed concessions were made on account of the uncertainty with which the existence of a state of war, undeclared, had come into existence. Bergbohm, *Bewaffnete Neutralität, op. cit.,* p. 68; Fauchille, *Ligue des neutres, op. cit.,* pp. 223–224.

[2] The looser phraseology of the Swedish treaty of 1670 made it quite reasonable to include naval stores in the category of "all other things necessary for warlike use," and such a construction was actually accepted also by Denmark, in the special convention of July 4, 1780. For text, Scott, *Armed Neutralities, op. cit.,* pp. 295–296.

[3] Malmesbury, *Diaries and Correspondence,* I, 269.

[4] Bernstorff to Guldencrone (Danish Minister at Stockholm), August 25, 1778, quoted by Thorvald Boye, *De Vaebnede Neutralitetsforbund, et Avsnit av Folkerettens Historie* (Christiania, 1912), pp. 142 ff.; printed in part only by J. B. Scott, *op. cit.,* pp. 48–49.

posal could have been fully discussed. An "American privateer" —the ship seems not yet to have been otherwise more specifically identified—appeared in the northernmost parts of the North Sea in July, 1778, and fell on eight British ships loaded with Russian cargoes plying the Archangel trade. It destroyed four of them, took three others in prize, and let the eighth go, after stripping it of gear, ballast and anchor—the crew were lucky enough to be picked up by fishermen in the neighborhood of Kola.[5] Incensed at this treatment of neutral cargo, Catherine II immediately proposed to Denmark, August 25, 1778, an alliance to protect the shipping of both countries by the use of separate cruising squadrons stationed along their respective coastal waters. This would have amounted to a special protection of British vessels against the depredations of American privateers, should any more appear in those distant waters, for no French carrier was venturing into the North Sea. Bernstorff perceived this, and in reply, September 29, proposed a more solid kind of alliance, which would extend protection to Russian and Danish shipping in all seas, according to a set of principles which he set forth in writing, after having drawn on papers left in the Danish Foreign Office by the distinguished jurist, Professor Max Hübner.[6] These were, practically word for word, none other than the principles subsequently proclaimed by Catherine II in 1780 as those of the Armed Neutrality. But in 1778 the Russian Minister of Foreign Affairs, Count Panin, advised against such an alliance, either with Denmark, or with Sweden, who would have been eager to join. He felt that Russia had no great maritime issues at stake, that Bernstorff's scheme consequently would serve only to assure Scandinavian neutral-carriage war profits; at the same time it might involve Russia in trouble with England unnecessarily, thus paralyzing the Empress's primary policy of advance in the direction of Constantinople. S the Bernstorffian proposal, though not rejected, was set aside and nothing more followed for the moment except a rather harmless Russo-Danish notification to the belligerents of a plan to patrol their respective coastal waters.[7]

[5] Bergbohm, *op. cit.*, p. 79.
[6] Boye, *op. cit.*, pp. 123–133.
[7] Bergbohm, *op. cit.*, pp. 79–103.

A dramatic chapter of occurrences made this feeble Russo-Danish "concert" of 1778–1779 the precursor of the more formidable Armed Neutrality of 1780. When Spain entered the war, she proclaimed a prize law more drastic even than that of England: *consolato del mare* plus the confiscation of neutral goods in enemy ships [8]; moreover all neutral vessels carrying cargoes of provisions or of materials of war destined ostensibly to Mediterranean ports, but suspected of being really intended for the besieged port of Gibraltar, were to be taken into Cadiz for sale of their cargoes to the highest bidder.[9] Soon a Dutch ship with Russian cargo was thus treated, and, before the Russian protests on this score could be answered, a Russian ship met a similar fate. These incidents precipitated the celebrated Declaration of Catherine II of February 28, 1780.

The court of St. Petersburg, from which this pronouncement descended *ex cathedra,* had been the stage for a spectacular duel between British and French diplomacy like that of The Hague. Confronted by a world of bitter enemies and nervous frowning neutrals, Great Britain had sent to Russia her most brilliant diplomatist, young Sir James Harris, to secure an alliance if possible. Catherine II and her powerful favorite, Prince Potemkin, treated Harris in a most flattering way, but the English Ambassador was not deceived by these caresses. He realized that it was difficult for the Empress to override the advice of her old and indolent but cautious minister, Count Panin, not to swerve from neutrality, not to be lured into a war which could do Russia no possible good but which might do her much harm. On the other hand, French diplomacy was active at all the northern courts, trying to stimulate allied neutral opposition to Great Britain. The idea of such a concert, even an armed league of neutrals, was not original with Vergennes,[10] but he had seized

[8] Ordinance of July 1, 1779, Hennings, *Sammlung, op. cit.,* II, 299.

[9] Bergbohm, *op. cit.,* pp. 106–109.

[10] Vergennes's first suggestions to his diplomatic representatives at the northern courts to stimulate such a concert were not made until September 17, 1778 (Fauchille, *op. cit.,* p. 211), whereas, as will be seen from the dates mentioned in the above text, Bernstorff had already made overtures to Sweden, and Russia had already proposed a Danish alliance.

hold of it and actively pressed it from the moment Bernstorff had first envisioned it in the summer of 1778; and the French representative at St. Petersburg was urging this as a means of blocking Harris's efforts for a British alliance. When news reached that capital of the Spanish captures,[11] Catherine II, acting independently of Count Panin, and apparently under the impulsion of her favorite Potemkin, a man whom Harris believed bound to himself, gave orders to the Admiralty for the immediate preparation of a naval armament.

The astonished diplomatists were at a loss to know against which belligerent the armament was designed. Potemkin joyfully assured Harris, who had urged vigorous action against Spain for these spoliations, that it was intended for use against Spain. He asserted that this threat to one of Great Britain's enemies was equivalent to the addition of twenty ships-of-the-line to the British navy. To the nonplussed Panin the Admiralty order also suggested naval coöperation with England against Spain, with all the entangling involvements such action was sure to bring. What must have been his consternation when he received sudden orders from the Empress to prepare a statement to the world explaining the Russian naval armament: namely, that it was to be used to protect neutral Russian commerce against *all* belligerents, according to a definite code of neutral rights which he was instructed to formulate and announce to the powers at war. At the same time an indignant protest was to go out to Spain, and Panin was to suggest to the French and the Prussian ambassadors that they advise Spain to yield and reform her prize law. The neutral maritime nations, Portugal, the Netherlands, Sweden, Denmark–Norway, Prussia, and Austria, were to be invited to associate themselves with Russia for the protection of commerce and the guaranty of neutral rights. Panin, now realizing his chance in conformity with the Czarina's own instructions to frustrate the possibility of joint Russian action with England, hastily drew up the necessary papers. For the principles of neutral rights which

[11] It so happened that on the same voyage the Russian ship, the *St. Nicholas,* which had been taken into Cadiz by the Spanish, had been searched and let pass free by a British cruiser.

Catherine had directed him to indite, he merely copied off the Hübnerian dicta offered by Bernstorff in September, 1778, with modifications of the treaty definition of contraband.[12] The first three of these principles had already been written into the American "Plan of 1776" and the French-American treaty of commerce and amity of February 6, 1778, as well as into many a small-navy-power treaty of the seventeenth and eighteenth centuries. The fourth was a newly defined proposition. They were:

"1. That neutral vessels may navigate freely from port to port and along the coasts of the nations at war.

"2. That the effects belonging to subjects of the said Powers at war shall be free on board neutral vessels, with the exception of contraband merchandise.

"3. That, as to the specification of the above-mentioned merchandise, the Empress holds to what is enumerated in the 10th and 11th articles of her treaty with Great Britain,[13] extending her obligations to all the Powers at war.

"4. That to determine what constitutes a blockaded port, this designation shall apply only to a port where the attacking Power has stationed its vessels sufficiently near and in such a way as to render access thereto clearly dangerous.

"5. That these principles shall serve as a rule for proceedings and judgments as to the legality of prizes." [14]

These rules Catherine II proclaimed in a Declaration addressed to the Courts of London, Versailles, and Madrid. Following the advice and example of France, Spain accepted the Russian demands, including the principles of the Armed Neutrality, as her prize law. Great Britain, without accepting the principles, promised *to observe her treaty obligations.* At the same time, the Em-

---

[12] The modifications were in the third article, in which Bernstorff had made the definition of contrabrand according to that "now practised by France (as elucidated in articles 19 and 20 of the treaty of Utrecht, as well as our ancient treaties with France and England)." Bernstorff's fifth article had read originally: *"Que ces principes soyent rendus public pour servir de regle manifeste, comme aux armateurs [sic], décidant sans autre procédure et forme de procès,* etc." Bergbohm, *op. cit.,* p. 136, compares the two documents in parallel columns.

[13] Of June 20, 1766, stipulating free ships free goods, and a limited enumeration of contraband, not including naval stores. Article XXIV of the Franco-American treaty of 1778 specifically stated that naval stores and provisions should never be contraband.

[14] Text in J. B. Scott, *op. cit.,* p. 274.

press formally invited the specified neutrals to enter into conventions with her to accept and enforce the code. The code itself was the image of Bernstorff's state paper, but it was accepted by the Danish Council of State only over his protests, for the Danish Foreign Minister had recently succumbed to the persuasion of the British resident, Sir Morton Eden. A Russo-Danish Convention of July 9, 1780, accepted the principles, but on Denmark's part subject to the definition of contraband according to the Anglo-Danish treaty of 1670 (which had been elucidated by the special secret [15] Anglo-Danish explanatory convention of July 4, 1780), and the Franco-Danish treaty of 1742,[16] thus adding naval stores to the contraband list, but adopting the principle of free ships free goods. Sweden made a like convention with Russia, August 1, 1780, with a similar reservation as to the definition of contraband as by her treaties of 1661 with England and of 1741 [17] with France. Appropriate declarations merged these conventions into a tripartite alliance for mutual armed assistance, if necessary for the protection of these neutral rights, against all belligerents. Subsequent understandings closed the Baltic Sea to all belligerent operations.[18]

Being nearest the wrath of England, and having more at stake in colonies and ocean trade than the other neutrals, the States General of the United Provinces hesitated to accept the Russian invitation received on April 3, 1780, without writing into the proposed convention a guaranty of their colonial possessions. The remainder of the year was consumed in unsuccessful negotiations at St. Petersburg by a special mission sent there to do this. It

[15] For the details of this secret negotiation, which was not revealed until several weeks later when the British navy began to enforce it, see Fauchille, *op. cit.*, pp. 402–452. The resulting commotion among the armed neutrals and at the Danish Court cost Bernstorff his office.

[16] This treaty included naval stores specifically as contraband; but provided free ships free goods (except contraband), and unfree ships unfree goods. Hauterive and Cussy, *Recueil des traités de commerce et de navigation de la France* . . . , 10 vols. (Paris, 1834–1844), I, 305.

[17] The treaty of 1741 contained no stipulation in regard to contraband or neutral rights. That of 1661, as above noted, included as contraband "all other things necessary for warlike use."

[18] Texts of these declarations, conventions, and relevant diplomatic notes in the compilation of J. B. Scott, *op. cit., passim.*

proved impossible. On November 20, 1780, amid their difficulties with England, the States General resolved to accede to the Armed Neutrality without the desired condition. The act of accession was consummated at St. Petersburg, January 4, 1781.[19] The British Ministry was resolved to declare war on the Dutch rather than see them join the Armed Neutrality and perhaps receive its protection for the carriage of naval stores to France and Spain.[20] As belligerents the United Provinces would be far less formidable than as protected neutrals. At the moment when the Netherlands were about to be received into the new League of Neutrals, an opportune, preposterous, but none the less serviceable pretext [21] unexpectedly presented itself to George III to declare war for reasons not ostensibly connected with the Armed Neutrality. This pretext had been afforded by the irresponsible negotiation of William Lee and Jean de Neufville at Aix-la-Chapelle, two years previously.

These negotiations followed rather disparately some overtures which the American Commissioners at Paris had attempted, a few weeks after the signature of the Franco-American treaties of February 6, 1778. Franklin, Arthur Lee, and John Adams (who had now replaced Silas Deane on the Commission at Paris) on April 10, 1778, instructed Dumas to present to the Grand Pensionary of Holland a copy of the treaty of commerce and amity, to be communicated to Their High Mightinesses, along with the expression of a desire "that a good understanding may be cultivated, and a mutually beneficial commerce established between the people of the two nations, which, as will be seen, there is nothing in the above-mentioned treaty to prevent or impede." [22] Failing

[19] Edler, *Dutch Republic, op. cit.,* pp. 144, 158, 163.

[20] "If the States second the wishes and views of our enemies by joining in what is called a neutral League, and make a Declaration the object of which is to give an undue Extension to the Claims of neutral States, whilst any Neutrality is, on the part of the Republic, a Breach of Treaty, if such should be their conduct, it must and would have the most serious consequences." Lord Stormont's account to Yorke, August 8, 1780, of an interview with the Dutch Ambassador, Count Welderen, cited by Colenbrander, *Patriottentijd, op. cit.,* I, 181.

[21] Lord Stormont to the King, Oct. 12, 1780, *Correspondence of King George the Third,* V, 140.

[22] Wharton, II, 547.

to elicit any response from that dignitary, Dumas gave a copy to the burgomasters of Amsterdam, who espoused the Patriot, anti-Stadhouder cause. They quickly acknowledged the document with the encouraging expression of their regret that it was not within their power to conclude a similar treaty with the United States.[23]

Just at this time the Carlisle peace commission had embarked from England in its effort to negotiate a reconciliation with America and thus to frustrate the ratification of the French treaties. The Amsterdam authorities feared that such a reconciliation might result in excluding all non-British trade from America. In August, 1778, the burgomasters discussed this subject with their Pensionary, van Berckel. The secret minutes of the conference are missing, perhaps intentionally destroyed. The burgomasters empowered van Berckel to draw up with "Mr. Lee" the draft of a treaty of commerce to take effect as soon as the independence of the United States should be recognized by Great Britain. They instructed van Berckel that he was to do this only under the understanding that the Americans meanwhile should not have made any treaty harmful to Dutch commerce. William Lee, brother to Arthur Lee the Commissioner in Paris, was now in Frankfort, on his way back to the French capital from Vienna. He had been commissioned by Congress, in an onslaught of "militia diplomacy" against the courts of central Europe, to negotiate treaties of commerce and amity with the Emperor and with the King of Prussia. If only because these two powers had just gone to war, when Lee reached Vienna in May, 1778, this commission proved a mistake, for not unnaturally neither of them would be eager to treat with an envoy who was also commissioned to treat with his enemy, even if there were no other reasons (such as recognition) to cause them to refuse. But Lee found the Court of Vienna entirely deaf to his pleas for recognition, and politely refusing even to allow the French Ambassador to introduce him. Believing that neither the Emperor nor his enemy the King of Prussia would recognize him, during the War of the Bavarian Succession, Lee left Vienna and postponed his

[23] Van Berckel, Pensionary of Amsterdam, to Dumas, July 31, 1778, Wharton, II, 674.

journey to Berlin.[24] From Frankfort he had some correspondence with Dumas,[25] through which he became known to the Amsterdam authorities, though it is doubtful whether they distinguished him from his brother, Commissioner Arthur Lee, the colleague of Franklin and Adams. Van Berckel delegated one Jean de Neufville, an adventurous and none too respectable business man of Amsterdam, to meet with "Mr. Lee."

At Aix-la-Chapelle the two drew up the draft of a treaty "to be entered into between Their High Mightinesses the States of the Seven Provinces of Holland and the Thirteen United States of America." It followed rather closely after the articles of the Franco-American treaty of commerce, and it did not express the original stipulation of the burgomasters to van Berckel that it was not to come into operation until the independence of the United States should be recognized by Great Britain.[26] Obviously enough this treaty was no more than the dream of two dilettante diplomatists. William Lee had no power to treat, and the American Commissioners at Paris pointedly so stated to him when they acknowledged receiving a copy of his draft.[27] Everybody knew that the burgomasters of Amsterdam had no authority to draw up treaties with foreign powers, just as everybody knows to-day that the London County Council cannot draft treaties to bind the

[24] W. Lee to the Committee of Foreign Affairs, Paris, September 12, 1778, Wharton, II, 714. See also Hanns Schlitter, *Beziehungen Österreichs, op. cit.,* and introductory remarks to same author's "Die Berichte des ersten Agenten Österreichs in den Vereinigten Staaten von Amerika, Baron de Beelen-Bertholff, an die Regierung der österreichischen Niederlande in Brüssel, 1784–1789," in *Fontes Rerum Austriacarum,* XLV band, II (Wien, 1891). W. Lee's correspondence has been edited by W. C. Ford, *Letters of William Lee,* 3 vols. (Brooklyn, 1891).

[25] Dumas to van Berckel, August 17, 1778, Wharton, II, 687.

[26] The document closed with this description: "This is the rough draft of a treaty of commerce, which, in fulfilment of an appointment and commission from Mr. Engelbert François van Berckel, councilor and pensionary of the city of Amsterdam to me Jean de Neufville, citizen of the said city of Amsterdam, I have considered and drawn up with William Lee, delegate of the Congress, to put into operation between their High Mightinesses the States General of the Seven United Provinces and the United States of America. Jean de Neufville." Translation from the copy printed by van Wijk, *De Republiek en Amerika, op. cit.,* p. 50, from the Dumas Papers, II, 315–334.

[27] Franklin, [A.] Lee, and Adams to W. Lee, September 26, 1778, Wharton, II, 744.

British Empire. De Neufville, by not inserting the condition that the draft itself was contingent upon the recognition of the independence of the United States by England, had so far exceeded his own anomalous commission from van Berckel that the latter person, on October 6, 1778, thought it desirable to make an explanatory statement of the real intention of the burgomasters on this point. Dumas appears to have been imperfectly acquainted with the details or perhaps even the existence of the Aix-la-Chapelle negotiations—he later said that he was absolutely ignorant of them—and he took pains to enlighten the burgomasters as to William Lee's lack of powers. The American Commissioners at Paris never considered the draft of any binding value. Nor did the burgomasters. It would never have appeared in history except for the capture of Henry Laurens, the representative of the Continental Congress, two years later on his way to The Hague in 1780.[28]

Joan Derck van der Capellen had sent to American men of mark, particularly to Governors Trumbull and Livingston, who read Dutch, copies of his protest in December, 1775, in the assembly of Overyssel on the affair of the Scottish Brigade, thus establishing a political correspondence with them. In October, 1779, copies of several of the Dutch radical's letters, and another from Lieutenant-Colonel Joan G. Dircks, a Dutch officer in the American service, on leave in Holland, suggested that the time might soon be ripe for the placing of an American loan in Amsterdam. After some brief deliberation Congress appointed on November 1 its former president, Henry Laurens of South Carolina, as Commissioner of the United States to the United Provinces, for the purpose of securing a loan of $10,000,000 and negotiating a treaty of commerce and amity. Straightway Congress characteristically began to draw drafts on him in anticipation of the money he was expected to borrow![29]

---

[28] The most penetrating account of this episode is that of the late Dr. van Wijk, *op. cit.*, pp. 48–60. Cf. F. P. Renaut, *La politique de propagande . . . , op. cit.*, II, 139–146.

[29] *Journals*, 1779, pp. 1167, 1168, 1180, 1197, 1198, 1236; as cited by van Wijk, pp. 87–88.

Laurens did not embark until August 13, 1780.[30] His ship was taken by H.M.S. *Vestal* frigate, September 3, 1780.[31] What he thought the more important of his papers he burned or sunk while his vessel was under pursuit, but a few others he held till the last moment and then threw them overboard, insufficiently weighted. The English captain had the pouch hooked out of the sea and its contents sent on to Downing Street. Laurens himself was imprisoned in the Tower of London. Among his papers was a copy of the old Lee-de Neufville treaty draft of 1778.

The Foreign Office pounced on this curious document. Was it not evidence that the United Provinces were negotiating a treaty with the American rebels? The States General were engaged in their final deliberations on joining the Armed Neutrality, without the stipulation of a guaranty for the preservation of the Dutch East and West Indies. Yorke presented a sudden ultimatum, November 10, 1780, demanding a formal disavowal of the conduct of the Amsterdam authorities and the punishment of van Berckel. On November 20, that sovereign body resolved to accede unconditionally to the Armed Neutrality. A week later it naturally disavowed any responsibility for the Amsterdammers' presuming to draft a treaty but made no move to punish van Berckel. As soon as news of the resolution of accession to the Armed Neutrality arrived, the British Government directed Yorke to quit his post without taking leave. Before the Dutch plenipotentiaries at St. Petersburg actually signed the act of formal accession to the Armed Neutrality, George III issued, December 20, 1780, a carefully timed [32] hostile manifesto against the United Provinces, accompanied by an order-in-council for general reprisals against their ships and cargoes. The retiring Dutch Ambassador attempted to present to the Foreign Office a copy of the resolution of accession to the Armed Neutrality, but it

---

[30] This was because the harassments of the British navy and military operations in the Carolinas actually prevented him from getting a ship that could get away from ports in that region. He finally sailed from Philadelphia. D. D. Wallace, *The Life of Henry Laurens* (New York, 1915), pp. 355–359.

[31] Wharton, IV, 56; Wallace, *op. cit.*

[32] Lord Stormont to the King, Dec. 18, 1780, *Correspondence of King George the Third*, V, 166.

was studiously and elaborately refused on the ground that the
two countries were already at war.[33] Thus technically the British
went to war *before* the Dutch accession. The reasons for hostilities, as enumerated in the manifesto, were: (1) refusal of the
casus foederis, and secret assistance to the enemy; (2) assistance
via St. Eustatius and elsewhere to the rebel Colonies; (3) attempts to raise up enemies against Great Britain in the East
Indies; and (4) "they have concluded a secret treaty with our
rebel subjects." [34] The real reason was the Armed Neutrality.

One of the immediate advantages to Great Britain of war with
the Dutch was the wiping out of that foyer of contraband traffic,
St. Eustatius. Admiral Rodney promptly descended on the island,
the inhabitants of which had not yet heard of the war, and completely rooted out this nest of active traders, who had been so
helpful to the American insurrectionists. He sent home twenty-
four shiploads of plunder only to have them recaptured by French
cruisers and American privateers before they reached England.
Presently French forces recaptured the island itself. But Rodney
in fulfilment of his drastic orders had done his devastation so
thoroughly that this Dutch colony was of no further use during
the war to his master's enemies.[35]

The North Cabinet had rightly estimated that the Armed Neutrals would not come to the support of the Netherlands, if furnished with a plausible pretext for not doing so. Actually Catherine II never intended to be led into hostilities for the defense
chiefly of the shipping of the Netherlands and Scandinavia. The
Armed Neutrality was a not ineffectual gesture, at a psychological moment, designed to give weight to further diplomatic endeavor in the shape of a Russian or an Austro-Russian mediation
which would bring peace and thus a solution of all maritime questions. So far as real force is concerned, the Armed Neutrality was
an Armed Nullity, as Catherine herself described it to Sir James
Harris.[36]

[33] Lord Stormont to the King, [?1780], *ibid.,* V, 14.
[34] The manifesto and relevant documents are in Piggott and Omond, *Armed
Neutralities, op. cit.,* pp. 288–290.
[35] J. F. Jameson, *op. cit.*
[36] *Diaries and Correspondence of Lord Malmesbury,* I, 355.

By the American Revolution a situation was created which engaged the Netherlands in the war. Only indirectly did this misfortune arise from any Dutch involvement with the United States. It was a European situation produced and manipulated by French diplomacy which brought war to the Netherlands. If the States General had accepted the British offer to compromise the opposing Anglo-Dutch treaties of 1674 and 1678 by waiving claim to the protection of naval stores, the United Provinces could easily and honorably have avoided disaster.

Though it had little actual sanction, the Armed Neutrality was of essential significance. It fulfilled the hope of Vergennes to isolate England completely. The several enemies of that country incorporated into their prize law the principles worked out by Hübner nearly two decades previously—independently formulated in large part by the Continental Congress of the United States in 1776—proposed by Bernstorff in 1778 and proclaimed by Catherine II in 1780. Except for the independent north Italian states, and the Pope, and Turkey, the other neutral maritime states, all of which had Atlantic commerce, acceded one after another to the Armed Neutrality conventions: Prussia, May 19, 1781; and then next Austria, October 9, 1781; Portugal, July 24, 1782; the Two Sicilies, February 21, 1783. It should be observed, however, that Portugal and the Two Sicilies acceded only after peace negotiations were well under way; and that the final exchange of ratifications for Prussia (though Frederick proclaimed the code on April 30, 1781) was not completed until May of 1782. Thus these accessions came rather late, some of them after hostilities had slowed up and England was seeking peace, all of them while Russia and the Empire were attempting mediation.[37] At the tag-end of the war it was safe to accept the principles of this League of Neutrals without danger of being called upon to back them by force, and with a hope of seeing them written by the mediators into the general peace settlement. Nevertheless the Armed Neutrality was portentous for Great Britain

[37] The several acts of accession and proclamation are printed in J. B. Scott, *ibid.* The accession of Prussia and Austria was not without significance, because the neutral traffic formerly carried by Dutch vessels was now seeking protection of those flags. *Correspondence of King George the Third*, V, 267.

and not without influence on her maritime measures. To that extent it was helpful to France. With the principal carriers, the Dutch, no longer protected neutrals, the new British naval instructions, though in no whit accepting the principles, enjoined privateers to observe the several specific treaties between Great Britain and the following neutrals: Portugal (treaties of January 29, 1641–1642, and July 10, 1654); Denmark (treaty of July 11, 1670); and Russia (June 20, 1766).[38] Further orders went out against "making prize of, stopping or detaining any ships and vessels within the Baltic." [39]

Because Great Britain captured most of the privateers of her enemies, and because her own orders-in-council greatly restricted the operations of British privateers, this type of commerce-destroying greatly diminished during the last months of the war, and Bergbohm hazards the conjecture that if the conflict had endured longer it is not unlikely that the several belligerents might have been induced to suppress privateering altogether.

As for the would-be mediators, we shall see in our concluding chapters that they were brushed aside in the peace negotiations and consequently were not able to write the new code into the peace treaties, though France did so partly and indefinitely by renewals of the treaty of Utrecht. The Armed Neutrality subsided practically lifeless at the end of the war. We cannot dismiss the subject, however, without a word as to the policy of the United States toward this League of Neutrals.

[38] The Portuguese treaties (Dumont, VI, pt. I, 238; pt. II, 82) sanctioned the rule of the *consolato del mare* and said nothing about contraband. The other treaties have already been analyzed above. For British instructions to naval commanders, Nov. 20 and Dec. 21, 1780, see J. B. Scott, *op. cit.*, pp. 328–335.

[39] April 20, 1781, *ibid.*, p. 391.

CHAPTER XII

The United States and the Armed Neutrality

The first prize law of the United States followed instinctively British precedent, though the model treaty, fashioned according to the "Plan of 1776," and embodied in the Franco-American treaty of 1778 adopted as ideals the dicta of small-navy belligerents and neutrals. When news arrived of the Russian declaration of Armed Neutrality, Congress, in conformity with suggestions conveyed from Vergennes, ordered the issuance of a set of instructions to naval commanders in line with the principles of that declaration.[1] The same resolution empowered the ministers plenipotentiary of the United States, if invited, to accede to such regulations conforming to the spirit of the Armed Neutrality as might be agreed upon by a congress expected to assemble in pursuance of Catherine II's invitation.[2] The Russian declaration was directed to the three European belligerents, but not to the United States, since the Empress took pains to commit no act which would violate her consistent policy of eschewing any recognition of the new American republic.[3] Nevertheless the new neutral combination seemed to Congress to present an opening for more widespread recognition of American independence, particularly by Russia, through adherence to the Armed Neutrality by formal treaty. In pursuance of this advantage it appointed as minister to Russia one of its former members, Francis Dana of Massachusetts, at the time serving as John Adams's secretary. At the court of the great Semiramis of the North this emissary was to endeavor to secure

[1] The actual instructions were adopted November 27, 1780, and a formal proclamation was issued April 7, 1781. *Journals,* XVIII, 865, 1097–1098; XIX, 361.

[2] John Adams on March 8, 1781, delivered copies of this resolution to the States General, and to the French, Russian, Danish, and Swedish diplomatic representatives at The Hague, Wharton, IV, 277.

[3] E. Albrecht, "Die Stellung der Vereinigten Staaten von Amerika zu bewaffneten Neutralität von 1780," *Zeitschrift für Völkerrecht,* VI, 441.

an invitation to the United States "to accede as principals and as an independent nation to the said convention," and if possible to negotiate with the Empress a treaty of amity and commerce.[4] This was an ill-considered mission, if only because the United States as a belligerent, even if recognized by Russia, could not become a member of a league of *neutrals*.

Dana proceeded to the Russian capital but accomplished nothing during two years of humiliating and unrecognized hanging-on. Catherine II was then in the midst of her diplomacy of mediation conjointly with her new ally, Joseph II. The basis of this policy was to find a formula by which Great Britain could negotiate with the revolted Colonies separately and independently and at the same time negotiate a European peace without recognizing their independence.[5] Any recognition of the United States by the Empress would have been as fatal to the possible success of her pretentious diplomatic endeavors as it would have been repugnant to her autocratic conceptions of the duties of subjects toward divine-right monarchs.[6] Vergennes gave orders to his minister at St. Petersburg to abstain from supporting any diplomatic propositions of Dana.[7] Anxious as he was for a Russian mediation to save him from the defection of Spain threatened by the Cumberland negotiations,[8] he was unwilling to antagonize the Czarina by

---

[4] Instructions to Francis Dana, "in Congress, Dec. 19, 1780," Wharton, IV, 201. F. P. Renaut, *La politique de propagande des Américains*, . . . *Francis Dana à Saint Pétersbourg* (Paris, 1922), treats of this subject, utilizing correspondence of the French Foreign Office and Dana's correspondence as published in Wharton. See also Paul Fauchille, *Ligue des neutres, op. cit.*, pp. 393–400.

[5] See below, Ch. XIII.

[6] F. A. Golder, "Catherine II and the American Revolution," *A.H.R.*, XXI, 92–96. See, for Dana, *Précis sur les rélations de la Cour Imperiale de la Russie avec les Etats-Unis d'Amérique sous la regne de l'Impératrice Catherine II*, facsimile in Library of Congress from State Archives at Leningrad XV, No. 214, *circa* 1784.

[7] F. P. Renaut, *La politique de propagande . . . Dana à St. Petersbourg*, I, 119, is repeated in his *Les relations entre la Russie et les Etats-Unis, 1776–1823*, Vol. I, *Catherine II et les insurgents: la mission Dana (1776–1783)* (Paris, 1923). See also J. C. Hildt, *Early Diplomatic Negotiations of the United States with Russia* (Baltimore, 1906), Ch. 1; and W. P. Cresson, *Francis Dana, A Puritan Diplomat at the Court of Catherine the Great* (New York, 1930).

[8] Doniol, IV, Ch. IX. See my *Hussey-Cumberland Mission, op. cit.*

urging her to recognize the independence of France's ally, an act which would instantly have rendered her mediation unacceptable to England. Dana was still at St. Petersburg when the preliminary peace treaty between the United States and Great Britain was signed; but even several months after Great Britain had recognized the independence of the United States, in the preliminary articles of November 30, 1782, the Russian Court contemptuously refused to have anything to do with him.[9]

Already the signing of the preliminaries of peace had led to debates in Congress on the expediency of continuing the Dana mission, since its principal purpose had been that of acquiring new supports, no longer really needed, for American independence. At that moment the Netherlands, coping alone with Great Britain after all the other belligerents had made preliminaries of peace, was trying in vain to write the Armed Neutrality principles into the peace treaty. When this proved impossible, they tried to get the United States either to accede to the treaty of armed neutrality already concluded between some powers of Europe or to enter into a similar engagement with France, Spain, and the United Provinces; or, in case France and Spain should refuse such a connection, to make a separate convention to that effect with the Netherlands. In a report to Congress on this proposal, the Secretary for Foreign Affairs,[10] Robert R. Livingston, ingeniously interpreted Dana's original instructions as restricted to the duration of the war.[11] Congress resolved, June 12, 1783,

[9] In an interview with the Vice-Chancellor, Osterman, April 23, 1783, that official orally laid down these conditions for the reception of a minister from the United States:

1. The conclusion of a definitive treaty between France, Spain, and Great Britain.

2. The American Minister must present letters of credence bearing date later than George III's recognition of American independence (Dana's had been of December 19, 1781).

3. The letters of credence must be dated later than Catherine's formal recognition of the United States.

4. Previous reception of an American Minister by the Court of London.

Dana to Livingston, No. 25, St. Petersburg, April 25, 1783, Wharton, VI, 392. This refusal was due to the energetic representations of Sir James Harris. *Diaries and Correspondence of Lord Malmesbury*, 4 vols. (London, 1844), II, 36.

[10] For evolution of this office, see above, pp. 32–33.

[11] Wharton, VI, 482.

against joining the "league," on the ground that such a step was no longer useful, and besides, might "entangle" the United States "in the politics and controversies of European nations." [12] Thus ended the relation of the United States to the Armed Neutrality,[13] with significant words that at once recall Tom Paine and adumbrate the paragraphs of George Washington's Farewell Address. Young Alexander Hamilton, who later was to be largely responsible for the phraseology of that famous address, played a prominent part in these debates of 1783 [14] and in the formulation of the anti-entanglement report.

The diplomatic relations between the thirteen United States of North America and the seven United Provinces of the Netherlands during the remainder of the war must be told briefly. In October, 1778, partly upon the advice of John Adams, one of the three Commissioners at Paris, Congress abolished that joint commission and placed relations with France in the hands of one minister, the competent Franklin. Adams returned home, after having done much to put the details of war purchases and such affairs in France on a more business-like basis. Arriving there, he found himself soon elected plenipotentiary of the United States for the conclusion of peace. We shall note in another place [15] his

[12] "Whereas the primary object of the resolution of October 5, 1780, and of the commission and instructions to Mr. Dana, relative to the accession of the United States to the neutral confederacy no longer can operate; and as the true interest of these states requires that they should be as little as possible entangled in the politics and controversies of European nations, it is inexpedient to renew the said powers either to Mr. Dana, or to the other ministers of these United States in Europe; but, inasmuch as the liberal principles, on which the said confederacy was established, are conceived to be in general favourable to the interests of nations, and particularly to those of the United States, and ought in that view to be promoted by the latter as far as will consist with their fundamental policy:

"*Resolved,* That the ministers plenipotentiary of these United States for negotiating a peace be and they are hereby instructed, in case they should comprise in the definitive treaty any stipulations amounting to a recognition of the rights of neutral nations, to avoid accompanying them by any engagements which shall oblige the contracting parties to support those stipulations by arms." *Journals,* XXIV, 394.

[13] See W. S. Carpenter, "The United States and the League of Neutrals of 1780," *Am. Jour. International Law,* XV, 511–522; and E. Albrecht, *op. cit.*

[14] Cf. Hamilton's resolution of May 21, 1783. *Works of Alexander Hamilton,* J. C. Hamilton, ed., II, 248. Madison also played an important part in the formulation of this resolution.

[15] See below, Ch. XIII.

services in this connection before he was superseded by a commission of five members. During the year 1780 he visited Holland to reconnoiter for diplomatic support which he believed would be less subservient to France. He was not successful in this—we have intimated how thoroughly France controlled Dutch diplomacy, at least so far as the United States was concerned—but he was able to feel out the situation in the Low Countries [16] somewhat and to furnish Congress with illuminating, if prolix, despatches [17] on European affairs in general. The delay of Laurens's departure caused Congress to place Dutch affairs temporarily in Adams's care, and after the capture of the South Carolinian it commissioned in his stead the man from Massachusetts.[18]

With the assistance of Dumas, Adams diligently applied himself to a campaign of propaganda, at first with meager results. France opposed any recognition by the Netherlands of American independence during the period of Dutch neutrality, for fear that this would cause the valuable neutral carrier to be involved in war as a less valuable belligerent. Even after the English declaration of war the Stadhouder's court was persistently opposed to recognition of the United States. French diplomacy also was at first apathetic in supporting with the new Dutch co-belligerent the interests of France's American ally, presumably because of Vergennes's vehement dislike of the independent and truculent Adams, perhaps because the United States was competing with France for loans in Amsterdam. Finally the circumstances of common belligerency, assisted by vigorous American campaigning for the favor of public opinion, and a desire on the part of France to forestall any separate Dutch peace negotiations [19]

[16] He found that it was still impossible to negotiate a loan with Dutch bankers. Dr. P. J. van Winter, *Amsterdamsche Handel, op. cit.,* pp. 29–58, has traced the various unsuccessful efforts to secure a loan before 1782, including that of South Carolina's representative, Alexander Gillon.

[17] Van Wijk regards Adams's despatches as of great source value for Dutch history at this time.

[18] *Journals,* XVII, 535 (June 20, 1780); XVIII, 1205 (December 29, 1780).

[19] In February, 1782, toward the fall of the North Ministry, Paul Wentworth, valued and capable secret service man of the British Government, visited Holland to make feelers for a separate peace. He had conversations with a member of the Amsterdam Government, one Rendorp, whom he gave to understand that no peace was possible with England if the American envoy were recognized. Van Wijk, *De Republiek en Amerika, op. cit.,* pp. 158–163.

brought French coöperation. On November 5, 1781, France borrowed 10,000,000 *livres* from the States General for the United States and guaranteed payment thereof. Adams was recognized as minister plenipotentiary on April 22, 1782. Recognition soon enabled him, June 11, to place a direct loan for which he had long been negotiating with a consortium of Amsterdam bankers, Nicolas and Jacob van Staphorst, and de la Lande and Fijne—a ten-year contract for 5,000,000 guilders at 5 per cent.[20] This was the first of several such loans negotiated by the United States government throughout the next ten years in Holland, loans which at first were the sole effectual support to languishing American credit and which barely enabled the government of the Confederation to survive the peace, to function until the recognition of Washington's new national government under the Constitution of 1787.[21]

Meanwhile Adams was negotiating a treaty of commerce and friendship. This document he signed on October 8, 1782. It followed largely the provisions of the Lee-de Neufville draft of 1778, which in turn was modeled on the Franco-American treaty of 1778, which again rested on the famous "Plan of 1776" which John Adams and Franklin, as members of the Continental Congress, had helped to formulate. That was the same plan which

[20] A 4½ per cent commission also exacted, plus 1 per cent for receiving and paying off annual interest, in addition to the interest. Van Wijk, *op. cit.,* p. 167; van Winter, *op. cit.,* p. 65; and Adams to Livingston, The Hague, July 5, 1782, Wharton, V, 594.

[21] Dr. van Winter's monograph, *op. cit.,* is a most scholarly history of these loans and of the share of Amsterdam trade in the foundation of American nationality. The loans by Dutch bankers were as follows:

1782	guilders	5,000,000
1784	"	2,000,000
1787	"	1,000,000
1788	"	1,000,000
Total	"	9,000,000

(approximately $3,600,000)

The last three of these loans were used to pay interest charges on the first loan and those following. After the establishment of the new government under the Constitution of 1787, Secretary Alexander Hamilton, in Washington's presidency, borrowed more money from Dutch bankers to take up arrears on the debt to France. The Dutch bankers exchanged their credits in 1795 for United States bonds, and this debt, like the debt to the French Government, disappeared in that way.

reached its roots back to the small-navy liberal principles of free ships free goods, limited contraband, and freedom of neutrals to trade on these principles with unblockaded belligerent ports, or between unblockaded belligerent ports, that same plan, in fine, which contained the first three principles of the Armed Neutrality of 1780. It was the American doctrine of freedom of the seas.

The origin of the Armed Neutrality has furnished an historical problem which has occupied many able minds. It will readily be apparent to the reader of these pages that the first three of the principles had already been subject to treaty practice in the seventeenth and eighteenth centuries, and that they had been picked out of that practice by the committee of the Continental Congress and incorporated in its plan of model treaties. The principles formulated by Bernstorff had already been worked out by Martin Hübner in 1762; the first three were proposed for treaties by Congress in 1776. Catherine II assumed the responsibility of declaring to the world a set of principles of neutral rights. Panin exploited the opportunity given him by Catherine II to incorporate in the Declaration of February 28, 1780, the Hübnerian principles put in diplomatic motion by Bernstorff in 1778. Vergennes supported them in his diplomacy with the United States and with the Northern Courts. It is difficult therefore to attribute them exclusively to any single person. Even without Hübner, who first grouped them into the formula which later came up through the Armed Neutrality, they would have been formulated in much the same way (except for blockade) by the Committee of the Continental Congress.

Franklin had by now called Adams to Paris to assist in the peace negotiations. As soon as he signed the Dutch treaty, he hastened thither, leaving the affairs of the United States in the hands of a chargé d'affaires, none other than the faithful Dumas, who installed himself in the *Hôtel des Etats-Unis* at The Hague, the first legation building actually to be owned abroad by the United States. This staunch and meagerly rewarded friend of American independence, who never set foot on the soil of his *nieuw vaderland,* exchanged, in the name of the United States, ratifications of the treaty of commerce between the two republics on June 23, 1783. On the same day the first Dutch Minister to the United States, Pieter Joan van Berckel, a burgomaster of Rotterdam, brother to the Pensionary of Amsterdam, set sail for Philadelphia.[22] The new minister traveled in a Dutch warship, for, although the other belligerents had signed preliminaries of peace with the common enemy, the Netherlands and Great Britain as yet had been unable to agree on peace terms. It will now be our task to review the negotiations which had ended the war and established the independence of the United States in the eyes of all the world.

[22] He was received by Congress, October 31, 1783, as minister plenipotentiary. For the ceremony, see *Journals* for that date and *Dip. Corres. of U. S., 1783–1789,* 3 vols. ed. (1837), III, 389–397.

CHAPTER XIII

The Imperial Mediators and France in 1781

The peace which fixed American independence was a major European settlement involving the interests of all the great powers. It was preceded by a long prelude of mediation which served as the sounding-board for the reverberations of the American war in far-away Vienna and distant St. Petersburg. These preliminary movements have certain instructive implications for American independence and for the later crystallization of American foreign policy. They led to the formulation by the Congress of the United States of its terms of peace. Before describing the peace negotiations of 1782–1783 we may properly review the attempts at mediation. These began with Spain's offer of 1779.

We remember that one of the points of the Spanish ultimatum of 1779 was that Great Britain during an armistice should treat, under Spanish good offices, with plenipotentiaries of the American Congress, that *during the negotiations* the "American Colonies" should be regarded as independent *de facto* (as the British Carlisle peace commission had been instructed to consider them in 1778, only *during the negotiations*); that the basis of the peace was to be a long-time truce *uti possidetis,* that is, the Colonies on the one hand and Great Britain on the other hand were to remain in possession of the territory in North America held by their respective military forces, at the date of the cessation of hostilities. This for the Colonies, with Gibraltar for Spain, remained Floridablanca's formula for peace during the Cumberland negotiations of 1780. In those later negotiations of 1780 the Spanish Foreign Minister did not urge that British and American commissioners treat through the good offices of any outside power. He suggested that Great Britain make her arrangements directly and separately with the Americans on the basis of the actual war-map in North America and what amounted to home rule within the Empire. If the Americans themselves accepted such a compromise in place of independence, France's obligations to them could be considered at an end, and she might need no longer to withhold herself from a peace in Europe which would fulfil the bond of the Franco-Spanish convention of Aranjuez by securing Gibraltar for Spain. Because Great Britain would not make under Spanish direction another offer to the "Colonies" like that of the futile Carlisle commission, and because she was also unwilling to let go Gibraltar, these complicated and secret maneuvers of Floridablanca, abetted by the priest Hussey, broke down.

This "middle road" of the Spanish Minister was to be essentially the pathway to peace along which the Austro-Russian mediators of 1781 would endeavor to lead the varying interests of Spain, France, Great Britain, and the "American Colonies"—at the expense of complete American independence. As with Spain's subtle proposals for mediation, it was also to be part of these Austrian démarches, professedly to save England's face, that the plenipotentiaries of the "Colonies" and of Great Britain should deal with each other directly and separately, though at the same peace conference, while the European belligerents were settling their own difficulties; but that the Anglo-American reconciliation should proceed *pari passu* with, and be dependent for its validity upon, the conclusion of peace between the European powers.[1] Here again the formula was to fail, due to the obstinacy of George III. But the idea of separate Anglo-American negotiations was to come to life again under interesting and greatly altered circumstances in the final peace negotiations of 1782.

Before we note the manner in which Austrian and Russian policy began to touch the diplomacy of American independence it is best to have in mind the American terms of peace. The first statement of them was in belated response to the Spanish proffer of mediation of 1779. Vergennes declared at that time that he had asked Franklin whether the United States would accept a peace in which independence would be assured tacitly by a truce, instead of positively by a definitive treaty. Franklin saw no objection. Vergennes thereupon instructed his representative in

[1] See my *Hussey-Cumberland Mission, op. cit.,* p. 118.

America, Conrad Alexandre Gérard, to request Congress to send Franklin full powers and appropriate instructions as representative of the United States in any peace congress which might follow Spain's offer of mediation, particularly empowering him to consent to a long-time truce, if necessary. This request precipitated in the Continental Congress a debate of no less than five months' duration, as we have already noticed in an earlier chapter, during which Gérard did his best to induce Congress to sanction Spain's claims as to boundary and navigation in the Mississippi Valley, to forego any unabatable claims of its own to the fisheries in the remaining British parts of North America, and to put its plenipotentiary under the control of French advice.[2] The fisheries question, as much as the matter of the required western boundary, prolonged the deliberations of Congress. They finally closed without any surrender on the matter of the western boundaries or the navigation of the Mississippi, but with a removal of the fisheries from the category of *sine qua non* for peace, if necessary relegating this issue to the condition of an indispensable article of any sequent treaty of commerce with Great Britain. Instead of Franklin, Congress elected John Adams, a reliable champion of New England interests, as plenipotentiary to negotiate a treaty of peace and, after that, one of commerce with Great Britain. He departed for France as John Jay left for Spain. Franklin remained the regularly accredited minister of the United States at Versailles.

Adams's instructions, dated August 14, 1779, laid down as indispensable conditions of peace the points of independence and the necessary boundaries of the United States. Very pointedly they forbade the plenipotentiary to enter into any negotiation, unless Great Britain should first agree to treat with the United States as sovereign, free, and independent. Independence must

[2] Vergennes to Gérard, No. 8, Versailles, Dec. 25, 1778, Archives des Affaires Etrangères, *Correspondance Politique, Etats-Unis*, V, 142. For Gérard's despatches on this subject, see *ibid.*, Vols. V–X. The subject is covered by Corwin, *French Policy and the American Alliance, op. cit.*, pp. 217–263, and P. C. Phillips, *The West in the Diplomacy of the American Revolution* (Urbana, Illinois, 1913), pp. 108–149. I can find no other evidence than Vergennes's statement to Gérard, Dec. 25, that Franklin acquiesced in the idea of tacit independence by truce.

also be "assured and confirmed by the Treaty or treaties of peace, according to the form and effect of the Treaty of Alliance with his Most Christian Majesty." The required boundary was to be the St. John River in the east and, roughly, the present northern boundary of New England and New York to the St. Lawrence at 45° north latitude; thence in a straight line to the southern end of Lake Nipissing (the boundary of Quebec before 1774); from Lake Nipissing straight to the source of the Mississippi (then unknown); on the west the Mississippi River; on the south the line of 31° north latitude from the Mississippi to the Chatta-hoochee, descending that stream to its junction with the Flint, thence straight to the source of the St. Mary's and down that river to the Atlantic Ocean.[3] If the line from Lake Nipissing to the source of the Mississippi could not be secured, the boundary might be drawn between that lake and the Mississippi anywhere north of 45°. If the designated eastern boundary between Nova Scotia and Massachusetts could not be agreed to, it might as a last recourse be left to a joint commission to determine. "Although it is of the utmost importance to the peace and Commerce of the United States that Canada and Nova Scotia should be ceded, and more particularly that their equal common right to the Fisheries should be guarantied to them, yet a desire of terminating the war hath induced us not to make the acquisition of these objects an ultimatum on the present occasion." With the consent of France, an armistice might be accepted, but only in case "all the forces of the enemy shall be immediately withdrawn from the United States."[4] "In all matters not above mentioned," concluded the instruction, "you are to govern yourself by the Alliance between his Most Christian Majesty and these States, by the advice of our allies, by your knowledge of our Interests, *and by your own discretion, in which we repose the fullest confidence.*"[5]

Gérard's only success in modeling the American instructions

[3] See map 4 opposite p. 228.
[4] This, presumably, meant the United States according to the boundaries laid down in the instructions.
[5] *Journals,* Aug. 14, 1779. Italics mine.

had been to get the fisheries thrown out of the requirements *sine qua non*. To these fisheries the French alliance had never applied, either in letter or in spirit.[6] Nor had that alliance ever set forth the boundaries of the United States whose independence it guaranteed; these were to be fixed at the peace. Congress left other matters to the judgment and discretion of the plenipotentiary himself, and not to the absolute control of France. On the same ship that took Jay to Spain, Gérard sailed home. The next French minister, La Luzerne, was to be more successful.

By the time Congress had finished debating, had voted instructions, and had appointed the plenipotentiary, the Spanish mediation had failed and Spain had declared war. When Adams returned to Paris,[7] Spain was already secretly engaged, as we have just observed, in the Hussey-Cumberland negotiations with the enemy.[8]

John Adams was a most resolute, unbending, and pertinacious American. As a diplomatist he deserves better of his country than many historians have been ready to admit, but we must acknowledge that his irascible temper did not ingratiate him with Vergennes, who not unnaturally looked upon the United States as another client state, like the Netherlands, Sweden, or Turkey. He was already prepared not to like Adams, whose acquaintance he had made during the American's previous sojourn at Paris as a member of the United States's diplomatic commission to France in 1778–1779. At that time Vergennes had advised Adams that the United States should devote its principal energies to winning the war and leave the management of diplomacy to France. Perusing the despatches of his envoys from Philadelphia, he had identified the American patriot with a putative party in Congress headed by Samuel Adams and Richard Henry Lee which he con-

---

[6] Simultaneously with voting these instructions, Congress passed a resolution empowering Franklin to conclude an explanatory article to the treaty of alliance, an article against any molestation by Great Britain, after the peace, of citizens of the United States or subjects of France "taking fish on the Banks, seas, and places formerly used and frequented by them, so as not to encroach on the territorial rights which may remain to her after the termination of the present war." *Journals*, XIV, 965. Nothing ever came of this.

[7] For his first mission, see above, p. 156.

[8] See note 1, above.

sidered opposed in principle to the French alliance and eager to
undertake a separate negotiation with England, even perfidiously
to substitute for the existing French alliance an eventual understanding with the enemy.[9] He welcomed the envoy with scarcely
concealed distrust and rather studied disdain. He even allowed
himself almost to insult Adams by saying to him that he would
delay a conference until after he received from Gérard the content
of Adams's instructions![10]

Vergennes's attitude became the more confirmed when Adams,
finding the Spanish mediation a vanished expectation, proposed
to communicate his powers directly to the British Government,
even to go to London. If the English wished to stop the war and
accept the terms of the allies, Adams proposed that they be given
the opportunity; such a move at least would react favorably on
British public opinion, said he. Adams's "shirtsleeves diplomacy"
did not appeal to Vergennes. He saw in it a demonstration to the
enemy of a rift in the Franco-American alliance, rather than a
chance to win Britain to the terms of the United States and
France. He flatly disagreed. If Vergennes were suspicious of
Adams's fidelity, the latter on his part began to be puzzled, though,
at this time not yet wholly disabused about Vergennes's good
faith. These perturbations of spirit contrasted with the more
supple and ingratiating qualities of the regular minister, Franklin. To have a person from Braintree, Massachusetts, declare un-
diplomatically to the French Foreign Office in Paris, France, the
fact that the United States was as useful to France as France was
to the United States was not the conventional conduct to expect
from the representative of a republic which Louis XVI had chosen
to deliver to history. When Adams made the mistake of going
beyond the purview of his instructions and began to argue about
the general interests of the two allies, Vergennes cut him off by
reminding him that Franklin was the accredited minister through
whom all regular business was done. Adams smarted under this
rebuke and began to suspect that France was selfishly blocking

[9] La Luzerne to Vergennes, Philadelphia, No. 5, October 8, 1779, Archives
des Affaires Etrangères, *Correspondance Politique, Etats-Unis*, X, fol., 197.
[10] Wharton, III, 496, 503.

America's real interests. In some dudgeon he went off to the Netherlands with a hope of cultivating diplomatic support that would be independent of France. He was to find only that France then controlled Dutch diplomacy, too.[11] But he still remained the official American peace plenipotentiary. Vergennes set about undermining him by suggesting to Congress that Adams be required to pay more attention to the advice of Louis XVI's ministers, or perhaps be supplanted by a more amenable agent.[12]

An opportunity to press this suggestion presented itself after the neutral Continental powers made their offers of mediation in 1780 and 1781.

Immediately following the Franco-Russian mediation at Teschen[13] in the summer of 1779, Austria had offered her good offices to France and England, professedly as a grateful return of the "service" which France had rendered in bringing peace to the mother country of Marie Antoinette. The real reason, of course, was Austria's desire to return coup for coup. The Emperor Joseph II and his celebrated Minister of Foreign Affairs, Prince Kaunitz, desired to maintain the balance of power by preventing England from sinking too low in the scale, above all to forestall the prestige which might come to the bitter rival, Prussia, or to the more friendly Catherine II, from a mediation by which either of those powers might pose as the arbiter of European affairs.[14] The offer was conveyed also to Spain. Both of the Bourbon allies at this time evaded the suggestion of mediation. England did not reject it.[15]

---

[11] For the correspondence between Adams and Vergennes see Wharton, III and IV, notably III, 814 and 854, and Franklin's report to Congress, IV, 21 (Aug. 9, 1780); *Works of John Adams,* C. F. Adams, ed. (Boston, 1852), Vol. VII.

[12] Vergennes to La Luzerne, No. 8, August 7, 1780, Archives des Affaires Etrangères, *Correspondance Politique, Etats-Unis,* XIII, 101; Doniol, IV, 417, 423.

[13] Above, p. 74.

[14] Flassan, *op. cit.,* VI, 280; Hanns Schlitter, *Beziehungen, op. cit.,* pp. 12–13; d'Arneth and Geoffroy, *Correspondance secrète entre Marie Thérèse et le cte. Mercy-Argenteau* (Paris, 1874), III, 327, 333, 336–337, 344, 347, 349, 357.

[15] Dánvila, *Reinado de Carlos III, op. cit.,* V, 332–338. The offer to Spain, also, shows that Austria had more at heart than a maternal solicitude for France's best interests. Text of the Austrian note to Spain, in Archivo Histórico Nacional, *Estado, legajo* 4116.

The next move came from the Empress of Russia. England's rather desperate efforts to counterbalance French and Spanish intervention by an Anglo-Russian alliance had failed to ensnare the Czarina. Catherine, who had an able mind if an unstable temperament, was a woman of great vanity, and the prospect of gratifying this weakness often threatened to prevail over more ponderable interests. It would have been the Empress's best policy to allow France and England, natural defenders of the Turks, to bleed themselves white while she matured her undisguised projects for the domination of Constantinople. But already, at Teschen, Catherine had posed to her satisfaction as the guarantor of central European stability, even of the peace of Westphalia itself.[16] A successful mediation between the western maritime belligerents might bring her the prestige of protector of all Europe. Attracted by such abstract and ephemeral prospects of glory, she ignored her real eastern interests sufficiently to attempt another European peace. The Czarina personally, as well as her ministers and favorites, repeatedly intimated to the British Ambassador, Sir James Harris, during 1779 that she would be eager to mediate. She continually advised England to make peace.[17] This the Russian Ambassador at London also suggested.[18] Vergennes received similar suggestions at Versailles.[19]

Every belligerent at first eluded these Russian feelers. Great Britain evaded them because she hoped to bring Russia to some significant declaration [20] that might threaten Britain's enemies if peace were not made soon according to English ideas; that is, to offset Spain's recently attempted anti-English mediation by an anti-Bourbon mediation on the part of Russia. Spain and France dodged them in 1779 because, in the honeymoon period of their alliance, they wished to reserve for themselves the advantages

---

[16] France and Russia were made guarantors of the peace of Teschen, which confirmed that of Westphalia. Catherine thus became a guarantor of that fundamental political structure set up in 1648. See Hanns Schlitter, *op. cit.*, pp. 2-3.

[17] Malmesbury, *Diaries and Correspondence, op. cit.*, I.

[18] F. F. Martens, *Recueil des traités et conventions conclus par la Russie avec les puissances étrangères* (St. Petersburg, 1874), X, 294-295.

[19] Doniol, III, 779-780.

[20] Malmesbury, *op. cit.*, I, 247-262.

which they had marked out at Aranjuez.[21] The declaration from Russia, for which England so fondly hoped, turned out to be the Armed Neutrality. It was part and parcel of Catherine's mediation policy. She calculated not only to enhance the prestige of the Empress by a pronouncement of lofty principles but by pressing England about with unexceptionable difficulties to induce her to accept a mediation in which this code might be brought forward for incorporation into the law of nations by the final treaty of peace.[22] In December, 1780, having brought the northern neutrals together, the Czarina finally made formal proposals, through her diplomatic representatives in London, Versailles, and Madrid.[23]

The Russian offer was the signal for careful maneuvering by each of the three belligerents to protect its own interests. Great Britain was about to declare war on the Netherlands (Dec. 20, 1780), really because of that power's decision to join the Armed Neutrality; it was not advisable further to oppose the Czarina's efforts by a refusal of her mediation. Accepting the offer in principle, the British Ministry took the opportunity to reflect on France's absence of alacrity in accepting the previous Austrian invitation and further requested that Austria serve with Russia as co-mediator, thus deferring to the earlier *démarche* of that power. The British reply also made it plain that any peace depended on the withdrawal of French forces from North America and the termination of the Franco-American alliance; and England soon informed Kaunitz that the treaty could contain no stipulation in regard to the revolted Colonies.[24] Lord Stormont, Minister for Foreign Affairs, presently dispatched a confidential offer to Catherine of the cession of the island of Minorca, if the Empress would use her influence as mediator to secure a peace for

[21] Doniol, III, 779.

[22] Bergbohm, *Bewaffnete Neutralität, op. cit.*, pp. 204–206; Fauchille, *Ligue des neutres, op. cit.*, p. 358; Malmesbury, *op. cit.*, I, 359.

[23] Doniol, IV, 523; Urtasún, *Historia diplomática, op. cit.*, II, 472; Schlitter, *op. cit.*, pp. 18–20.

[24] Draft of answer to Mr. Simolin's note, December 26, 1780, R.O., State Papers Foreign, Class 91, Vol. 106; Stormont to Sir Robert Keith, "secret and confidential," March 16, 1781, Record Office, *F.O.*, Class 7, Vol. I, fol. 61.

Great Britain according to these requirements.[25] We must antic-
ipate a step to say here that the Empress quite judiciously refused
the bribe.

Because of the ominous military and financial situation Vergennes was now really anxious for peace. He preferred Russian
mediation to having Floridablanca's formula imposed on him
through the medium of the Hussey-Cumberland negotiations then
under progress in Spain. Rather than buckle to Spain, he made
ready, in these the blackest days of the war, to accept the same
"middle-road" formula for peace, provided it were brought forward by the mediators instead of by his ally. A succession of
calamitous war news [26] arriving at Versailles during the winter of
1780–1781 convinced the French diplomatist that it would be
necessary to keep ajar the conveniently opened Austro-Russian
door of mediation to a compromise peace, in case during the
summer of 1781 the military situation should collapse in America
or on the sea. Meanwhile he mustered the remainder of France's
resources, and what could be secured from Spain's peninsula-
hugging fleet, for a last campaign.

Characteristically Vergennes noted down his policy in a confidential memorandum, dated February, 1781. It remains a most
revealing document for the history of the Franco-American alliance. The essence was that France as a last desperate expedient
would not oppose closing the war, so far as the United States and
Great Britain were concerned, by means of a long-time truce *uti
possidetis* between Colonies and mother country. This would be a
truce accepting the actual war-map at the beginning of 1781.
British forces were then in possession of the ports and much of
the interior of North Carolina, South Carolina, and practically
all of Georgia. They held New York City and Long Island. They
occupied the mouth of the Penobscot River, and thus could claim
control of most of Maine. They were fortified at Lake Cham-
plain, Oswegatchie, Oswego, Niagara, Detroit, and Michilimackinac, from which posts they could claim the territory now

[25] Stormont to Harris, St. James's, Jan. 20, 1781, Malmesbury, *op. cit.*, I, 373.
[26] *Hussey-Cumberland Mission, op. cit.*

comprised in the States of Minnesota, Wisconsin, northern Illinois, northern Indiana, Michigan, northern Ohio, northwestern New York, and northern Vermont. In fine, the British held the important seaports of New York, Charleston, and Savannah, still clung to Maine, and dominated the Great Lakes country and the far northwest. And Spain in January, 1781, was in possession of West Florida and the east bank of the Mississippi up to opposite the mouth of the Arkansas, with consequent claims still farther north. A Spanish raiding party had driven a British garrison from the post at St. Joseph, Michigan, hoisted the Spanish colors there, and claimed the Illinois valley also for Charles III.[27]

Not unconscious of the fact that to leave British troops in occupation of important portions of any of the thirteen American States would be an abandonment of the American cause, and not oblivious to the significance of this for the stipulations of the Franco-American alliance, Vergennes stated:

"One may therefore presume to say that the King would be lacking in delicacy, that he would be somewhat violating his engagements, that he would be giving the Americans just cause for complaint or at least distrust, if he should propose to Congress to sign a truce leaving the English what they possess on the continent. Therefore only the mediators, bound by no such ties, could make a proposition so painful to the United States."

Let the mediators, however, bring forth the *uti possidetis* except for New York, and France would accept. France herself could propose no such thing. The King could do no more than induce the United States to attend the mediation Congress, Vergennes piously decided.[28] It requires very little imagination to see that in a mediation opened under such auspices, the cards would be hopelessly stacked against American independence.

[27] For war-map of June, 1781, which corresponds to the above situation except that by then the British had lost their hold on the interior country of the Carolinas, see map 1 opposite p. 182. In February, 1781, news had not reached Europe of the Spanish raid to Ft. St. Joseph. For the raid, see Ch. VIII, note 17, above.

[28] "Memoir [of Vergennes] on the ways and means of concluding a truce with Great Britain, minuted in part by Rayneval." Archives des Affaires Etrangères, *Correspondance Politique, Etats-Unis*, XV, 269–278.

The first, temporizing answer of France to Russia, pending a crystallization of Vergennes's policy of a compromise peace and the preparation of the Americans for this contingency, was that while France welcomed the good offices of the Empress, the King would first need to consult his respective allies, the United States and Spain. Floridablanca on his part replied that Charles III preferred not to abandon the direct negotiations then (publicly) under way with Cumberland, but that if insurmountable difficulties should arise in the course of those discussions, the assistance of Russia would be welcomed.[29] Presently those separate Spanish negotiations ended. Presumably because of the new British interest in Russian mediation,[30] Cumberland received orders to quit Spain. Floridablanca immediately and complacently turned to the Austro-Russian mediation, taking proper caution to protect the paramount interests of Spain: Gibraltar, Florida, Honduras.[31] After Cumberland left Spain, Vergennes's ardor for a Russian mediation cooled somewhat,[32] at least pending the developments of the final campaign of 1781.

Russia meanwhile had quickly assented to the co-mediation of Austria—the two powers were even then maturing an alliance pivoted on a mutual arrangement of the Eastern Question—and readily acquiesced that Vienna might be the seat of the congress. The cautious replies of England, France, and Spain to the formal proposals of the joint mediators did not discourage Kaunitz.[33] In the agreeable rôle of a patriarch of European diplomacy the Aus-

---

[29] Dánvila, op. cit., V, 346.

[30] Stormont to Sir Robert Keith, No. 26, "most secret," March 16, 1781, Record Office, F.O., Class 7, Vol. I, fol. 62.

[31] Dánvila, op. cit., pp. 348–350. The despatch recalling Cumberland was dated Feb. 14, 1781, and received by him Mar. 11. He left Madrid Mar. 24. Record Office, State Papers Foreign. 94, Vol. 209.

[32] Vergennes to Montmorin, May 31, 1781, Doniol, V, 11.

[33] As a matter of fact the British Minister at Vienna, acting on instructions, had informed him that though the termination of the Franco-American alliance and the withdrawal of all French forces from America was a *sine qua non* of peace, it was not a condition precedent of entering into a negotiation; nevertheless he was careful to say that Great Britain would not allow any foreign power to arrange a settlement between herself and her revolted colonies. See Stormont's "secret" despatch to Sir Robert Keith, of February 27, 1781, and his two despatches, "secret and confidential" and "most secret," of March 16, 1781, Record Office, F.O., Class 7, Vol. I, folios 7, 49, 62.

trian Chancellor proceeded to compose some preliminary articles to offer to the several belligerents as the basis for peace negotiations at Vienna under Austro-Russian mediation, articles based on his principle that no party should propose to his enemy anything which he felt he could not grant if he were in his enemy's place.[34]

As the mediators eagerly proceeded to the task at hand it was necessary for Vergennes to prepare the Americans to be led, if necessary in the last extremity, to the *abbatoir* at Vienna. Already following the umbrageous interviews with John Adams, Vergennes had taken the first step to make France's ally ready for such a fatal sacrifice of American independence to the exigencies of European diplomacy and, after all, of the military situation. He had instructed La Luzerne to intimate to Congress that Adams was not the right man to be entrusted with the negotiation of peace. He continued to stress this. After composing the revealing February memoir, he sent further instructions to La Luzerne, March 9, 1781, that the Austro-Russian mediation had been proposed and was in the way of eventual acceptance by the several belligerents. Though France had pleaded the necessity of consulting her allies, he wrote, there might not be any legitimate excuse for declining the mediation of the two imperial courts. It was therefore indispensable that Congress inform the King of its intentions as to such a mediation, authorizing His Majesty to communicate them to Austria and Russia, and that Congress further declare its willingness to accept a mediation. That assembly, the Minister vouchsafed, might count on the justice of the sovereign mediators and on the defense of its interests by the King. It would not now be possible to supplant Adams, Vergennes stated, but further instructions by Congress could and should subordinate him to the advice and control of the King, "and to let himself be directed by me or the person who shall be in charge of the negotiations." Further, Congress under the existing circumstances ought to make its peace terms as moderate as possible.

But before any answer could come from America, a final crisis

[34] Flassan, *op. cit.,* VI, 293; d'Arneth, *Joseph II und Katharina von Russland: Ihr Briefwechsel* (Wien, 1869), p. 35. L. von Ranke has a most interesting passage on Kaunitz's elevated personal sphere at this time, in *Die deutschen Mächte und der Fürstenbund,* I, 50.

might occur in Europe. In this case, notwithstanding the fact that Congress actually had in Europe a duly accredited plenipotentiary for peace negotiations, Vergennes was resolved *to take charge of affairs for the United States even without their permission.*

"You will advise the President of Congress that in case the mediation offer of the two imperial courts should take such a turn as that His Majesty might be obliged to give a categorical answer, His Majesty will accept conditionally for himself and for the United States; this step will be so much the less inconvenient since nothing now hinders them from following the example of the King in placing their interests in the hands of mediators so just and enlightened, and a refusal to do so might bring on disastrous and incalculable results." [35]

The mediators, whom Vergennes in his own heart considered neither just nor enlightened, by a joint note dated May 20, 1781, and immediately delivered to the Courts of Great Britain, France, and Spain, but not to the United States (which might so well trust its interests to them), laid down the following articles as a basis for the negotiation of a peace:

1. The negotiation at Vienna, by the united good offices of the two imperial courts, of all such objects necessary to the establishment of peace as the belligerent parties should deem fit to propose to the mediators.

At the same time a negotiation should take place between Great Britain and the American Colonies without the intervention of either of the other belligerent parties, nor even of the two imperial courts, unless formally requested and granted.

2. The separate peace between Great Britain and the Colonies was not to be valid unless signed conjointly with the other peaces.

Both pacifications were to be guaranteed by the mediatory courts and by any other neutral power whose guaranty the belligerent courts might think proper to claim.

3. "A general armistice between the two parties for the term of one year" for the purpose of negotiation.[36]

It will be observed that the mediators carefully refrained from

[35] Vergennes to La Luzerne, No. 14, Mar. 9, 1781, Archives des Affaires Etrangères, *Correspondance Politique, Etats-Unis,* XV, fol. 90; Doniol, IV, 556.
[36] English text in Wharton, IV, 861.

mediating between Great Britain and the "American Colonies," thus giving to Great Britain (as well as to the "Colonies") a free hand to arrange a separate settlement without the intervention of a foreign power.

When these articles appeared Vergennes felt it expedient to consult, perhaps to persuade, Adams. For the latter still remained under his original instructions, modified to enable him to accept independence by truce,[37] the sole American plenipotentiary for peace negotiations.[38] At Vergennes's request Adams hurried from The Hague to Paris. Another interesting exchange between the two men occurred, in which Adams completely and luminously saw through the whole scheme of mediation and the whole disingenuous design of the French Foreign Minister. He declared that the United States could not consider any truce until British troops withdrew from American soil. He was willing to treat separately with Great Britain relative to truce or peace, at a congress of mediation and in the manner proposed, but only under conditions which would not call into question the independence or sovereignty of the United States; therefore only, "if the two Imperial Courts would acknowledge and lay down as a preliminary the sovereignty of the United States, and admit their minister to a congress." [39] This is precisely what neither of the mediating powers proposed to do. Reflecting on the incident in after life, Adams believed that his reply to Vergennes "defeated the profound and magnificent

[37] Instructions of October 18, 1780, also enjoined: (1) avoidance of a short-time truce; (2) no long-time truce with implied recognition of independence, *except on condition of French acquiescence,* and of removal of all British land and naval armaments from the United States; (3) in any truce "to hold up the United States to the world in a style and title not derogatory to the character of an independent and sovereign people"; (4) no stipulation for the readmission of exiled Tories, nor any compensation for their confiscated property, except on equivalent and full compensation for property of American citizens wantonly destroyed by British armies; (5) no obligation to admit British subjects to any rights and privileges of American citizenship, nor (without consent of the French Minister as a means of ending the war) to an equality with French citizens in the United States. Wharton, IV, 101.

[38] News of a new peace commission of June 15, 1781, and its altered instructions, had not arrived in France.

[39] Adams to the Count de Vergennes, Paris, July 13, 1781, commenting on the proposed mediation articles. *The Works of John Adams,* VII, 436.

project of a congress at Vienna for the purpose of chicaning the United States out of their independence. It moreover established the principle, that *American ministers plenipotentiary were not to appear without their public titles and characters, nor to negotiate but with their equals, after an exchange of full powers."* [40]

For this principle American plenipotentiaries waged a victorious fight presently in 1782.

There is no denying the force of these reflections of John Adams. The primary reason for the failure of the mediation proposal was not the unwillingness of Vergennes to accept terms which would have tricked the United States out of its independence, and would have left great parts of the country in the possession of the common enemy, quite in violation of the terms of the Franco-American Alliance. That trick failed because of the dogged British obstinacy of George III. He and his advisers construed the invitation as a foreign intervention in the domestic affairs of his own subjects and rejected it. The United States was consequently saved, for soon thereafter arrived the new instructions from Congress that had been inspired by Vergennes and that would have prevented Adams from taking such an independent tone. Pending more decisive military events the mediators dropped their mediation. It was not to come up again except in a mildly decorative way at the final signature of the definitive peace. [41] Yorktown, that lucky victory, soon occurred, October 17, 1781. When direct peace negotiations with England began in 1782 under victorious skies there was no temptation for the French ally to equivocate on the issue of American independence. To use a

[40] *Ibid.*, VII, 452.

[41] The correspondence of the Austrian Court relating to the attempted mediation has been extensively edited under the leadership of Alfred d'Arneth and others: d'Arneth and Geoffroy, *Marie-Antoinette, Correspondance secrète entre Marie-Thérèse et le cte. de Mercy-Argenteau, avec les lettres de Marie-Thérèse et de Marie-Antoinette,* 3 vols. (Paris, 1874); d'Arneth and Flammermont, *Correspondance secrète du comte de Mercy-Argenteau avec l'Empereur Joseph II et le Prince de Kaunitz,* 2 vols. (Paris, 1889); d'Arneth, *Joseph II und Katharine von Russland; Ihr Briefwechsel;* A. Beer, *Joseph II, Leopold II, und Kaunitz, Ihr Briefwechsel* (Wien, 1873); A. Beer and J. Ritter von Fiedler, *Joseph II und Graf Ludwig Cobenzl, Ihr Briefwechsel,* in *Fontes Rerum Austriacarum,* LII band (Wien, 1901).

metaphor of our own times, Vergennes during the parlous period of 1781 had reached for a parachute, but he was not obliged to pull the rip-cord before his Franco-American biplane came out of the fog and the two allies soared not ungracefully down to the landing field of victory.

CHAPTER XIV

The Beginning of Peace Discussions

In the final negotiations for peace in 1782 the American plenipotentiaries were bound by the new instructions from Congress of June 15, 1781, which Vergennes had insinuated. His new minister in Philadelphia, La Luzerne, with his great talent and the judicious use of money, quickly established an extraordinary ascendancy over Congress,[1] which did his will. If we are to believe his reports to Vergennes, he actually procured the election of Robert R. Livingston as Secretary of Foreign Affairs, who was very grateful to him for it, and who appointed a French officer as his assistant.[2] At the close of the war when Livingston retired, La Luzerne, describing the former's career as Secretary, stated that, although unfortunately Livingston could act in no essential matter without the sanction of Congress, he, La Luzerne, had concerted with him the drafts of instructions which went out from his office.[3]

In the new instructions of June 15, 1781, voted by Congress before Livingston's election, Adams found himself grouped in a commission of five: Benjamin Franklin, minister to France; John Jay, unrecognized minister to Spain; Henry Laurens, the minister designate to the Netherlands, now a prisoner in the Tower of London; and Thomas Jefferson, who did not set out from his homeland early enough to participate in the negotiations. At the peace congress the commissioners were to have "liberty to secure the interest of the United States, *in such a manner as cir-*

---

[1] La Luzerne ascribed his success with the instructions partly to the influence of General John Sullivan of New Hampshire. La Luzerne to Vergennes, No. 147, June 11, 1781, Archives des Affaires Etrangères, *Correspondance Politique, Etats-Unis,* XVII (Stevens Transcripts). Sullivan was financially indebted, at least, to La Luzerne. B. Faÿ, *L'Esprit revolutionnaire, op. cit.,* p. 88.

[2] La Luzerne to Vergennes, No. 191, Nov. 1, 1781, Archives des Affaires Etrangères, *Correspondance Politique, Etats-Unis,* XIX.

[3] Doniol, V, 303.

cumstances may direct and as the state of the belligerent and the disposition of the mediating powers may require." These new instructions removed even the boundaries from the category of *sine qua non* and placed the American Commission, except for the point of independence, entirely under the advice and control of the French court.[4]

"Blush, blush, America," wrote James Lovell to John Adams, commenting on these instructions. "Consult and Immediately concur in everything with the Ministers of his most Christian Majesty, the independence of the United States according to the tenor of our alliance kept sole ultimatum."[5] This is how the instructions appeared to at least one member of Congress, who had concerned himself with foreign affairs. So it appeared also to others. Arthur Lee tried in vain to get the instructions reconsidered, after Yorktown, and tightened. Congress with engaging but naïve loyalty clung to its confidence in the Court of France and continued to trust the subtle Vergennes to treat the interests of the United States as if they were those of his own sovereign. Never in history has one people voted to put its entire destiny more absolutely, more trustfully, under the control of a foreign government. Jay immediately, and Adams later, protested manfully against these trammels which their principals had laid on their action.[6]

Yorktown did not at once destroy George III's determination

---

[4] Wharton, IV, 505. The italics are mine. After Yorktown, Robert R. Livingston, Secretary of Foreign Affairs, wrote to Franklin January 7, 1782, some detailed arguments, which reflected debates in Congress, for the support of boundary and fishery claims and against compensation for or restoration of confiscated estates to Loyalists, and in favor of reparation for injuries wantonly done to American citizens and property. This advice did not alter the actual instructions of June 15, 1781. It is very enlightening, and possibly suggestive of Livingston's close relations with La Luzerne, to note that, after he had fortified the Commissioners with arguments for the boundaries originally laid down in Adams's instructions, he observed that if these could not be secured and a restricted boundary should be required by the mediators, then the independence of the Indians to the west might be guaranteed by four powers, Great Britain, France, Spain, and America, with free trade for all with them. *Ibid.*, V, 87–94.

[5] Burnett, *Letters*, VI, 125.

[6] Jay to the President of Congress, S. Ildefonso, Sept. 20, 1781, and to Livingston, Madrid, April 28, 1782; Adams to Livingston, The Hague, September 6, 1782; and Paris, October 31, 1782. Wharton, IV, 716; V, 373, 703, 838.

never to yield American independence. As the rising tide of opposition in the House of Commons portended the immediate overthrow of the Administration, if the war should continue in America, the collapsing North Ministry made desperate eleventh-hour efforts to open separate negotiations with the Netherlands, with France, and with the "plenipotentiaries of Congress." It offered to the Netherlands, in return for a separate peace, the *uti possidetis* (provided no Dutch colonies recaptured from British forces by the French were retained by the latter), with an explanatory article to the maritime treaty of 1674 fixing naval stores and ship's timbers as contraband, as in the case of Denmark.[7] To France it offered the *uti possidetis,* with suppression of the servitude on Dunkerque, and concessions in India.[8] By separate overtures to Franklin and his colleagues [9] the tottering British Government hoped desperately to salvage a peace short of independence.[10] These attempts to break down the now solid diplomatic front of the victorious anti-British combination ignobly failed.[11]

At last the "fatal day" was come for the King. The eloquent attacks of Fox, Dunning, Conway, Sheridan, and others carried an opposition majority against further continuation of the war in America. They forced North to resign, March 20, 1782, after the Ministry had been repudiated and an address carried without division declaring enemies of their country all those who should advise or in any way attempt to prosecute an offensive war in America for the purpose of reducing the Colonies to obedience by

[7] Colenbrander, *Patriottentijd,* I, 219.

[8] Vergennes to La Luzerne, No. 31, March 23, 1782, Archives des Affaires Etrangères, *Correspondance Politique, Etats-Unis,* XX, fol. 143, and Vergennes to Montmorin, March 22, 1782, *ibid., Espagne,* Vol. 606, fol. 185.

[9] See correspondence of J. Adams and Benjamin Franklin, with Alexander, Digges, Hartley, *et al.,* printed in Wharton, V, 50–293, *passim;* see also G. H. Guttridge, *David Hartley, op. cit.,* pp. 294–296; *Correspondence of King George the Third,* V, 104–105.

[10] "Peace with America seems necessary, even if it can be obtained on no better terms than some Federal Alliance, or perhaps even in a less eligible mode." Lord North to the King, January 21, 1782. *Correspondence of King George the Third,* V, 337.

[11] Franklin and Vergennes exchanged complete information as to these overtures. Franklin to Rayneval, March 22, 1782, and Rayneval to Franklin, April 12, 1782, Wharton, V, 271, 298. The list of enclosures is contained in Archives des Affaires Etrangères, *Correspondance Politique, Etats-Unis,* XX, fol. 138. See also Doniol, V, 40.

force. Not that it would be wrong under this act to attempt to reduce them to obedience by peaceful means or by diplomacy, though considering the circumstances of the war no peace was possible without American independence. This was hard for the King to stomach, a public announcement to all the world by Parliament that Great Britain would fight no longer for the Colonies. Nevertheless the failure of the campaign in America, depleted finances, the "crazy state of our ships" (as Sir John Jervis put it some months later when advocating the acceptance of the preliminary articles of peace),[12] and disasters in both the West and the East Indies [13] recommended peace as indispensable to Great Britain in the spring of 1782.

Under these circumstances George III had to yield to the inevitable. He still refused to deal directly with the radical leaders of the opposition. Instead of approaching Richmond or Fox, the men who had favored independence rather than a continuance of the war in America, he offered the government to Lord Shelburne. Here was a man who had consistently opposed independence. Only military events made him consider it as the necessary price of peace, for the yielding of which certain equivalents might be gained from England's European enemies; perhaps something of the "Colonies" might yet be recovered by diplomacy. He hoped for the union of Great Britain and America under the same king, but with separate sovereign parliaments, a parliament for America like that just established for Ireland in April, 1782.[14]

[12] John Jervis, Arguments for peace, 1783, deduced from the state of the navy, Shelburne Papers, Vol. 72, 523 (Stevens Transcripts).

[13] The following is a list (not to mention Yorktown) of British reverses:
Surrender of Pensacola, to Spain .... May, 1781
Recapture of St. Eustatius and San Martin by France .... November, 1781
Recapture of Demarara and Essequibo by France .... January, 1782
Capture of San Cristobal, Nevis, and Monserrat by France .... February, 1782
Capture of Minorca by Spain .... February, 1782
Failure of Hughes to defeat Suffren at Pulicat and Ceylon ....
                                                February and April, 1782
V. Urtasún, *Historia Diplomática de América,* II, 499–500.

[14] "You will be startled, but it is my firm belief, that Lord Shelburne long thought, that America was more or less to be *recovered.* How much was to be recovered, he did not know; but, *bona fide,* he thought a great deal was to be recovered.—He now [*i.e.,* after the preliminary peace] [sees] that all of America that is to be recovered lies in her trade, and other circumstances, depending upon the spontaneous inclinations of her people. And to gain these,

Shelburne politically was a free-lance disciple of the departed Chatham. He had no substantial party following and therefore hesitated to accept in his own name the responsibility for forming a government. Rockingham, whose former ministry had repealed the Stamp Act in 1766, was the only man about whom the various elements of the opposition could assemble and whom the King could, morosely, accept. The sore and obstinate monarch, now on the point of abdicating his crown,[15] would not deal directly even with Rockingham. So Shelburne became the go-between and arranger of the new Rockingham administration. He was more than that: he was a sort of king's major-domo in this curious government in which the sovereign reserved the right of receiving the advice of Rockingham and of Shelburne, separately.[16]

Shelburne's nominal post in the Rockingham Ministry was that of Secretary of State for the Southern Department, which included home, Irish, and colonial affairs. The other remaining secretaryship, for the Northern Department, that is to say for foreign affairs, went to Charles James Fox (that of colonial affairs was now abolished as a separate office). He was the brilliant and magnetic spokesman for that wing of the opposition which championed parliamentary reform and a liberal Irish settlement, as well as independence for America, a program still too radical to command a stable majority in the House of Commons.[17] The two secretaries could not see eye to eye on matters of European diplomacy, on the Irish question, on domestic reform, nor on American independence. They speedily developed an acute personal jealousy and rivalry which presently became ventilated to all the world.

he must make the state independent: and win its subjects by justice, liberality and attention." Benjamin Vaughan [see p. 224 below] to his American brother in Philadelphia, Paris, December 15, 1782. Vaughan Photostats in W. L. Clements Library at Ann Arbor, Michigan.

For the idea of the separate "sovereign" parliaments, see George M. Wrong, *Canada and the American Revolution* (New York, 1935), pp. 351–353.

[15] He actually drafted an abdication. *Correspondence of George the Third,* V, 425.

[16] *Ibid.,* V, 447.

[17] The Rockingham Government contained five followers of Rockingham's own party, *i.e.,* the radicals, and five Chathamite adherents of Shelburne, plus one high Tory, Thurlow, whom the King was able to retain as Lord Chancellor. *Cambridge History of the British Empire* (London, 1929), I, 769.

Until the independence of the "Colonies" should be definitively recognized, the administration of American affairs remained in Lord Shelburne's department, rather than in the Foreign Office where Fox now presided. Shelburne's first peace move was to try to draw the Americans away from their French ally, by rather obvious maneuvers both in Europe and across the Atlantic.

After Yorktown, Franklin, Vergennes, and Shelburne were all anxious to open conversations.[18] An opportunity occurred on the 21st of March, 1782, for Franklin to send inconspicuously a suggestive note to Shelburne. It reached that nobleman just after he took office. He grasped at the chance to send an agent to talk with the American statesman. At the same time he resolved to feel out John Adams, then at The Hague, in order to verify a report of one of North's former agents that Adams might be willing to answer "confidentially and secretly" any questions that might be put to him.[19]

Studiously Shelburne chose his agents. For parleys with Franklin he took Richard Oswald, a Scottish merchant who had amassed a fortune dealing in human misery, but who had the reputation of being a peaceable, patient, ingenuous, and "sensible" man. Certainly he was an elderly personage who had no political ambition to gratify. He had made his money as an army contractor in the Seven Years' War and as a slave merchant out of Bristol to the Sierra Leone River and the Colonies before the American Revolution. Henry Laurens, now one of the American Commissioners, had been one of Oswald's correspondents in this business and had disposed of cargoes of slaves for him on a 10 per cent commission in Charleston. In his youth Oswald had lived in Virginia, and he had family connections and estates in America. He was of a

---

[18] Franklin to Wm. Hodgson, Nov. 19, 1781, to D[avid] H[artley], Feb. 16, 1782, Shelburne Papers, Vol. 72; Correspondence of du Pont (secret French observer in London) with Vergennes, Archives des Affaires Etrangères, *Correspondance Politique, Angleterre*, Vol. 536. See also H. Doniol, "Tentatives de l'Angleterre en 1781 et 1782 pour amener la France à traiter de la paix," *Rev. d'hist. diplomatique*, XIV (1900), 161.

[19] Copy in the King's handwriting of memorandum of Mr. Digges [the agent of the North Ministry who had visited Adams a few weeks previously], March 30, 1782. *Correspondence of George the Third*, V, 432. See also "Mr. Digges's account of what passed between him and Mr. Adams, March 30, 1782," Shelburne Papers, Vol. 72.

philosophic disposition, calculated to soften the tamer of light-
nings. Adam Smith had introduced him to Shelburne. Both sub-
scribed to Smith's new teachings against monopoly.[20] The British
were now reduced to the expedient of cultivating and flattering
the man so contemned by the recent ministry and the King. They
even hoped that an appeal to ancient ties and old friendships, to
the Philadelphian's homely human benevolence, might elicit his
good-will and place bygones in the way of being bygones, at least
until the French alliance should be broken up.

To confer with Adams, Shelburne used Henry Laurens. He
had recently cultivated the South Carolinian and let him out on
bail from the Tower of London, the bail being furnished in part
by Oswald, Laurens's old business friend. To his satisfaction
Shelburne discovered to the King that Laurens was "fundamen-
tally averse to France." [21] In fact, Laurens during his incarcera-
tion had mentioned his former respect and attachment though not
present loyalty to the British Crown and had made a plea on that
basis for ameliorating the severity of his imprisonment.[22] No
evidence has so far appeared to prove that he suggested any desertion of France.

Oswald and Laurens crossed the Channel together to Ostend,
where they parted, each on his respective mission. Oswald had
his first meeting with Franklin at the latter's suburban residence
in Passy, April 12. He learned that the Americans were indeed
willing to treat for peace, though only in concert with their allies,
and that nothing could be done until the several plenipotentiaries
could be assembled. Franklin then took Oswald to Vergennes,
from whom the British agent learned that France was also willing

[20] See *Dictionary of National Biography*, "Oswald." There is a valuable
pen portrait of Oswald's personality and character in the MS. letter of Benjamin Vaughan to James Monroe in *Monroe Papers*, VIII, 964, Library of
Congress. Vaughan took credit for suggesting Oswald's appointment. For Oswald's activities in the slave trade see Elizabeth Donnan, *Documents Illustrative
of the Slave Trade to America* (Carnegie Institution of Washington, 1930–1935,
4 v.), II, 111n., 537, 540n., 565n., 657; and D. D. Wallace, *Laurens, op. cit.*,
pp. 72–94.

[21] Shelburne to the King, April 5, 1782. *Correspondence of King George the
Third*, V, 442.

[22] Wallace, *Henry Laurens, op. cit.*, puts the best possible light on this un-
dignified petition.

to treat for peace, but only after consulting with her allies; that a general treaty was indispensable and that France certainly would have some special demands of her own to present. Before returning to London, Oswald held further converse with Franklin, who allowed him to take back a confidential paper, never revealed to Vergennes, suggesting that the cession of Canada to the United States would be an ideal solution of the outstanding problems; that same Canada, as Oswald conveniently had remarked, which had served to encourage the American insurrection when ceded to Great Britain in 1763. This Franklin felt would promote a sweet reconciliation of a durable nature by at once removing possibilities of all further friction. The vacant lands in those vast domains might likewise provide funds to indemnify American citizens whose property had been wantonly destroyed by the British military or even afford compensation for the confiscated property of British Loyalists. Oswald manifested his sympathy for this idea.[23] Franklin immediately perceived that the Scotchman would make an ideal negotiator. He sent word back to Shelburne to that effect.[24]

In Franco-American relations, throughout the history of the alliance, Canada had been a delicate subject. It might easily have been a fatal embarrassment to the two allies if Choiseul and Vergennes had not renounced ambitions of resurrecting another colonial empire. France had brought European civilization to Canada. The land had borne the name of New France for over a century and a half before its conquest in the Seven Years' War. Its population was still overwhelmingly French-speaking and devoted to the memory of the previous generation, though a stroke of British statesmanship, conspicuous for its political wisdom in a period of English government otherwise pretty empty of that quality, had introduced, in the Quebec Act of 1774, a little more of contentment into the political lot of the French Canadians dwelling there, stilling some of the restlessness for revolt in com-

---

[23] Franklin's *Journal*, Wharton, V, 541, 572. Thomas Hodgkins, *British and American Diplomacy Affecting Canada, 1782–1899* (Toronto, 1900), has signaled out the documents illustrating Oswald's complaisance about Canada, emphasizing the implications involved for the future of Canada.

[24] Wharton, V, 538.

mon with the Protestant colonies to the south.[25] Nevertheless, the French tradition and the French population there could not have been expected to resist very heartily an actual French invasion. The reëstablishment of French power in America, as Vergennes so clearly saw, would have provoked immediate alarm throughout the thirteen colonies in revolt, would have convinced them that the real object of France in intervening in the American Revolution was to repossess herself of Canada rather than to assure American independence. It would have strengthened tremendously the position of the Loyalists. For these reasons he had opposed any French, or even Franco-American, step toward Canada during the war.

Nervousness in the United States about the possible French repossession of Canada was not the less because Congress from the beginning had coveted that province as a fourteenth State in the Union. In 1775 Congress had issued an appeal to the inhabitants of Canada to join the revolt. It had dispatched the unlucky expeditions of Montgomery and Arnold for the conquest of Montreal and Quebec in the winter of 1775–1776. It had supported that unsuccessful enterprise with a diplomatic mission of Benjamin Franklin, Samuel P. Chase, and Charles Carroll, "three wise men from the South," accompanied by the Jesuit brother of Carroll, John Carroll, who they hoped might help to shake the allegiance of French Catholic subjects in the St. Lawrence Valley. The mission failed, as the campaign collapsed, but it had the result of fixing Canada as a quest in Franklin's subtle mind.[26] The treaty with France projected by the "Plan of 1776" called for French agreement not to make any conquests on the continent of North America. The alliance of 1778 stipulated this renunciation, so far as the continent and the Bermudas were concerned, leaving France

[25] R. Coupland, *The Quebec Act, A Study in Statesmanship* (Oxford, 1925).

[26] The Montgomery-Arnold campaign, though a failure in achieving the conquest of Canada, had a vastly favorable and unexpected strategical result that can be seen better by the historian than it could be perceived by contemporaries. It drew to Canada British troops originally intended for Boston or New York, thus dividing the King's forces and presaging the British catastrophe of the Saratoga campaign, which was an attempt to unite the two armies. In this sense the Montgomery-Arnold failure was a great strategic success which made possible American independence.

a free hand in the other islands including Newfoundland. Finally we have observed that the instructions of Congress to the peace commissioners had enjoined them to get Canada if possible.

From the beginning Vergennes had been aware of the significance of the American attitude toward Canada in relation to his policy of intervention.

We recall that he sent Bonvouloir on his secret mission in 1775 to tell Congress, among other things, that France did not want to get Canada back. "They [the Americans] don't want to shake off the mother country's yoke only to take on that of another power," he had told the King in 1777. Taking the final step of actual intervention, the Foreign Minister had come to realize that it would be better to leave Great Britain in Canada in order to furnish a necessary makeweight against the United States and to keep the latter attached to French interests. This makeweight would be equally lost if the United States independently took Canada for itself, but Vergennes was too wise ever to go so far as actively to oppose such a project. He readily agreed to the restrictions on Canada that were written into the alliance. In the diplomatic contact of the two allies during the war Vergennes had frowned on plans for the conquest of Canada, jointly or independently by the United States, without ever going so far as to take a position positively opposed to the latter. Gérard, setting out for Philadelphia in 1778, had instructions not to encourage the conquest of that province, but to acquiesce in good grace, without committing France to any coöperation, if the Americans proved determined to attempt it.[27] D'Estaing, leaving with his fleet for American waters at the same time, had been told carefully that France sought nothing for herself on the North American continent, though she would not be averse to acquiring the island of Newfoundland as a defense for her fisheries. If Congress should press him for assistance in any campaign against Nova Scotia, he might go no further than to aid them with a cruiser or an *attaque de poste,* providing France and Spain should share in any fishing privileges there; and he was allowed to make an appeal to the

[27] Doniol, III, 156.

Canadian people to warm up their former attachment for France.[28]

Canada's attraction for Lafayette, if given a free rein, might easily have imperiled the alliance. Burning for glory and craving an independent command, he had proposed to d'Estaing, upon the arrival of the fleet, a joint expedition of American troops to be led by himself and carried by the French fleet for an attack under its support on Halifax or some other British port. It was a youthful and foolhardy conception, but there is some indication that d'Estaing was tempted by the idea [29] Lafayette had hastened from Boston to Philadelphia to secure the consent of Congress for such a campaign. That body referred the proposal to Washington, who immediately objected. In a public letter to Congress he argued against it on strategical grounds. In a private communication to the President of Congress he gave his principal objection as political: it would present to France too great a temptation to reëstablish her power in a country still filled with memory for her, and attached to her by all the ties of blood, habits, manners, religion, and former connections of government. The possession of Canada by France, together with her influence over the Indians and her alliance with Spain, would give her a means of "awing and controlling these States, the natural and most formidable rival of every maritime power in Europe." [30] Congress followed Washington's advice and shelved the idea. In discussing the matter, Gérard had been consulted. He frowned gently on the project. Washington's advice to Congress had been entirely in line with the wishes of France. Vergennes approved his minister's action. "You have done wisely," he wrote, "to elude the overtures made to you concerning Halifax and Quebec. Your instructions embody the King's way of thinking on that subject; and His Majesty has changed the less because he has reason to believe that it enters into the policy of Spain as well as our own to maintain the English in possession of Nova Scotia and Canada." [31]

[28] Doniol, III, 191–193.
[29] Doniol, III, 412–413; IV, 40–41.
[30] *The Writings of George Washington,* W. C. Ford, ed., VII, 239–262.
[31] Doniol, III, 616.

Later, in the dark months of the autumn of 1780, when the French expeditionary force was immobilized at Newport, Washington in desperation had changed his mind. He suggested to La Luzerne that the French troops might possibly be used in some joint expedition against Canada. But French policy had not changed. La Luzerne dissented. The object of the alliance, he said, as Gérard had said before him, was to secure the independence of the United States, not to make territorial conquests for them; that object could be best secured by efforts to dislodge the enemy from the southern States.[32] With this review in mind of Canada as a factor in the diplomacy of the French alliance, we are not surprised, as we come to the peace negotiations of 1782, to see Franklin endeavoring to persuade the British to cede the country to the United States. We shall expect to see Vergennes prefer otherwise, now that the war there was drawing to a successful conclusion without the American conquest of Canada.

Franklin was not the only one of the commissioners who was alert for Canada in the approaching negotiations. John Adams, too, was thinking of it, when Henry Laurens met him at Haarlem on April 15; if the cession of Canada and Nova Scotia were not attainable, he wanted at least the elimination of any garrisoned or fortified frontier. Canada struck Laurens, too, as not impossible of attainment. He reported many people in England to be in favor of cession. Adams incidentally noted Laurens to be "perfectly sound in his system of politics." [33] To Shelburne, Laurens took back a confirmation of the reports of Lord North's previous agents, only to the extent that the American Commissioners were indeed empowered to treat for a peace or truce on the basis of independence and a strict adherence to the French alliance. It was apparent that neither Adams nor Franklin was open to easy beguilement. Even Laurens came back *"changed,* touchy and conceited, and vulgarly so. . . . An acknowledgment of Independ-

---

[32] Doniol, IV, 555–556. On the subject of Canada, see, in addition to Doniol, the remarks of Corwin, *French Policy and the American Alliance, op. cit.,* pp. 200–201; and particularly the able and sparkling study of A. L. Burt, *The Province of Old Quebec* (University of Minnesota Press, 1933), pp. 176–247.

[33] To Franklin, April 16, 1782, Wharton, V, 543.

ence must be a Preliminary, and no proceeding whatever without France." [34]

While he was preparing to sound out in Europe the plenipotentiaries of Congress, Lord Shelburne did not overlook the chance of separate peace negotiation with the "Provinces" on American soil. An approach in America, though it could not escape the attention of the vigilant French Minister there, would be more comfortably distant from the infinite resources of the Comte de Vergennes. Might not Congress, or the individual state governments across the ocean, less directly in touch with the requirements and commitments of the distant European scene, be more likely than its commissioners in Paris to yield to the temptation of an immediate peace rather than to continue the war for uninteresting and unprofitable objectives in Europe, Asia, and Africa, of France and her Spanish ally? At least might not Congress be brought to soften its instructions to the commissioners? Sir Guy Carleton, now being sent to prepare the evacuation of British forces from the Atlantic seaboard, and Admiral Digby, naval commander on the American station, received instructions, April 4, 1782, to convey to Congress the late proceedings of the House of Commons,[35] as showing the dispositions of the government and people of Eng-

[34] Lord Shelburne to the King, April 24, 1782, *Correspondence of George the Third*, V, 487. Adams had refused to give Laurens a copy of his full powers as a peace Commissioner so long as he remained technically a prisoner. Franklin however sent him a copy on April 12, and after Laurens's release from parole he showed it to Shelburne. Wharton, V, 544, 547.

In the exchange of news between Adams and Franklin which followed these interesting interviews both agreed that a truce was no longer in order. Adams insisted on explicit recognition of American independence, either in the treaty to be eventually signed, or by virtue of Great Britain's treating with plenipotentiaries of the United States specifically so denominated. Franklin mentioned to Adams that he had suggested, in this written memorandum for Shelburne's eyes, the cession of Canada; it had been a favorite project with him ever since he left Philadelphia in 1776, in fact ever since the unsuccessful journey to Montreal of the "three wise men from the South" (Burt's good phrase) in 1775–1776. Wharton, V, 542–550. For Franklin's first sketch of peace propositions, in 1776, see Smyth, *Writings of Franklin*, VI, 452. See also P. B. Morris *Peacemakers* (1965) 516, n. 77.

[35] The proceedings of February 27 to March 4, 1782, with an address to the King in favor of peace, and a copy of the bill enabling the King to conclude a peace or truce with the revolted "Colonies" in America.

land toward America.[36] In vain General Carleton tried to conclude with General Washington a one-sided armistice—applying only to land warfare and only along the seaboard—to cover the intended evacuation of British troops. Washington refused to convey to Congress the resolves of Parliament which the British commander wished to forward through him. Congress itself refused to provide a passport for a messenger to deliver them direct from the hands of Carleton and alertly passed a resolution of rigid adherence to the French alliance, "against the insidious steps which the Court of London is proposing." [37] The State of Maryland, its legislature then in session, resolved against any local peace parleys, leaving everything to Congress—which left everything to its commissioners in Europe in tight concert with the Court of France.

These maneuvers so far had spoken only of provinces in America and His Majesty's subjects there. Later Carleton conveyed to Washington a statement that the British Government had begun negotiations for peace in France and was prepared to acknowledge independence "in the first instance." This move was calculated, both in America and (as we shall see presently) in Europe, to detach the Americans from France by persuading them that there should be nothing more to fight for after their independence were acknowledged. Washington was in no way deceived, nor was Congress, nor a single State. Carleton finally had his correspondence with Washington published in an effort to stimulate public opinion against sticking to the French alliance, but in the hour of victory the American leaders were not taken in by this transparent blandishment.[38]

[36] "You must . . . lose no time to avail yourself of the change of measures which has lately taken place, for the purpose of reconciling the minds and affections of His Majesty's subjects, by such open and generous conduct, which may captivate their hearts, and remove every suspicion of insincerity. . . . You may state every circumstance, if occasion offers, which has passed or is passing here, which can tend to revive old affections or extinguish late jealousies." Instructions to Carleton and Digby, J. Sparks, *Writings of George Washington* (Boston, 1835), VIII, 297.

[37] *Journals*, May 14, May 31, 1782.

[38] The correspondence may be found scattered through the Sparks and the Ford editions of the *Writings* of George Washington; the *Correspondence of King George the Third;* the Sparks, Bigelow, and Smyth editions of the *Writings* of Benjamin Franklin; Wharton; the *Journals;* etc.

Nor were these first British efforts to split apart the allies at first more successful in Europe.

The first interviews with Oswald justified Franklin in summoning his fellow commissioners to the interesting work at Paris. Jay set out straightway from Madrid, not arriving in Paris until June 23, 1782. Laurens, although released from parole at Franklin's behest, avoided service with the peace Commission until the last moment, a maneuver not easy to explain with full credit to himself.[39] He participated in the negotiations only at the last hour, in the following November, after having been specifically ordered to his task by Congress itself. Adams was obliged to tarry in Holland in order to wind up the highly important contract for a loan and to complete the negotiation of the treaty with the Netherlands.[40] He did not reach Paris until October 26. The aged but perfectly functioning [41] Franklin was thus left alone to cope with any immediate developments.

Oswald's reports that the allied enemies were at least willing to treat led to the opening of formal negotiations at Paris. Both sides preferred to negotiate directly without the mediators. But we must abridge in these pages the earlier phase of the negotiations in May and June during the short-lived Rockingham Ministry. Remember that the British Ministry was badly strained between the rival secretaries: Shelburne, who esteemed himself to be the real leader of the government, and Fox, the man who had been so conspicuous in the movement for the overthrow of North. Shelburne, acting as home and colonial secretary, sent Oswald, for whom Franklin had expressed a preference, back to Paris to talk peace to Franklin; and Fox sent a plenipotentiary, Thomas Grenville, to Versailles to treat with Vergennes, but also to ply

[39] See his correspondence on the subject in Wharton, V, 559–560.

[40] See above, pp. 168–169.

[41] Franklin was now in his seventy-sixth year. In 1780 he had requested leave to resign, because of age and infirmities. John Jay wrote from Madrid, April 21, 1781: "The letters I have received from him bear no marks of age, and there is an acuteness and sententious brevity in them which do not indicate an understanding injured by years." On arriving in Paris, Jay wrote to Livingston, June 25, 1782: "He [Doctor Franklin] is in perfect good health, and his mind appears more vigorous than that of any man of his age I have known." Wharton, V, 517, 648n.

Franklin.[42] It was the effort of both to mollify the American Commissioners, particularly the philosophic Franklin, by appeals to natural affinity and indissoluble love for "old England." The Ministry decided to make American independence the principal equivalent of an offer of peace to France.[43] They hoped that France straightway would demand impossible terms for herself, that Spain would add to these, and that thus it would appear that, with Great Britain ready to grant independence, the principal object of the Americans was being frustrated by the exorbitant requirements of France and Spain in Asia, Africa, and Europe.[44] If the Americans could be persuaded that France was prolonging the war, for example, only to secure Gibraltar for Spain, they might quit and make a separate peace. Oswald and Grenville reported that at times Franklin appeared to glance in that direction.[45] With the Americans out of the way, it should then be possible to secure better terms from the remaining enemies.

These tactics failed,[46] if only because the experienced Vergennes met them with a formula already fashioned during the diplomacy of the previous year in regard to mediation. Let Great Britain and the United States negotiate directly their own peace. It were sufficient, he declared, that the two negotiations (French and American) proceed at an equal pace, provided that the final efficacy of each depended upon the signature of the other.[47] In this way he easily parried the first British move. In thus eluding the British attempt to separate the Americans, by persuading them that a peace of independence now depended on exorbitant and impossible non-American demands of their ally and of their ally's

[42] Lord John Russell, *Memorials and Correspondence of Charles James Fox,* 4 vols. (London, 1853-1857), I, 360.

[43] *Correspondence of King George the Third,* V, 448.

[44] *Ibid.,* VI, 31-32.

[45] *Ibid.,* VI, 41; Russell, *op. cit.,* I, 343-359; IV, 174-213; Lord Fitzmaurice, *Life of William Earl of Shelburne,* 2d ed., 2 vols. (London, 1912), II, 128-136; Franklin's *Journals,* Wharton V, 544-566.

[46] French minutes of the conferences of Vergennes with Grenville are to be found in Archives des Affaires Etrangères, *Correspondance Politique, Angleterre,* Vol. 537 (W. L. Clements Library photostats).

[47] Russell, *op. cit.,* IV, 209; Vergennes to Montmorin, No. 33, Archives des Affaires Etrangères, *Correspondance Politique, Espagne* 607, fol. 135 (Stevens Transcripts).

ally, he steered the Anglo-American negotiations into a separate channel. These negotiations had not advanced beyond the opening stage when Rockingham died, July 1, and Shelburne became Prime Minister. Immediately he united the control of British diplomacy under his own direction. Fox resigned.[48] Meanwhile had occurred Rodney's great victory over the French fleet in the West Indies, April 12, 1782, which had the effect of softening Vergennes's original intention of using these negotiations to undo the Peace of Paris of 1763 in Africa and India. By the time the British Cabinet was reorganized under Shelburne the French were in a more reasonable mood for peace than appeared on the surface.

[48] When it was evident that these tactics for splitting apart the allies had failed, Fox (following a suggestion of Grenville), put through the Cabinet a decision, May 23, "to instruct Mr. Grenville to propose the Independency of America in the first instance, instead of making it a condition of a general treaty." Fox believed that once possessed of independence the United States would not continue the war to assure French, Spanish, and even Dutch *desiderata*. The King and Shelburne interpreted the Cabinet decision of May 23 to mean only an assurance that independence would really be granted as a price of final peace—no peace, no independence. The Cabinet sustained this interpretation. Fox did not resign until he realized that his rival was to be the new prime minister. *Correspondence of King George the Third, VI*, 44, 45; Fitzmaurice, *op. cit.*, II, 133–166. See also the Duke of Grafton's *Memoirs*, from his diary, concerning divisions in Lord Rockingham's Cabinet, June, 1782, in Lord Mahon's *History of England . . . 1713–1783* (London, 1854), VII, Appendix, xix.

CHAPTER XV

The repeated overtures for mediation, followed by the stunning victory of Yorktown and the downfall of the North Ministry, had finally clarified the terms of peace on the part of all the belligerents, but the awkward enmity of Fox and Shelburne had stultified the British negotiations. The elimination of Fox simplified matters, at least for Great Britain. For the next ten months Lord Shelburne, in full control of the government, was to have barely time to salvage the Empire by making a peace with the powerful enemies which ringed England about. Then Fox and his old and bitter enemy North, the former Prime Minister, were to unite and overthrow Shelburne for the work he had done to save his King and country. But it is not with this curious chapter of English politics that we are concerned as much as with the negotiation of the major European, and American, peace settlement of 1782–1783.

Several weeks of delay ensued, during July and August, 1782, while Shelburne was adjusting his new administration to his own control of the entire British part of the negotiation. Oswald, whom Shelburne had designated to treat with the "Colonies," remained in Paris near Franklin. His immediate superior henceforth was Thomas Townshend, the new Secretary of State in charge of home and colonial affairs. In the Shelburne Ministry the American negotiations were thus significantly colonial business. Alleyne Fitzherbert repaired to Paris from his post at Brussels to replace Grenville, who had resigned with his friend Fox. Fitzherbert received his instructions from Lord Grantham, the new Secretary of State for foreign affairs. During this lapse of time, while an act was moving through Parliament to enable a peace and Oswald was awaiting the arrival of his actual full powers, Franklin consented to further confabulations with him.

It was in these informal talks, which Oswald requested of Franklin "as a friend," even "as a friend of England," that the Doctor allowed his elderly Scottish crony to listen to the reading from a confidential memorandum of a set of American terms of peace, designed to be imparted to the British Ministry, not as coming from Franklin himself but as suggestions from Oswald to his own principals. Oswald reports them in his own words as what Franklin considered "advisable for England to offer for the sake of reconciliation and her future interest, viz:—

"1st. Of the first class *necessary* to be granted, Independence full and complete in every sense, to the Thirteen States, and all troops to be withdrawn from thence.

"2d. A settlement of the boundaries of *their* colonies and the loyal colonies.

"3rd. A confinement of the boundaries of Canada; at least, to what they were before the last Act of Parliament, I think in 1774, if not to a still more contracted state, on an ancient footing.

"4th. A freedom of fishing on the Banks of Newfoundland and elsewhere, as well for fish as whales.

"I own I wondered he should have thought it necessary to ask for this privilege; he did not mention the leave of drying fish on the shore at Newfoundland, and I said nothing of it. I don't remember any more articles which he said they would insist on, or what he called necessary for them to be granted.

"Then as to the advisable articles, or such as he would, as a friend, recommend to be offered by England, viz:—

"1st. To indemnify many people who had been ruined by towns burned and destroyed, the whole might not exceed the sum of five or six hundred thousand pounds. I was struck at this. However, the Doctor said, though it was a large sum, it would not be ill-bestowed, as it would conciliate the resentment of a multitude of poor sufferers, who could have no other remedy, and who without some relief would keep up a spirit of secret revenge and animosity, for a long time to come, against Great Britain; whereas voluntary offer of such reparation would diffuse a universal calm and conciliation over the whole country.

"2d. Some sort of acknowledgment, in some public Act of Parliament, or otherwise, of our error in distressing those countries so much as we had done. A few words of that kind, the Doctor said, would do more good than people could imagine.

"3d. Colony ships and trade to be received, and have the same privileges in Great Britain and Ireland as British ships and trade. I did not ask any explanation on that head for the present. British and Irish ships in the Colonies to be, in like manner, on the same footing with their own ships.

"4th. Giving up every part of Canada."

"Upon the whole [said Oswald] the Doctor expressed himself in a friendly way towards England, and was not without hopes, that if we should settle on this occasion in the way he wished, England would not only have. a beneficial intercourse with the Colonies, but at last it might end in a foederal union between them. In the mean time we ought to take care not to force them into the hands of other people. . . ."[1]

In reporting these terms Oswald expressed a belief that the "Colonies" might conclude them separately, to take effect only upon the ratification of an Anglo-French peace; and he hoped that England could accept, certainly, the "necessary" group; in that case, he thought, "They will not be any way stiff as to those Articles he calls *advisable,* or will drop them altogether."[2]

Hardly had Oswald received these ideas than Franklin, having heard reports that the change of ministry in London meant—contrary to assurances previously received from the departed Grenville—a new policy of attaching conditions to independence, forbade him to consider any such terms of peace until further explanation should be forthcoming from Shelburne on the point of independence.[3] "I did understand from him [Grenville]," Franklin took care to state in writing, without referring to the memorandum that he had just read to the Scot, "that such an acknowledgment [of independence] was intended before the commencement of the treaty; and until it is made and the treaty formally begun, propositions, and discussions seem, on consideration, to be untimely, nor can I enter into particulars without Mr. Jay, who is now ill with the influenza."[4]

In view of much historical discussion about Franklin's having been persuaded only by the advice of his associates Jay and Adams

[1] Oswald to Shelburne, Paris, July 10, 1782, Russell, *Memorials and Correspondence of C. J. Fox, op. cit.,* IV, 239–241.
[2] Oswald to Shelburne, July 11, 1782, Russell, *op. cit.,* IV, 251.
[3] Oswald to Shelburne, Paris, July 12, 3 P. M., 1782, Russell, *op. cit.,* VI, 253.
[4] Franklin to Oswald, July 12, 1782, *ibid.,* p. 258.

to negotiate the preliminary terms of the treaty, somewhat independently of French advice, it behooves us at this point to note: (1) that Franklin had first confidentially suggested the cession of Canada without any consultation with Vergennes; (2) Franklin himself mentioned the detailed American terms of peace to Oswald quite independently of Vergennes and carefully covered up his own responsibility for them, so that the only record we have is Oswald's report of what he could remember of the memorandum as it was read to him; (3) he made it plain that there must be a preliminary acknowledgment of American independence before the treaty; (4) he reserved any commitment pending conference with Jay (whom Oswald had not yet seen). Is it not plain that the Sage of Passy, whom historians have unanimously represented as overpersuaded by his more youthful and downright colleagues, had been the first to take the path, which all presently trod, to a violation of their instructions to proceed only under the full confidence and advice of the French Minister?

The desired further explanations on the point of independence were at hand when a copy of Oswald's intended commission arrived on August 8. It forecasted the phraseology of the actual document, which still had to await the official signatures and seals to be imposed by certain British dignitaries loitering in the country.[5] By this advance text of a still unsigned commission Oswald was to be empowered to treat, agree, and conclude with "any commissioner or commissioners, named or to be named by the said colonies or plantations, or with any body or bodies, corporate or politic, or any assembly or assemblies, or description of men, or any person or persons whatsoever, a peace or truce with the said colonies or plantations, or any of them, or any part or parts thereof."[6] This commission, so carefully worded as not to recognize any plenipotentiaries of the United States, and even to divide the "Colonies" among themselves, was a sufficient explanation that the Shelburne Ministry was not yet ready to recognize independence before the treaty should be signed. Oswald's accompanying in-

[5] Franklin to Vergennes, August 8, 1782, Wharton, V, 651.
[6] It was actually the text of an order from the King to the Attorney General, directing that a commission be made out in the phraseology therein laid down. It is printed in Wharton, V, 613.

structions confirm this explanation.[7] In case no treaty should result, having employed such cautious powers as these the British Government certainly would have formally acknowledged nothing. Franklin, Jay, and Vergennes discussed the text of Oswald's commission on August 10. Vergennes, very anxious to have the several peace negotiations "tied together," though proceeding separately, advised accepting the commission as soon as the authenticated document should arrive. So long as independence were made an article of the final treaty, he said, the form of the commission was unimportant: France herself did not object to treating with a British plenipotentiary who presented full powers with the traditional phrase denominating the King of England as also King of France! If the commissioners wished to protect themselves, let them be mindful to require Oswald to exchange formally full powers with them; by receiving their commissions as plenipotentiaries of the United States of America he would have committed himself to that form.[8] Vergennes turned to Franklin and asked what he thought about it. The Doctor said he thought it "would do," but the legalistic Jay said that he did not like it and thought it best to proceed cautiously.[9] When presently the

[7] A draft is in Shelburne Papers, Vol. 71, 1–18. The instructions were enclosed in Townshend to Oswald, August 3, 1782. Record Office, F. O., *France,* Vol. 479.

[8] This accords perfectly with the reasoning of a confidential memorandum in the French Foreign Office, analyzing the problem, under the title of "Reflexions sur l'acte du 25 Juillet, 1782" [*i.e.,* on the advance text of Oswald's commission] : *"Assuming that it is important to tie up* [lier] *the negotiations in some way or other,* one may ask if, to avoid all false inductions on the part of England, the act of protestation above mentioned is necessary; or whether the delivery and acceptance pure and simple by Mr. Oswald of the full powers of Messrs. Jay and Franklin would not fulfil the same object? It may be observed that the King of England in no part of his commission presents or names the Colonies as his subjects or vassals; while in the full powers of the Americans the Colonies are called United States of North America. It appears to result from this comparison that the acceptance of the commission of Mr. Oswald will not involve an admission of the supremacy of England over the Americans and that the acceptance of the full power of Messrs. Franklin and Jay will involve the indirect acknowledgment of the independence of the United States." Archives des Affaires Etrangères, *Correspondance Politique, Etats-Unis,* XXI, fol. 145 (Stevens Transcripts). I have italicized part of the first sentence quoted above.

[9] Vergennes concluded after this interview that it was agreed that the Americans should deliver a copy of their full powers to the British Commissioner, and that notwithstanding his solicitations they should defer entering into the subject until he produced the original of his commission. Vergennes to La Luzerne, Versailles, Aug. 12, 1782, printed in the E. E. Hales' *Franklin in*

two were alone after the interview, he argued vigorously with Franklin, pointing out that it was the interest of France to postpone American independence until French views and the objectives of Spain could be gratified by a peace. This explained Vergennes's advice, he said. Jay thought the French Minister was trying to slow up the Anglo-American negotiations on that ground. Franklin believed on the other hand that he was trying to hasten them, professed confidence in Vergennes's loyalty, and cited the instructions of Congress to take his advice.[10] Vergennes's confidential correspondence of the time shows that Jay's caution was not excessive.[11]

Jay now worked on Oswald. He convinced the British plenipotentiary of the utter impossibility of ever treating with Great Britain on any other than an equal footing.[12] He asserted that this

France, op. cit., II, 155. In the Franklin Papers [No. 2594] in the Library of Congress is a formula to this effect conveyed from Vergennes in Lafayette's handwriting, with provision for complete renunciation of independence by the first article of the treaty.

[10] This is taken from Jay's account of the interview in Wharton, VI, 15.

[11] Floridablanca urged France that it was important to defer recognition of American independence until the general peace, lest the Colonies, being satisfied, might drop out of the war before Gibraltar were secured. Vergennes assured Spain that he was delaying the negotiation with England until the fate of Gibraltar should be determined. He did not pledge himself to block any premature recognition of American independence—that he could not guarantee —but it is significant that he argued with the Americans that it was proper to include actual recognition by Great Britain in the final peace, rather than to seek a preliminary recognition. Montmorin to Vergennes, July 8, Aug. 12, Vergennes to Montmorin, Aug. 10, 1782, Archives des Affaires Etrangères, _Correspondance Politique, Espagne_, 608, fols. 15, 113, 119, (Stevens Transcripts) ; Jay to Livingston, Nov. 17, 1782, Wharton, VI, 17. It is vastly more significant that he revealed to the British peace commissioner treating with France at Versailles, Alleyne Fitzherbert, that he had so advised the Americans! This, reported Fitzherbert to the Secretary [of the Northern Department] for Foreign Affairs, "certainly evinces clearly that Your Lordship was founded in your suspicion that the granting Independency to America as a previous measure is a point which the French have by no means at heart, and perhaps are entirely averse from." A. Fitzherbert to Grantham, Nos. 54 and 55, August 29, and September 11, 1782. Record Office, _F. O., France,_ Vol. 558, pp. 166 and 257 (Stevens Transcripts).

[12] "I told him plainly that I would have no concern in any negociation in which we were not considered as an independent people." Jay to Livingston, November 17, 1782, Wharton, VI, 16. Oswald describes these interviews with Jay and Franklin in great detail in his letters, with attached minutes, from August 7 to 21. See transcript of "Oswald's Journal" in Franklin Papers, in Library of Congress.

meant a preliminary recognition of independence irrespective of the treaty, as Grenville had promised in May—indeed, we may add, as Franklin had been careful to require. But Oswald, showing the fourth article of his instructions of August 3, 1782, to Jay (to acknowledge independence in the first article of a treaty irrespective of other articles), believed he had persuaded the latter "of the sincere intentions of His Majesty to make this grant in the precise way they desired." [13]

When the opinions of Jay and Franklin were reported to London, the Cabinet, August 29, agreed in principle to such a preliminary recognition as the two Americans had demanded, that is, if such recognition should prove to be unavoidable and provided the Americans would agree at the same time to make peace on the basis of the four "necessary" articles of Franklin's proposed terms.[14] But the King's ministers did not feel that they possessed authority without an act of Parliament. Therefore they agreed that the King should, *if insisted on by the American plenipotentiaries,* recommend to Parliament (then about to begin its third session) [15] an absolute and irrecoverable acknowledgment of independence. It was indeed a surrender in principle, shrewdly made in the hope of splitting the United States from its French ally. "Indeed I have reason to think," wrote Lord Grantham to Fitzherbert, September 3, 1782, "that even the independency of America, however ultimately disadvantageous to France, would not, if accepted now by the commissioners, be a measure agreeable to her, as the bond between them would thereby be losened before the conclusion of a peace." [16]

The American Commissioners did not insist on the advance

---

[13] Oswald to Shelburne, August 15, 1782, John Bigelow, *Works of Benjamin Franklin* (Boston, 1888), VIII, 150.

[14] *Correspondence of King George the Third,* VI, 118.

[15] Reference to the *Journals,* with the assistance of Dr. Leo F. Stock, shows that Parliament had been prorogued from July 11, 1782, which marked the end of the 2d session of the 15th Parliament, to September 3, 1782, then to October 10, 1782, then to November 26, 1782, then to December 5, 1782, when business was resumed. Adjournment followed on July 16, 1783, the end of the 3d session.

[16] *British Diplomatic Instructions, 1689–1789,* Vol. VII. *France,* Part IV, 1745–1789. L. G. Wickham Legg, ed. (London, Royal Historical Society, 1934), p. 184.

recognition ahead of a treaty. Jay had weakened and consented to go ahead provided Oswald's commission were altered to enable him to treat with plenipotentiaries of the United States of America. Franklin easily followed him.[17] If Franklin and Jay had stood firm and promptly followed up the advantage they had gained, by the former's subtle suggestions and the latter's earlier insistence, an advance recognition of independence might have been wrung from George III, and it is conceivable that preliminaries of peace might have been signed before news reached England, September 30, 1782, of the failure of the great assault on Gibraltar, an event which naturally raised British hopes and heightened British tone. Such preliminaries could have given the United States all that it secured under the articles of November 30—if we assume Franklin's overlooking of fish-drying privileges on shore in Newfoundland would have been caught up—and these without any mention of the status of private debts to British creditors, nor of British Loyalists in America; all these, of course, without Canada and Nova Scotia. Canada was not one of the "necessary" terms. Some curious delays now veiled this possibility to the American Commissioners, so that they never knew of it.

The despatches containing the new British offer reached Paris on September 4. In the accompanying instructions [18] Townshend bade Oswald, before showing his hand, at least to make an effort to persuade the Americans to accept independence as the first article in the treaty, offering as an inducement peace on the basis of Franklin's "necessary" articles pure and simple.

[17] John Adams, at this time in The Hague, felt strongly that no negotiation should be permitted without a preliminary recognition of independence, suspected Franklin (only) of having compromised on that point, and thought of resigning from the peace commission rather than participate in its labors after such a mistaken concession. This he says in a section, deleted before sending, of a letter to R. R. Livingston, August 18, 1782. The letter, without the deletion, is printed in Wharton, V, 665, but another copy has recently come to light to which Wharton did not have access. It gives the first draft in full.

[18] Memorandum, enclosed in Townshend to Oswald of September 1, 1782, Record Office, F. O., Series 95, Vol. 511 (Stevens Transcripts); Townshend to R. Oswald, Sept. 1, 1782, Shelburne Papers, Vol. 70, fol. 188 (in W. L. Clements Library, Ann Arbor, Michigan).

The fact that Oswald consumed a few days with this preliminary sparring delayed matters just enough for the appearance of a conjuncture of events which gave the negotiation quite another turn.

CHAPTER XVI

"The Point of Independence"

From the time he first set foot on European soil John Jay had developed a distrust of European diplomacy. The inquisitiveness of Conrad Alexandre Gérard, the French diplomatist who returned from Philadelphia on the same ship in which Jay voyaged to Spain, about his fellow traveler's instructions; the equivocal attitude of Spain; her refusal to recognize American independence; the secret Spanish treaty with France, the terms of which Jay either accurately suspected or positively knew—all this made him fear that France would now try to prolong the war beyond American independence for non-American objects like Gibraltar. After he arrived at Paris these feelings were deepened into suspicion of positive treachery by a combination of occurrences and intelligences which preceded and followed the interviews [1] with Vergennes about Oswald's powers. They may now be brought together.

The first of these happenings was Jay's contacts with Aranda, the Spanish Ambassador at Versailles, and, through him, with the French Court. When Jay left Madrid for Paris, Floridablanca told him that he had sent to Aranda all the papers relating to American matters and that Jay could get in touch with him there. Now that peace was imminent Floridablanca instructed Aranda at least to listen to Jay or any other agent of the United States and to negotiate with him or them on western boundaries and a general commercial arrangement, but to conclude nothing without referring it home.[2] Two days after arriving in the French me-

[1] When the authentic copy of Oswald's commission arrived, a second interview took place in which their divergence of view was more apparent. Wharton, VI, 17–18.
[2] Floridablanca to Aranda, No. 3, May 17, 1782, Archivo Histórico Nacional, *Estado, legajo* 4079.

tropolis Jay solicited an interview with Aranda,[3] who was careful to receive him as a private Spanish nobleman in order not to imply any recognition of the United States.[4] We must keep continually in mind that it was Spanish policy to defer any acknowledgment of American independence at least until Spanish objectives had been secured in the general treaty, and that Vergennes was deferring to this policy. Interviews followed during the month of August, in which Jay did not refuse to discuss boundaries, though Aranda could show no full powers to conclude anything.[5] Before Jay broke off these conversations on September 10, for lack of Aranda's powers,[6] some significant exchanges of view had taken place. Aranda had suggested a settlement of boundaries between the United States and Spanish possessions after the manner of give and take: the two would sit down at a table with maps before them, he said, and agree on some sort of a compromise boundary. With Mitchell's great map of North America,[7] of 1755, spread out before them, Jay insisted uncompromisingly on the Mississippi as the western boundary as far south as the line of 31° north latitude, which was the old northern boundary of West Florida from 1763 to 1764, and which he now claimed as

[3] Jay to Aranda, June 25, 1782, Wharton, VI, 21.

[4] Aranda to Floridablanca, No. 2241, Paris, July 6, 1782, Archivo Histórico Nacional, *Estado, legajo* 6609.

[5] Aranda in fact wrote to Floridablanca, anent Jay's request for an exchange of full powers, that the time to treat American representatives as those of other sovereign powers would be only after preliminary discussions should have shaped things more definitely and when Great Britain herself should have recognized the independence of the United States. Aranda to Floridablanca, No. 2301, Paris, Sept. 15, 1782, *ibid.*

[6] Jay to Aranda, Paris, Sept. 10, 1782, *ibid.*, also Wharton, VI, 28.

[7] Those who wish to delve into the maps used in the negotiations will find useful directions in J. Winsor, *Narrative and Critical History of America,* VII (Boston, 1888), 171–184; John Bassett Moore, *History and Digest of the International Arbitrations to Which the United States Has Been a Party* (Washington, 1898), I, 152–161; and Lt. Col. Dudley A. Mills, "British Diplomacy and Canada," with map illustrations, in *United Empire,* Vol. II (New Series) [Oct., 1911], 683–712. Colonel Lawrence Martin, Chief of the Division of Maps in the Library of Congress, who has helped me on this and numerous other occasions with guidance as to maps, is preparing for publication a book on Mitchell's Map, the preliminary draft of which he kindly allowed me to consult. The essential portions of these data are published in a long note explanatory of the Anglo-American convention of 1827 in Vol. III (1933) of the Hunter Miller edition of *Treaties and Other International Acts of the United States,* pp. 328–351.

the southern boundary of the United States. Aranda claimed for Spain, by right of conquest, West Florida up to its established boundaries—since the British proclamation of 1764 these had been the latitude of the mouth of the Yazoo River (present Vicksburg, Mississippi) on the north, and the Chattahoochee on the east. He further claimed the east bank of the Mississippi all the way north to the Ohio, even to the Great Lakes.[8] The Spaniard asserted a line which began at the western end of Lake Superior and, following the southern shore of that lake, continued around the shore-line of Lake Michigan and Lake Huron to the western end of Lake Erie, thence by a straight line to the confluence of the Kanawha and the Ohio, thence southwesterly to the region of the headwaters of the Flint River, whence it diverged to the southeast to lose itself near the source of the St. Mary's River on the confines of East Florida.

The two lines were highly irreconcilable. Aranda now appealed to Vergennes to intervene on behalf of Spain's interests in America. Vergennes thought the Wabash-Maumee line would be a proper boundary for Spain on the east, for the territory north of the Ohio; if the Americans would not listen to reason, perhaps the problem could be solved by setting up some kind of neutral Indian buffer state between the United States and the Mississippi. He referred Aranda to his private secretary, Rayneval, who was thoroughly familiar with the boundary, as well as the fisheries and all other American questions, if only from perusal of the despatches of La Luzerne and the voluminous memoranda of the active young secretary of legation at Philadelphia, Barbé Marbois. The Franco-American alliance never promised to get the fisheries for the United States, nor did it guarantee American territory itself until it should have been fixed by the peace. It was now in the act of being fixed. These were the critical days in which the fate of the West was to be determined.

We cannot blame Vergennes for not wanting to continue the war for the sake of securing for the United States these western domains, at the possible displeasure of Spain, his other ally, any more than we can condemn the American representatives for

[8] See above, p. 102. For the suggested boundaries, see map 2 opposite p. 216.

not wishing to prolong the war after American independence to get Gibraltar for a power which had never been willing to recognize that independence. But we must remember that, quite apart from the exigencies of the war or of Franco-Spanish diplomacy, Vergennes had been opposed to American acquisition of Canada,[9] and this despite the fact that the Franco-American alliance gave the United States a free hand there. Under these circumstances we can hardly disapprove Franklin's keeping secret from the French Court his efforts to get Canada, or Jay's refusing to follow the advice of Vergennes's confidential aide for the western boundary. Presently we shall see that, when Vergennes did learn that the Americans and British were at odds on boundaries, fisheries, and Loyalists, he caused it to be intimated to Shelburne confidentially that France would not support them on at least the first two of these points. Certainly the two American Commissioners would have been at a great disadvantage if either had interpreted his instructions to require them to seek and then to follow Vergennes's advice at every turn of the negotiations.

Rayneval and Aranda put their heads together and worked out a startling compromise to present to Jay as Rayneval's "personal ideas." If Vergennes himself never urged it formally and personally, it certainly had his countenance. The reports of Aranda make that clear. Reinforced by *ex parte* historical arguments of Rayneval, it proposed a line which zigzagged, by various convenient rivers, from the mouth of the Cumberland in a general southerly direction to the "eastern angle" of the Gulf of Mexico, at Apalachicola Bay. This line would have kept American territory away from the Mississippi from the Ohio River south, and Rayneval would next have excluded the United States from all the region north of the Ohio by recognizing that as British. The Indians to the west and south of Rayneval's line and east of the Mississippi were to be free and under the protection of Spain; those to the east of the line were to be free and under the protection of the United States, or the United States might make such arrangements with them as it should see fit. The Indian trade was

[9] De Circourt, *Histoire de l'action commune de la France et de l'Amérique pour l'indépendance des Etats-Unis,* 3 vols. (Paris, 1876), III, 290, 311.

to be free to both parties. Rayneval argued that Spain had no pretensions to territory north of the Ohio; the disposition of that region was to depend entirely on Great Britain. If this French proposal, which so pleased the Spaniards, had been adopted, the United States would not have secured from Great Britain title to the region now composing the present states of Ohio, Indiana, Illinois, Michigan, Wisconsin, and Minnesota, and would have lost to Spain the western part of Kentucky and Tennessee, Mississippi, and part of Louisiana, together with most of Alabama.[10] Rayneval delivered to Jay on September 6 a memoir of more "personal ideas" which embodied these propositions.[11]

These proposals, we repeat, left the Mississippi south of the Ohio under exclusive Spanish control and kept the United States far away from its entire length.[12] As Franklin remarked, it looked

[10] For western boundary lines, see map 3 opposite p. 218.

[11] It appears to have been drawn off from a much longer document which the French diplomatist placed in Aranda's hands the next day, together with a brief arguing that the United States could not derive from the British proclamation of October, 1763, any title to land beyond the Ohio. In the more voluminous document Rayneval had suggested that Spain might concede to the United States a privilege of navigating the Mississippi, with an *entrepôt* or free port on its lower reaches, so necessary for new American settlements on the Ohio, in return for American acknowledgment of the proposed boundary. In the earlier drafts of this longer memorandum we have the line beginning at the mouth of the Tennessee instead of the Cumberland. As turned over to Aranda the memorandum started the line farther north at the Cumberland (as proposed to Jay); but it left the Cumberland-Tennessee-Apalachicola Bay line as the *absolute* boundary of Spanish possessions, without mention of any Spanish protectorate over independent Indians west of the line. Rayneval also made in the longer memorandum the assertion that the ephemeral incursions of George Rogers Clark into the Northwest region could not be seriously advanced as an American claim "nation to nation." So far as the documents relating to the entire negotiation reveal, such a claim was never made on the basis of Clark's conquests. As a matter of fact he had at this time withdrawn his garrisons to the falls of the Ohio River, and the Northwest was "no man's land."
I realize that there is a voluminous literature arguing that by virtue of Clark's earlier conquests and his position on the Ohio he was in strategic control of a portion of the Old Northwest in 1782. Even if one admits the force of these arguments, which I do not, by far the greater part of that territory was more subject to the influence of British garrisons at Detroit and Michilimackinac than to Clark's at Fort Nelson.

[12] Aranda's account of his negotiations with Jay and with Rayneval concerning the American West is detailed at length in his despatches to Floridablanca, No. 2207, June 1, No. 2241, July 6, No. 2266, August 10, No. 2274, August 18, No. 2290, September 1, No. 2301, September 15, No. 2314, Octo-

as though Spain desired "to coop us up within the Alleghany Mountains." [13]

Rayneval's "personal ideas" fired Jay's suspicions, already warmed by Vergennes's complaisant attitude toward Oswald's unacceptable commission. He next heard (September 9) that Rayneval had departed on a secret trip to London. The following day the British opportunely put into his hands a copy of an intercepted ciphered despatch from Barbé Marbois to Vergennes, strongly arguing against stretching the alliance to support American claims to the inshore fisheries of Newfoundland. [14]

All of these things taken together persuaded Jay that the object of Rayneval's secret trip was to suggest to the British Ministry: (1) that France did not countenance American demands for independence previous to incorporating it as an article in the final peace treaty; (2) to sound Lord Shelburne on the fisheries and discover whether Great Britain would agree to divide them with France, to the exclusion of all others; (3) "to impress Lord Shelburne with the determination of Spain to possess the exclusive navigation of the Gulf of Mexico, and of their desire to keep us

ber 4, 1782, with enclosures of *billets* (as he studiously called them) between himself and Jay (printed in Wharton), including a lengthy diary of the conversations (printed in Yela, *España ante la independencia de los Estados Unidos, op. cit.*, II, 355–364), all in Archivo Histórico Nacional, *Estado, legajo* 6609. Rayneval's longer memorandum on boundaries is to be found: (1) in Archives des Affaires Etrangères, *Correspondance Politique, Etats-Unis*, XXII, fols. 309–317; (2) in *ibid.*, *Angleterre*, vol. 537, fols. 389–399, endorsed "Juillet, 1782"; (3) in Archivo Histórico Nacional, *Estado, legajo* 6609, attached to Aranda's No. 2295 of Sept. 8, 1782. There is a transcript of the first of these in the Library of Congress, and a photocopy of the third. Of the second there is a photostat, which is a duplicate of one in the W. L. Clements Library at Ann Arbor, Michigan. An inaccurate English translation of the memoir handed to Jay is printed in Wharton, VI, 29–31, as a part of Jay's letter to Livingston of November 17, 1782. The original French exists, in copy, in Vol. 110 of the Papers of the Continental Congress.

13 Franklin to Livingston, August 12, 1782, Wharton, V, 657.

14 The despatch, dated March 13, 1782, is printed in English translation in Wharton, V, 238. Marbois affirmed to Madison in 1783 that it was spurious, and several historians have accepted this statement. There is a quintuplicate of the despatch in the French archives, Archives des Affaires Etrangères, *Correspondance Politique, Etats-Unis*, XX, 407–417, which proves it genuine. Marbois later admitted its authenticity. (J. Jay [the grandson], "The Peace Negotiations of 1782–1783," in Justin Winsor, *Narrative and Critical History of America*, VII, 120.) There is a copy of the despatch in the archives of the British Government. Record Office, *C. O.*, 5/40.

from the Mississippi; and also to hint the propriety of such a line
as on the one hand would satisfy Spain and on the other leave to
Great Britain all the territory north of the Ohio"; (4) "to make
such other verbal overtures to Lord Shelburne as it might not be
advisable to reduce to writing, and to judge, from the general
tenor of his Lordship's answers and conversation whether it was
probable that a general peace, on terms agreeable to France, could
be effected in order that, if that was not the case, an immediate
stop might be put to the negotiation." [15]

Jay's suspicions were not ill-founded. While it is true that the
principal object of Rayneval's journey concerned French and
Spanish peace objects in Europe and Africa and Asia—notably
with a report brought from Shelburne by the paroled prisoner
Admiral de Grasse, that Great Britain might give up Gibraltar—
he nevertheless took occasion to insinuate to Shelburne what he
had already more pointedly told to Fitzherbert,[16] that the Americans had no real claim to fishery rights anywhere outside their
own territorial waters, except on the high seas. He further very
subtly suggested to Shelburne that English definitions and pre-
cedents themselves (as construed by Rayneval) quashed the
claims of the United States to the territory beyond the Ohio.
More than this, Rayneval secretly promised Shelburne that France
would not reveal prematurely any preliminary articles that England, France, and Spain might conclude, and even said that the

---

[15] Jay to Livingston, November 17, 1782 Wharton, VI, 29.

[16] Fitzherbert reported in his No. 53 of Aug. 21, 1782, to Grantham that
Vergennes in emphasizing France's "exclusive" rights to certain parts of the
Newfoundland fisheries, meant thereby to secure himself against any American
claim to enter the fisheries of such coasts. In his No. 54 of Aug. 29, 1782, reporting a conversation with Rayneval, Fitzherbert said that Rayneval "signified to me in pretty plain terms that nothing could be farther from the wishes
of this Court than that the said [American fishery] claim should be admitted,
and moreover that he thought we, on our parts, were not only bound to reject it, but that we might do so consistently with the strictest principles of
Justice . . . a ground of right which he said farther was no way invalidated
by our admission of the French to a share in the said Fishery, it being expressly declared in the Treaties which allow it them, that they hold it as a
concession from us. Though upon mentioning this, Mo^r. de Raineval added
that he said it merely from himself, and without any kind of authority from Mo^r.
de Vergennes, I think it right nevertheless to communicate it to Your Lordship." Record Office, F. O., 27, III, fols. 141, 165 (Stevens Transcripts).

Americans might be put off the trail by keeping them ignorant of what went on between England, France, and Spain.[17] "The point of Independence once settled," wrote Shelburne to the King late at night after the first conference with Vergennes's secretary, "he appears rather Jealous than partial to America upon other points, as well as that of the Fishery." [18]

[17] "Conférences de M. de Rayneval avec les Ministres Anglais," September 13, to September 18, 1782, Archives des Affaires Etrangères, *Angleterre*, Vol. 538, fol. 146 (Stevens Transcripts). Printed by H. Doniol in *Revue d'histoire diplomatique*, VI (1892), 62–89. One is in danger of misunderstanding Rayneval's allusion to boundaries if one does not read in connection therewith his memoir of September 6, above mentioned. In that memoir and in the historical memoranda from which it was drawn (see Note 11 above) Rayneval emphasized that in the negotiations attending the opening of the Seven Years' War, Great Britain had admitted French claims as far south as the Ohio. In the conversations with Shelburne, Rayneval, on the subject of a boundary for the United States, records: "I merely said that the English Ministry ought to find in the negotiations of 1754 relative to the Ohio the limits which England, then sovereign of the thirteen United States, thought she ought to assign them." Doniol, V, 619. See below, p. 232.

In his memoir (Wharton, VI, 25) delivered to Jay on September 6, 1782, immediately before departing for the conferences with Shelburne in London, Rayneval had sought to show that, in the negotiations attending the outbreak of the Seven Years' War, "*according to the very propositions of the Court of London,* almost the whole course of the Ohio belonged to France" (italics mine). This seems to me abundant evidence of what Rayneval had in mind when talking to Shelburne. Of course we cannot say positively whether Shelburne got the idea; but in the text above is quoted Shelburne's comment to the King:—"he appears rather Jealous than partial to the Americans upon other points, as well as that of the Fishery," and we shall see presently how Shelburne stood out for the line of the Ohio. I do not vouch for Rayneval's interpretation of the negotiations at the beginning of the Seven Years' War; on that more research needs to be done; but what he was hinting to Shelburne seems clear from these memoranda.

On the point of secrecy, Rayneval said anent a conference of Saturday the 14th: "We spoke about observing secrecy in case we should succeed in establishing preliminaries. I assured him it would be most faithfully guarded on our part. My Lord fears gamblers in the public funds and would be extremely desirous to frustrate their endeavors. I said we could arrange to conclude in the greatest secrecy so as to throw the curious off the scent. My Lord fears the Americans and Dutch: I repeated that there would be a way to put them off the track principally by keeping them ignorant of the negotiation between France, Spain, and England. Lord Shelburne has this article infinitely at heart."

[18] *Correspondence of King George the Third,* VI, 125. The same sentiment is reflected in Vaughan's subsequent correspondence with Shelburne, notably his letter of October 29, 1782. *Mass. Hist. Soc. Proc.,* 1903, 2d series, XVII, 419.

Thirteen years later Benjamin Vaughan (see second paragraph below) answered from Basel an inquiry of James Monroe, then Minister of the United States to France, to be informed, on the basis of Vaughan's intimacy with

Alarmed at this prospect of French diplomatic collusion with the enemy, Jay gave up the demand for an immediate and unequivocal recognition of independence as a condition precedent for further negotiation. He now made quick efforts to bring affairs to a conclusion. He suddenly told Oswald (September 9) that if he could get his commission altered so as to recognize independence *constructively* by empowering him expressly to treat with the Commissioners of the United States of America, this would be adequate. Providing Franklin would agree, they would accept this in place of an explicit preliminary recognition. Later Oswald asked Jay if Franklin had agreed. Jay said yes. Oswald was much pleased. He wrote to London urgently requesting the change in his commission.[19]

To block these French designs, Jay next made a counter-move of his own. Without consulting Franklin, whom he thought over-

Shelburne's policy in 1782, what grounds and motives the American peace Commissioners at Paris may then have had for "suspecting the liberality of the French Court with regard to boundaries, fisheries, etc.," whether these suspicions were not excited by the address of the English negotiators. Vaughan remembered "that the American negotiators were *well authorized* to suppose that France, on the subjects in question, took part with England. The evidence arose from the manner in which Count Vergennes recommended moderation to the American negotiators, respecting their demands on the head of boundaries, fisheries and refugees." But, explains Vaughan, Shelburne headed off this French intrigue by treating ingenuously with the Americans, particularly by agreeing to the revision of Oswald's commission as demanded by Jay and represented to Shelburne by Vaughan in his special trip to London. Vaughan also calls attention to the then recently published instructions of 1793 to Genêt to confirm Jay's suspicions of 1782. Benjamin Vaughan to James Monroe, September 18, 1795. Monroe Papers, VIII, 964, Library of Congress. It is noteworthy that Monroe, who was seeking evidence to blacken English and whiten French diplomacy, made no use of this interesting letter.

Other statements of Vaughan supplement this. He wrote to Shelburne from Paris, December 17, 1782: "Your Lordship may thank the Court of France, whose intrigues made it [the Anglo-American preliminary articles], and Dr. Franklin, who [so says Vaughan, to emphasize the value of his putative intimacy with Franklin] first established the personal attachment here to Your Lordship." In an undated paper entitled "Miscellaneous Remarks" (Vaughan Photostats, W. L. Clements Library, Ann Arbor, Michigan), Vaughan stressed French willingness to enter into arrangements with England to limit American territory, as a justification for the separate signature by the Americans of the preliminary articles and also alluded to previous French willingness to achieve a peace short of perfect independence for the United States. In these sentiments Vaughan appears to reflect Jay's suggestions.

[19] Oswald to Townshend, Paris, Sept. 10, 1782. "Oswald's Journal," transcript in Franklin Papers, Library of Congress.

trustful of unwavering French support, he dispatched a messenger of his own to Shelburne. This was none other than a young Englishman, Benjamin Vaughan. This person was related by marriage to the London family of Henry Laurens's daughter-in-law, a friend of Franklin, but also a confidant whom Shelburne had sent over to Paris, after the death of Rockingham, to cultivate the Americans and to pick up such useful information as he could find. Vaughan mingled continually with the American Commissioners and sent to Shelburne a prolix and ill-digested series of private despatches. At first inclined to intrigue, his easily impressionable character presently led him completely under the spell of Franklin and Jay,[20] later Adams too. By suggestion they were able to make him their spokesman who supplemented Oswald's official despatches with a series of private letters to Shelburne replete with arguments in favor of the particular American demands and the several American viewpoints. It is doubtful whether, except in the especial case we are to mention, Shelburne paid much attention to Vaughan's lengthy and disjointed epistles. Certainly George III placed no value on them.[21] Jay requested Vaughan to say, more suggestively, to the Ministry what he and Franklin [22] had actually given the Scot to understand: that there could be no treaty without a commission to Oswald empowering him to treat with Commissioners of the United States of America; that as Great Britain could not conquer the United States it was to her interest to conciliate them; that it was the interest of France, but not of England, to postpone the recognition of American independence to the final treaty. It followed that "it was the obvious interest of Britain immediately to cut the cords which tied us to France, for that, though we were determined faithfully to fulfil our treaty and engagements with this court, *yet it was a*

[20] "Had a long Conversation with Mr. Vaughan on the State of the Negotiation—we agreed in all things." *Diary* of John Jay, October 25, 1782.

[21] For some printed letters from Vaughan to Shelburne, reflecting the influence on him of his intimacy with Franklin, Jay, and Adams, after his return to Paris, Oct. 3, 1782, to Jan. 12, 1783, and a biographical note, see *Mass. Hist. Soc. Proc., op. cit.,* pp. 409–438.

[22] Franklin to Grantham, Sept. 11, 1782, *Works* of Franklin, J. Bigelow, ed. (New York, 1887–1888), VIII, 170.

different thing to be guided by their or our construction of it"; that the United States would not stay in the war to satisfy the demands of Spain; that America would not make peace without the fisheries—such a settlement would irritate and inflame, and lead to resentment and consequent restraints on British commerce; that it was to the advantage of Great Britain to see the United States extend to the Mississippi, because by arranging free commerce by the St. Lawrence and Mississippi she would have as a market for her manufactures the multiplying populations of American citizens who would take up these hinterlands.[23]

One consistent effort of British diplomacy had been to bring the Americans to a separate peace, or at least to separate preliminaries. It was now apparent that the latter was distinctly possible.

Oswald's earnest letters and Vaughan's reports convinced Shelburne that it would be desirable to alter the commission as Franklin and Jay required[24] if the negotiation with them were to go forward. Shelburne's Cabinet already on August 29 had voted *if necessary* to advise the King to ask Parliament to recognize American independence unconditionally before the treaty and irrespective of further negotiations. It was easy to vote the lesser concession now that the Americans had failed to insist on the more radical recognition. Immediately it was resolved, September 19, "that a new Commission be made out under Your Majesty's Great Seal for enabling Mr. Oswald to treat with the Commissioners appointed by the Colonys, under the title of Thirteen

[23] Jay to Livingston, November 17, 1782, Wharton, VI, 31.

[24] Oswald to Shelburne, September 10, 11, 1782, enclosing draft of letter by Jay of September 10, representing that the Americans could not treat except on equal terms, etc., the Hales' *Franklin in France, op. cit.*, II, 131–144; Wharton, *Digest of International Law* (Washington, 1887), III, 945–949. See also *Correspondence of King George the Third*, VI, 128. My doubt that Vaughan had anything to do with influencing the decision disappeared after reading the Townshend Papers in the W. L. Clements Library, Ann Arbor, Michigan. See particularly Ashburton to Shelburne, Spitchwell Park, Sept. 16, 1782; and Shelburne to Townshend mentioning important "private letters from Paris" (presumably by Vaughan), dated Wycombe, "Monday." The inquisitive reader might also consult Fitzherbert to Grantham, No. 55, September 11, 1782, received September 14, Record Office, F. O., 27, III, fol. 257 (Stevens Transcripts); and Oswald to Shelburne, September 10, 1782, in transcript of "Oswald's Journal," Franklin Papers, Library of Congress.

United States, inasmuch as the Commissioners have offered under that condition to accept the Independence of America as the First Article of the Treaty." [25]

This curious language, still dragging in the word *Colonies,* was by no means a clear-cut recognition of American independence. It is doubtful whether even Oswald's new commission [26] to treat with the Commissioners of the United States of America constituted such a recognition beyond recall. Though Europe generally took it as a recognition, the British Government (with the possible exception of the Lord Chancellor) did not so admit,[27] and it is quite probable that, if the ensuing negotiations had broken down, Great Britain would have maintained obstinately that she had never recognized the independence of the United States.[28] In demanding and accepting Oswald's new commission Jay and Franklin deserted that ground on which they had once stood for an explicit and unequivocal preliminary recognition of American independence, as their first instructions had required, a recognition which on August 29 the Cabinet had been willing to advise the King to recommend to Parliament. Into this concession they had been hastened by their reaction to Rayneval's conduct. If it had not been for their quite understandable suspicions, the American Commissioners might have forced Oswald's hand, under his instructions of September 1, before the first good news from Gibraltar reached London on September 30. In that case they could

[25] *Correspondence of King George the Third,* VI, 131.

[26] Text in Wharton, V, 748.

[27] "They came unanimously and without hesitation to the resolution which is contained in the minute which I enclose to your Lordship; it not appearing to them that the making such an alteration in the commission was of importance enough to put a stop to the negotiation or that it by any means amounted to a final acknowledgment of Independence, it only giving them during the negotiation the title which they wished to assume." Draft of letter of Townshend to the Lord Chancellor, September 20, 1782, Townshend Papers, in W. L. Clements Library. Like the Lord Chancellor, Lord Ashburton was also distant in the country and could not attend; but in a letter of September 16 to Shelburne from Spitchwell Park he expressed some doubt whether the altered commission would not constitute an express recognition; and further doubt whether it were right for the Executive to acknowledge Independence without a treaty.

[28] George III warmly expressed himself against William Pitt's speech on the American preliminaries themselves, in which he assumed that independence was now irrevocable, even though the present treaty proved abortive. *Correspondence of King George the Third,* VI, 175.

have had their preliminaries two months earlier and without mention of Loyalists or debts and on the basis *at least* of Franklin's "necessary" articles. These articles would have limited Canada to the Nipissing line, that is, present Quebec and northward; and Canada north of a line from the southernmost corner of Lake Nipissing to the source of the Mississippi. As it was, the negotiations were delayed unfruitfully, and Franklin and Jay by no means had yet secured even what they thought they were getting and what the Continental Congress of the United States joyously thought it was getting: a virtual acknowledgment of American independence.[29]

[29] Burnett, *Letters,* VII, iv–v.

CHAPTER XVII

THE PRELIMINARY ARTICLES OF NOVEMBER 30, 1782

Vaughan returned to Paris, September 27, with the courier who brought the new commission for Oswald.[1] The negotiations now proceeded in regular form at a lively pace. On October 5 they took shape in a set of preliminary articles of peace, drafted by Jay with Franklin's approval, to take effect only upon the signature of preliminary articles between Great Britain and France.

This draft [2] consisted of Franklin's "necessary" articles, plus a new article stipulating freedom of navigation and commerce by both parties on the Mississippi River, *and elsewhere throughout all their dominions on the terms of nationals.* They now laid down this boundary for the United States: on the north what we will call the Nipissing line; on the west the Mississippi; on the south the 31°-St. Mary's River line; on the east the Atlantic Ocean, including for the United States all islands within twenty leagues of the coast; on the northeast Oswald entered into a supplementary agreement with Jay and Franklin to leave the boundary to be settled by a joint commission after the war. Even with this concession on the northeast this line of October 5 corresponded with the original instructions to Adams of August 14, 1779.[3]

[1] Jay to Livingston, Paris, Nov. 17, 1782, Wharton, VI, 11–49; Fitzmaurice, *Shelburne, op. cit.,* III, 183.

[2] A copy of this draft was attested by Oswald on October 8, 1782, as a true copy which doubtless led Wharton (V, 805) to date the draft October 8. Fitzmaurice dates it October 5. Oswald's No. 74 to Townshend of October 7, 1782, enclosed the draft; and he explains that it was delivered by Jay in his own hand on October 5, Record Office, F. O., 27, II, fol. 665.

[3] See our Map 4 opposite p. 228. The various boundary proposals have been worked out with great care and thoroughness on Mitchell's Map of North America of 1755, the map used by the negotiators in 1782, by C. O. Paullin, *Atlas of the Historical Geography of the United States* (published jointly by the Carnegie Institution of Washington and the American Geographical Society of New York, Baltimore, 1932), pp. 52–54, and plates 89, 90. The agreement concerning the northeast boundary was made after the 5th and on or before the 8th of October, and added to the original draft.

Jay correctly divined that if the British could be sure of commercial vestibules [4] to the American West they would accept these boundaries. Quebec would be one of these side-door entries; Florida could be another. He urged on Oswald that Great Britain instead of Spain ought to retain West Florida at the final peace and might well remove her troops from New York and other American ports, still occupied, for reconquering that province. He argued to Vaughan [5] what he had persistently said to Oswald: that the United States, by consenting to the mutually free navigation of its several lakes and rivers, would afford for Great Britain an inland navigation to a great free market—in a way, a monopoly—for the sale of European manufactures to the anticipated millions of English-speaking settlers in the western hinterlands of the new American republic. By luring the British into West Florida as an easy entrance to the trade of the American West, Jay hoped to keep the Spanish away from the east bank of the Mississippi above West Florida. Incidentally he saw a means of drawing away the British garrison from the still occupied Atlantic seaports. Here, too, is the explanation of the separate article in regard to West Florida in the actual preliminaries.[6]

It is fortunate that Jay's preference for Great Britain instead of Spain as a neighbor in West Florida, a preference which apparently commended itself to Franklin [7] also, came to naught in the final peace. As Vaughan shrewdly pointed out to Shelburne, West Florida would have been a focus of expansion into the interior territory to the north and, under the circumstances of its possession by Great Britain, "the River St. Lawrence, the Lakes,

---

[4] Dr. Gerald S. Graham has emphasized the value of this inland trade in the views of the Shelburne Ministry in his scholarly essay *British Policy and Canada, 1774–1791, A Study in 18th Century Trade Policy* (London, 1930). See pp. 46 ff.

[5] Wharton, VI, 31; the Hales, *Franklin in France, op. cit.,* II, 170. Dr. George W. Brown has a cogent analysis of a phase of this point in "The St. Lawrence in the Boundary Settlement of 1783," in *Canadian Hist. Rev.,* IX (September, 1928), 223–228.

[6] Lord Shelburne later expressed himself to this effect to Rufus King, United States Minister to Great Britain, in 1802. C. R. King, ed., *Life and Correspondence of Rufus King* (New York, 1894–1900), IV, 93.

[7] Vaughan to Shelburne, Paris, Dec. 4, 1782, *Mass. Hist. Soc. Proc.,* 2d Series, XVII, 421.

the Ohio, and the Mississippi will form a trading coast at the back of the American Colonies, somewhat as the Atlantic does at the front." [8] Any one familiar with the process of American territorial expansion since 1783 will realize the estoppel which Jay's invitation and Franklin's complaisance in regard to Florida signified. Luckily the separate Florida article of the preliminary articles of peace dropped out of the final treaty. Meanwhile Jay had practically won his point of ejecting Spain from the West by committing Great Britain to the Mississippi as a boundary and letting her ships and commerce in there by the free navigation of that river, as he planned, in return for similar entrance of American ships and goods to British dominions everywhere.

But where was Canada now? Historians have wondered whether John Jay, by insisting on a revision of Oswald's commission, delayed affairs until after news of the successful defense of Gibraltar had raised the tone and stiffened the terms of the British. They have asked whether by this insistence John Jay upset the apple-cart in which Franklin had been so patiently and so gently trundling Canada. The answer is that Canada tumbled out of the American apple-cart when Jay was wheeling it single-handed during Franklin's indisposition, sometime between the arrival of Oswald's revised commission, on September 27, and October 5, when Jay and Oswald agreed on the draft of preliminary articles. Though favorable but not conclusive news from Gibraltar had reached London as early as September 30,[9] there is no indication that Oswald availed himself of it as an argument to exclude Canada from the treaty. Oswald and Jay discussed Canada,[10] but it was not included in Jay's draft of October 5, except insofar as the Nipissing line embraced the Ontario peninsula. Jay had be-

---

[8] Vaughan to Shelburne, Paris, October 3, 1782, *ibid.*, p. 409.

[9] *Correspondence of King George the Third*, VI, 138. This must be news of the failure on September 13 of the great bombardment by the Chevalier d'Arcon's floating batteries, which marked the climax of the besieging efforts. Lord Howe's fleet definitively relieved Gibraltar on Oct. 13, 1782. C. Fernández Duro, *Armada Española* (Madrid, 1901), VII, 319, 331.

[10] Oswald to Townshend, Paris, October 2, 1782, the Hales, *op. cit.*, II, 169. In a postscript to this letter Oswald says, "I hope to get clear of the advisable articles [*i.e.*, Franklin's "advisable" articles], as distinguished from his 'necessary' articles, but as to some of those in my instructions I doubt I shall not [*sic*] succeed."

come so frightened at Spain's claims to the east bank of the Mississippi and France's apparent support of them that he let go any hope for Canada and promised free navigation and trade into the American West from the Mississippi River and from the St. Lawrence-Great Lakes system. He did this particularly in order to push Spain out and make sure at least of the boundary which Congress had instructed the commissioners to get, but also keeping in mind the reciprocal concessions for American navigation and trade in British dominions *everywhere*. Learning of Spain's territorial pretensions in the Mississippi Valley and France's attitude toward them, Jay was anxious to secure a title from Great Britain which would help protect the West. To relinquish what at best must have been a remote chance of getting Canada, and placing Florida in British rather than Spanish possession was to him a cheap price to pay for this. After the Jay draft of October 5, which Oswald reported [11] had the approval of Franklin, we hear no more of Canada.[12]

This first draft of an actual treaty reached London October 11, twelve days subsequent to the arrival of the first encouraging news from Gibraltar, the failure of the great decisive bombardment of the 13th of September. In this new situation Shelburne was no longer willing, as he had been previously, to accept in principle a treaty based merely on the "necessary" articles of Franklin, without mention of Loyalists or pre-war debts owed to British creditors. Successes at Gibraltar immediately strengthened the British position at Paris and increased England's demands. Henry Strachey, Undersecretary of State in the colonial office, was dispatched to assist Oswald to make a fight for debts and Loyalists, particularly to have something on paper to show that a valiant effort appeared to have been made for the latter, although there were if nec-

[11] Oswald to Townshend, October 8, 1782, Record Office, *F. O., 27*, II, fol. 665 (Stevens Transcripts).

[12] When Adams, Franklin, Jay, and Laurens dispatched to Livingston the signed preliminary articles, Dec. 14, 1782, they reveal the motive for relinquishing Canada: "We knew this court and Spain to be against our claims to the western country, and having no reason to think that lines more favorable could ever have been obtained, we finally agreed to those described in this article; indeed they appear to leave us little to complain of and not much to desire." Wharton, VI, 132.

essary "other Resources" that might be used to satisfy them; to endeavor to restrict American fisheries to the high seas; and to get a better boundary, before signing any articles. "Urge the French boundary of Canada," Shelburne said to him. "Urge the boundary established by the Quebec Act [the Ohio], which was acquiesced in." Perhaps Shelburne was then thinking of Rayneval's hint a month previous that before the surrender of Canada to Great Britain, the French boundary had been acknowledged by the English at the Ohio. This suspicion is strengthened by Oswald's remark to Jay, on Strachey's arrival at Paris, that he (Strachey) "spoke of limiting our [American] western extent by a longitudinal line on the East of the Mississippi." Such Rayneval had suggested to Jay. Now Jay hears it from England, after Rayneval's visit there. Jay told Oswald it was useless to talk of peace if he insisted on this.[13]

As if to balance Strachey's appearance, John Adams, fresh from his diplomatic triumphs in the Netherlands, arrived at Paris October 26, 1782, to reinforce the American Commissioners. In correspondence with Jay he had already staunchly and spiritedly upheld his colleague's demand to treat with England only on equal grounds, even as he had taken that position with Vergennes in 1781 at the time of the proposed mediation congress at Vienna. Adams also was a lawyer, a stickler for form and for details, from Boston, city of sound credit and sacred cod.

We cannot trace here in detail the animated negotiations which ensued between October 28, when Strachey reached Paris, and the signature on November 3 of the preliminary articles. The principal issues in these discussions were: the precise boundary line to separate remaining British North America from the United

---

[13] See above, Ch. XVI, note 17. See Shelburne Papers, Vol. 87, pp. 194, 206; Minute of Cabinet, Oct. 17, 1782, *Correspondence of King George the Third*, VI, 143. Strachey's instructions are printed in *Appendix to Sixth Report of the Royal Commission on Historical Manuscripts*, p. 403, which contains a calendar of the papers of Henry Strachey remaining in the possession of the Strachey family. On the point of Loyalists Shelburne told Strachey: "The Refugees are of great Importance, but if the province of Main be left to Nova Scotia, and the Americans can be brought to join us in regard to West Florida, there are Resources which may satisfy them. But the Debts require the most serious attention—that *honest* debts be *honestly* paid in *honest* money." See also *Diary* of John Jay, Oct. 29, note 16 below.

States, the extent of fishery rights to be allowed to citizens of the United States as compared with their colonial status before the separation, the condition of British Loyalists in the United States, and whether the United States Government was to be responsible for the payment of private debts owed before the war to British creditors. As to the boundary, the British finally accepted the principle of some ancient limit of Canada as *before* the Quebec Act, though Strachey had been instructed to try for the Ohio River.[14] The Americans receded from the Nipissing line and offered a choice between the present familiar river-and-lake line from the St. Lawrence west to the Lake of the Woods, or the extension of the line of 45° from the Connecticut due west to the Mississippi.[15] Some torrid conversation [16] ensued between Strachey and the American Commissioners about Loyalists, debts, and fisheries. On the question of compensation to Loyalists the British made a tenacious fight to get what Shelburne long since had considered as a bargaining point if worse should come to worst, though he was determined to do them justice in some way or other. Oswald and Strachey took great pains to place themselves on record in writing to prove that a strenuous fight had been made on this point.[17] On the matter of debts, the Americans gave in, thanks to Adams.[18] They promised to validate all *bona fide* debts contracted before 1775.

Since Rayneval's departure for London in early September the

[14] A cogent memorial came to Shelburne in September from Lt. Col. John Connolly, well-known Loyalist officer in western campaigns, now in England as an exchanged prisoner. He pleaded for the boundary of the Ohio according to the established (1774) limits of Quebec: (1) to preserve the fur-trade, (2) to salvage a respectable portion of the Empire certain speedily to fill up with immigrants, (3) to provide land for suffering Loyalists, (4) to erect a barrier of protection for Canada to the north. Shelburne Papers, Vol. 72.

[15] Adams to Livingston, Nov. 6, 1782, Wharton, V, 856. Strachey to Townshend, Calais, Nov. 8, 1782, Record Office, *C. O.*, 5, VIII, 322 (Stevens Transcripts), in conveying treaty articles mentions choice of two lines, as marked on an accompanying map indicating all these lines. The map, presumably Mitchell's, has not yet been located.

[16] *Diary of John Jay during the Peace Negotiations of 1782*, F. Monaghan, ed. (Yale University, 1934), October 29, 1782.

[17] Oswald to the Commissioners, Nov. 4, 1782, and Strachey to the Commissioners, November 5, 1782, Wharton, V, 848, 850.

[18] Adams, *Diary*, November 3, 1782, in the *Works of John Adams*, C. F. Adams, ed., III, 301.

Americans and French had drifted away from full confidence in each other. Vergennes on his part was revealing nothing important of the negotiations which were proceeding between Great Britain, France, and Spain. On their part Jay, Adams, and Franklin grew more reserved toward him, particularly as he continued to urge them not to make the extreme claims for fisheries and boundaries a necessary condition of peace.[19] Franklin, who had already done many things without Vergennes's privity, agreed with his two colleagues, about November 1, to proceed without the full confidence and advice of the French Minister.[20] Thus the three Commissioners broke their specific instructions from Congress. Both Franklin and Jay had long since broken them. On November 5, after much difficult but not inimical chaffering, Strachey hastened to England with a second set of agreed articles which acknowledged independence and offered this boundary: on the east the St. Croix (instead of the St. John) ; on the north, the line of 45°, or alternatively the present river-and-lake boundary west,[21] from

[19] Jay notes in his *Diary*, "We retired with Rayneval. He asked us how matters stood between us and Oswald. We told him we could not agree about all our Boundaries. We mentioned the one between us and Nova Scotia. He asked, what we demanded to the north. We answered, that Canada should be reduced to its ancient bounds. He then *contested our right to those back Lands, etc. etc.*

"He asked what we expected as to the Fisheries. We said, the same right we had formerly enjoyed. He contested the propriety of that demand; adding some strictures *on the ambition and restless views of Mr. Adams,* and intimated that we might be contented with the coast fishery." William Jay, *Life of John Jay* (New York, 1833), I, 150–157.

"There is nothing in our treaties which obliges us to prolong the war to uphold the ambitious pretentions which the United States may make either on fisheries or on boundaries." Vergennes to Luzerne, Nov. 23, 1782, de Circourt, *Action commune, op. cit.,* III, 294.

[20] Adams, *Diary, op. cit.,* p. 336.

[21] The negotiators, using Mitchell's Map of North America of 1755, could not determine the source of the Mississippi because the northwest corner of this map was covered by an inset map of Hudson's Bay; the Mississippi flowed out from under the inset. The negotiators assumed that a line due west from the northwesternmost corner of the Lake of the Woods—the final language of the treaty—would strike the Mississippi; but actually the source of that river lies south of such a latitude. See my "Jay's Treaty and the Northwest Boundary Gap" in *Am. Hist. Rev.,* XXVII (April, 1922), 465–484. It is 151 miles from the latitude of the most northwestern part of the Lake of the Woods to the latitude of Lake Itasca, the source of the Mississippi.

It should be noted that Benjamin Vaughan called this defect to Shelburne's attention before the definitive treaty was signed and recommended that the phraseology of that part of the treaty be altered by substituting the words:

where the latitude of 45° strikes the St. Lawrence River to the Lake of the Woods and the Mississippi River; on the west the Mississippi; and on the south the 31°-St. Mary's line.[22] The Mississippi article was reduced [23] simply to a statement that the navigation of the river was to be free from its source to its mouth and nothing was said about commercial reciprocity. They then appended a separate secret article stating that, in case West Florida should be British at the end of the war, its boundary should be the latitude of the mouth of the Yazoo (about 32° 28′) instead of 31°. Loyalists were to be allowed six months to remove effects from any of the States, and it was left to the States to extend to them such amnesty and clemency as they might deem just and reasonable, with indemnity to those not affected by acts, judgments, or prosecutions actually passed or commenced a month previous to the evacuation of British troops. Further, as a compromise suggested by Oswald, it was agreed that Congress would merely *recommend* to the several States to correct, if necessary, their acts confiscating estates of British subjects. That this left the Loyalists with little resources within the treaty for redress was realized clearly enough on both sides of the Atlantic.[24] Fishery rights for American citizens as before the war,

"and from thence [Lake of the Woods], by a line which shall describe the shortest course for reaching the Mississippi" or "and from thence on a due south course to the Mississippi." Benjamin Vaughan to Shelburne, Feb. 21, 1783, Vaughan Photostats in W. L. Clements Library at Ann Arbor, Michigan. The article was not changed in the definitive peace.

Vaughan also recommended a change in the article providing for evacuation of British garrisons "with all convenient speed," so that the Canada merchants trading in American territory might have a long time to settle their affairs. The article was not changed, but British garrisons continued in the Indian territory south of the boundary until 1796. See my *Jay's Treaty: A Study in Commerce and Diplomacy* (New York, 1923).

[22] For these alternate boundary lines, see Map 4 opposite p. 228.

[23] Trade on equal terms in each other's dominions in all parts of the world, which had been a concomitant of this article in Jay's draft of October 5, was considered by the British to be in the nature of a commercial article, which they desired to postpone to the anticipated separate commercial treaty, which never was concluded. Brown, *op. cit.*

[24] Vaughan wrote Shelburne, Nov. 5, 1782, that he thought as much had been done for the refugees as Britain could expect. "But still the proper *refugees* are left, as I knew they were likely to be, to Britain to provide for; and the burden is not immense; as the number cannot be more than a few hundreds; and we have various means of disposing of them; but I shall last of all think of giving

with drying privileges on Sable Island, Cape Sable, and the unsettled regions of Nova Scotia and the Magdalen Islands, were stipulated. Debts to British creditors were validated before 1775, but nothing was said reciprocally as to debts to American creditors.

Omission from the articles of that clause of the Jay draft of October 5 which allowed reciprocal treatment as nationals to the ships and commerce of citizens or subjects of either party throughout the dominions of the other in all parts of the world greatly altered the structure of the proposed peace as it had first been built on a pediment of free trade. In that draft admission on a reciprocal basis of American ships and goods to all the dominions of the British Empire had been an equivalent for admission of British ships and goods to all parts of the United States, particularly to the prospective markets of the American West by the free navigation of the Mississippi River. This had reconciled Shelburne to leaving, if necessary, the region between the Great Lakes and the Ohio under American sovereignty. He was doubtless the more willing because of his sympathy for the free-trade ideas of Adam Smith. Complete reciprocity would have been one of those acts of "sweet reconciliation" which Franklin liked so much to talk about, tending to bind the two peoples the more closely in the future, and within the limits of his political situation Shelburne strove for that too. But the clause ran afoul of the British navigation laws and foreshadowed a heavy political risk in Parliament. The subject of commercial reciprocity was therefore left for further negotiations after the peace, and it remained long to spoil sweet reconciliation. The free navigation of the Mississippi, on the other hand, stayed in the treaty even after its equivalent had been removed. Conceivably the American negotiators did not want to jeopardize their territorial victory by holding out against what had now become a one-sided advantage to Great Britain.

The articles as now agreed made peace relatively certain as

them as neighbors to America, where they will make mischief to *both* of *us*, and to themselves." Vaughan Photostats in W. L. Clements Library at Ann Arbor, Michigan. See also Burnett's *Letters,* VII, vii.

soon as Great Britain and Spain could come to terms about Gibraltar, for meanwhile the French negotiations had advanced to a conclusive state.[25] Recognizing this, Shelburne sent Strachey back to make a last plea for the Loyalists and for restriction of fisheries.[26] If it proved impossible to get these, Oswald was to sign, provided Strachey and Fitzherbert in written opinions agreed. Fitzherbert on his part was to make what use he could of the parallel French negotiations to extract concessions from the Americans.[27]

Before they signed, the British negotiators secured some small advantages. In these last exchanges Franklin countered very effectively the British demands for indemnity for Loyalists by pulling from his pocket a long list of damages to American citizens, which he insisted on including if Loyalists were to be

[25] The King to Lord Shelburne, Nov. 10, 1782, *Correspondence of King George the Third*, VI, 154.

[26] Minute of Cabinet, Nov. 11, 1782, *Correspondence of King George the Third*, VI, 155; see also 156; Sense of Cabinet, Nov. 15, 1782, Hales, *op. cit.*, II, 180.

[27] On November 10, 1782, in response to a question from Vergennes as to how the negotiations with Great Britain were progressing, John Adams had said that they were divided on two points: Loyalists and the Penobscot. Adams, *Diary*. On November 15, when Rayneval left on his second trip to London, to see what Great Britain would take from France in exchange for Gibraltar to Spain (see below, p. 245), Vergennes instructed him to suggest to Shelburne that the American negotiation be cleared up by placing the unsettled boundaries in the hands of a mixed commission and by deferring the status of the Loyalists until the definitive treaty. By the time Rayneval reached London, Shelburne had already committed himself on boundaries and had resolved to forego compensation for the Loyalists if it could not be won at a last stand. He therefore (November 23) told Rayneval, to quote Shelburne's description of the interview to George III, "that there would be little difficulty about Boundarys [*sic*] with the American Commissioners, provided the Article relative to the Loyalists was express'd in so comprehensive a manner as to acquit Your Majesty towards every description, which had a right to Your Majesty's protection. That in regard to the Fishery, Your Majesty wish'd nothing more than to avoid every possibility of future dispute and desir'd it upon their account as well as our own. I found him uninformed of what had pass'd. He stated the reserve of the Commissioners towards them, to be owing to their refusing to support them in a variety of unreasonable demands, which I perfectly believe." Lord Shelburne to the King, Berkeley Square, November 24, 1782, *Correspondence of King George the Third*, VI, 161. This letter is significant because of conclusions which it affords: (1) that French diplomacy was still in confidential parley with the enemy opposing important American claims above bare independence; (2) that Vergennes, with France's interests taken care of, was now anxious for a quick Anglo-American agreement in order, we presume, to profit by its persuasive effect on Spain.

compensated. As to fisheries, Adams tolerated the introduction of the weakened word "liberty" to describe American inshore fishing privileges, as compared with the "right" to fish on the high seas. It was a word which the English had employed successfully once before, in the treaty of Paris of 1763, to vitiate a right which the French had previously claimed to the inshore fisheries of Newfoundland.[28] It was to cost a century of controversy. Henry Laurens, ill in body, weighted in spirit by the loss in battle of his brilliant son, and forced to obey the injunctions of Congress to get to his duty as a negotiator, appeared at the last hour and put in an article forbidding the carrying away of slave property by evacuating British armies.[29] It was easy enough for two old slave merchants like Oswald and Laurens to agree on this. The British chose the familiar, present-day, river-and-lake boundary on the north, in place of the line of 45° west from the Connecticut to the Mississippi. Presumably it was because the latter would have cut them off from the navigation of the Great Lakes.[30] This line conformed very reasonably with the requirements of the Commissioners' instructions from Congress. It was far more expansive than the Appalachian watershed which perhaps Congress might have accepted if hard pushed.[31]

The articles also stipulated that after the peace British forces would evacuate American soil "with all convenient speed." This loose phrase became a loophole for controversy; the natural boundary line also resulted in a long series of disputes as to details of locality; the fisheries clause was full of difficulties, because of the word "liberty," as instanced in a later century of controversy and litigation over it; and the debts article (the Americans gratuitously threw in, finally, all private debts without limitation of time),[32] though specific, created other difficulties that were not settled until 1802.

[28] Dallas D. Irvine, *Fisheries, op. cit., Can. Hist. Rev.*, XIII, 268–285.

[29] Wharton, V, 730–747; Wallace, *Henry Laurens, op. cit.*, pp. 390–419.

[30] Benjamin Vaughan to Shelburne, Paris, November 1, 1782, Vaughan Photostats in W. L. Clements Library at Ann Arbor, Michigan.

[31] Map 5 opposite p. 238 illustrates a conjectural minimum boundary. See note at end of my article "Canada and the Peace Negotiations of 1782–1783," *Canadian Historical Review*, XIV (Sept., 1933), pp. 265–284.

[32] Oswald to Townshend, Paris, Nov. 30, 1782, Hale, *op. cit.*, II, 194.

After these modifications as to detail, they quietly signed the articles without consulting the French, at Oswald's lodgings in Paris, on November 30, 1782.[33] The preamble explicitly described them as the treaty of peace "proposed to be concluded . . . but which Treaty is not to be concluded until Terms of a Peace shall be agreed upon, between Great Britain and France. . . ."

The evening before the signature Franklin had dispatched a note to Vergennes saying that they had agreed on preliminary articles.[34] The next day he promptly sent to Versailles a copy of the signed articles (except for the separate article on Florida, which was not to take effect unless Florida should remain English in the Anglo-Spanish preliminaries).[35] Vergennes received them with surprising equanimity, though in his next interview with Franklin he may have tried to give the impression that the abrupt signature had little agreeable in it for the King.[36] It was not until two weeks later that a passage occurred which ever since has been celebrated. Franklin then wrote Vergennes that the Americans had received a British passport for protection of a ship in which they intended to send despatches to America, obviously the recently signed preliminaries. During the negotiations Franklin, in his capacity of Minister of the United States at the Court of Versailles, had been pressing the French for another loan for the depleted money-chests of Congress. He now took occasion to say that this vessel offered a safe mode of conveyance for any part of the financial aids that had lately been requested. Vergennes suspected that, contrary to an understanding which he thought he had reached with Franklin, this presupposed an intention of the Commissioners to hold out to America a certain hope of peace "without even informing themselves of the state of the negotiation on France's part." For the first time the

---

[33] We reproduce in the Appendix the text of the preliminary articles of peace, taken from Hunter Miller's carefully collated edition of American treaties which is based on the original signed treaty in the British Archives. William Temple Franklin, the Doctor's grandson, who had received a formal appointment as secretary to the Commission, signed as witness. So did Caleb Whitefoord, Oswald's secretary.

[34] Wharton, VI, 90.

[35] Adams inadvertently disclosed to the Duc de la Vauguyon the existence of a separate article. *Diary*, Dec. 5, 1782, *Works*, III, 343.

[36] Such Vergennes stated to La Luzerne, Dec. 19, 1782. Wharton, VI, 150.

Minister, with perfect courtesy, complained to Franklin of the conduct of himself and his colleagues. Incidentally to the main point, he remarked that they had concluded the preliminary articles without any communication to the French Ministry, although their instructions from Congress prescribed that nothing should be done without the participation of the King of France. These were the instructions of Congress which had really been fashioned by Vergennes himself, though of course he could not say so.

Franklin's irresistible reply is one of his best diplomatic utterances: it was certainly incumbent upon the Commissioners to make as early as possible a report to Congress of their proceedings, which would think it extremely strange to hear of them by any other means; there was nothing in the preliminary articles contrary to the Franco-American alliance, because they were not to take effect until the Anglo-French preliminaries should be signed; besides all this, he had hoped to send the proceeds of the new loan by a protected ship. Then he gently admitted the indiscretion, the lack of *bienséance,* of himself and his fellow-Commissioners. In simple, happy sentences he went on to explain that it had not been for lack of respect to the honored and beloved King of France. He trusted that this one indiscretion on their part would not tear down the great structure then under erection: *"The English, I just now learn, flatter themselves they have already divided us.* I hope this little misunderstanding will therefore be kept secret, and that they will find themselves totally mistaken."[37]

The little misunderstanding would have remained secret from the enemy if a copy of Franklin's letter had not been promptly delivered to Fitzherbert by the American secretary and British spy, Edward Bancroft.[38] But this report did no harm. Before the signature of the Anglo-French preliminaries, the ship set out for

[37] Franklin to Vergennes, Dec. 15, 17, 1782; Vergennes to Franklin, Dec. 15, 1782; Wharton, VI, 137, 140, 143.

[38] Strachey had opened up communications with this dexterous agent of the North Government, and Fitzherbert made use of him. Shelburne Papers, Vol. 71, pp. 321, 333. See also "E. Edwards" to Strachey, Paris, Dec. 4, 1782. Record Office, *C. O.,* 5, VIII, 376 (Stevens Transcripts).

Philadelphia with the Anglo-American articles and with the first instalment of the last French loan of 6,000,000 *livres*. It carried a significant passport from George III to "the vessel called the *Washington,* commanded by Mr. Joshua Barney, belonging to the United States of North America." [39] At a time when the French Treasury was stopping payment on its own bills, Vergennes did not yet think it wise to refuse Franklin's request for more money. Not until the general preliminaries were safely signed did he stop the golden stream of loans.

In this exchange there was manifest no tone of anger or of resentment on the part of Vergennes. Is it not reasonable to guess that, in view of the general situation, the announcement of the American preliminaries was not unwelcome because of their influence in bringing Spain to the necessary relinquishment of Gibraltar, and thus in concluding the war and in sealing the perfect triumph of that skilful foreign minister's diplomacy?

In my narrative of the Anglo-American negotiations I have found ground for Jay's suspicions of Vergennes's opposition to American boundaries and fisheries. Vergennes also suggested to the Americans [40] to yield to the British claim for indemnification for the Loyalists. What was the motive for this? French strategy was, first, to tie all the negotiations together sufficiently to drag them along until the Gibraltar campaign had been decided; but to let the Anglo-American negotiations run in a separate channel *under French control* so that it could not seem to the American plenipotentiaries that their cherished independence was being held up until Gibraltar were secured for France's European ally. But when Vergennes heard through de Grasse that Great Britain might promptly cede Gibraltar, he sent Rayneval to London to arrange a quick peace on that basis, or at least to see what must be done should de Grasse's report about Gibraltar be inaccurate. In case of an immediate French-Spanish-British peace Vergennes did not want his movements held up by American demands for expansive boundaries, for inshore fishing rights in British territory, especially when these were not guaranteed by the Franco-American

[39] Wharton, VI, 137n.
[40] J. Adams, Journal of the Peace Negotiations, Wharton, V, 872.

treaties. Nor were Spain's desires to coop the United States up behind the Alleghenies incompatible with French policy. Finally Vergennes wanted the British to stay in Canada to make the United States more amenable to French policy in the future.

We must now finally examine the complications injected by de Grasse's twisted report of British peace terms and follow through the negotiations of the European belligerents to the final peace settlement of 1783.

CHAPTER XVIII

The Peace Settlement of 1783

By the time the Anglo-American preliminary articles were signed France, pressed for peace by collapsing finances,[1] had practically come to terms with Great Britain on all principal points. Spain still held out for Gibraltar. Now that the Americans had signed their preliminaries and achieved their ends so completely, could they be expected to wait too long for a definitive peace which would secure Gibraltar for Spain? Particularly after British arms had effectually relieved that fortress?

At first the two Bourbon powers had procrastinated in their negotiations with Fitzherbert to give time for their colossal operations to succeed against Gibraltar.[2] Before the fate of that place had been determined the Count de Grasse, returning to France on August 15 as an exchanged prisoner of war, related to Vergennes a conversation which he had with Shelburne, representing that minister to have outlined peace terms by which the principal French objects would have been satisfied and Spain would have received her conquests on the Gulf of Mexico (West

[1] Vergennes to Montmorin, Oct. 2, 1782, de Circourt, *Action commune, op. cit.,* III, 331.

[2] As early as May 19, Floridablanca outlined Spain's desires, to govern Aranda in any discussion of peace, but the purpose of the discussion with Grenville or Oswald was "to gain time,—that is what we need"; and he had no powers yet to conclude. Floridablanca to Aranda, Aranjuez, May 29, 1782, No. 1, "Instructions as to Peace," Archivo Histórico Nacional, *Estado, leg.* 4079. Montmorin reported to Vergennes, July 8, 1782, Floridablanca's reproaches at the precipitation with which France seemed to be pursuing the negotiations started at Paris; that the Spanish Minister did not like the fact that the English had recognized purely and simply American independence (as he believed), because Spain did not yet find herself in possession of Gibraltar. Vergennes answered, July 20, that if Aranda had studied carefully Vergennes's reply to Grenville of June 21, "he would have been easily convinced that far from proposing a plan to break off the negotiation it was drafted solely with the idea of prolonging it to the satisfaction of our own desires and the benefit of our allies." Archives des Affaires Etrangères, *Espagne,* 608, fol. 47 (Stevens Transcripts).

Florida) and either Gibraltar or Minorca by choice.[3] If this report were true it offered an opportunity for immediate peace, than which nothing could have been more welcome to France. It did not correspond with what Fitzherbert had been saying in Paris. It was to confirm this statement of de Grasse that Vergennes had sent his secretary on that famous mysterious mission to London. On this, his first trip to London, Rayneval succeeded in secretly laying the basis for a Franco-British peace, even though he found that de Grasse most erroneously had reported the matter of Gibraltar and other important details, which made it impossible for him to initiate an immediate settlement then and there. By the end of November, before the Gibraltar question could be settled, the Americans anticipated the French impulse; on their part they secretly signed conditional preliminaries first.

With the Anglo-French issues clarified and settled in principle and the American preliminaries actually signed Shelburne was reasonably sure of a general peace. The announcement of the American preliminaries—and this is why they must have been pleasing to Vergennes—made it pretty certain that Spain, in the existing military and diplomatic situation, could not hold up the general peace much longer. The conquest of Gibraltar was hope-

[3] Vergennes's memorandum of de Grasse's report was:
"For the United States of America.
"The most complete and absolute independence without conditions or modifications.
"For France.
"Restitution of Santa Lucia. Retrocession of Dominica and Saint Vincent.
"Abrogation of articles regarding Dunkirk in treaties since 1713.
"A sure, convenient and free fishery on the Grand Banks, with power to fortify it without the restrictions of the treaty of 1763.
"An establishment sufficient for the slave trade.
"Trade and establishments in the East Indies to be reëstablished on the footing either of 1748 or 1763, as shall be agreed on in the preliminaries.
"To Spain.
"Cession or definitive holding of her conquests in the Gulf of Mexico. Mahon [Minorca] or Gibraltar as she chooses, but England to have a fort in the Mediterranean for her commerce to the Levant.
"To Holland.
"The *uti possidetis* except for reciprocal cessions to be negotiated in the treaty.
"For all nations.
"Freedom of commerce according to the principles of the Armed Neutrality."
Doniol, V, 104, n. 1. The original document, dated August 17, 1782, in Archives des Affaires Etrangères, *Correspondance Politique, Angleterre*, Vol. 538, shows certain of these items crossed off, as if a later hand had checked them.

less. Vergennes made no scruple to the English that he would not support the exorbitant demands of Spain,[4] even as he had let it be known to Shelburne that he would not favor the American claims to expansive boundaries, inshore fisheries, or a preliminary recognition of independence before the treaty. But after all, France was bound explicitly not to sign a peace without securing Gibraltar for her ally. He pleaded anxiously with Aranda, and, in Madrid, Montmorin importuned Floridablanca to offer substantial Spanish territory for Gibraltar, which could not be taken by war.[5] Floridablanca confidentially instructed Aranda, November 23, 1782, to get the fortress by way of exchange and went so far as to state that, if the British should hold out against exchange, it would be worth while to see what other territory could be had for relinquishing Spain's demands for that rock.[6] He first tried to induce France to yield Corsica or some other French possession to England in exchange for the delivery of Gibraltar to Spain, France to be compensated in her turn by some Spanish possession overseas, perhaps the Spanish part of Santo Domingo. Vergennes would not do this, but he sent Rayneval on a second trip to London, November 15, to find out what Great Britain would take for Gibraltar.[7] After much deliberation and discussion which involved a trip of Rayneval to Paris to consult with Vergennes, the British Government proved not averse to arrange an exchange of Gibraltar for either (1) Spanish Porto Rico, (2) the French islands of Martinique and Santa Lucia, (3) Guadeloupe (French) and Dominica (British, occupied by France), plus the full value in money for the fortifications, artillery, and stores at Gibraltar, and the restoration of all other Spanish territorial conquests during the war.[8]

---

[4] Fitzherbert to Grantham, No. 63, October 24, 1782, Record Office, *F. O., France*, 27, III, fol. 513 (Stevens Transcripts).

[5] Vergennes to Montmorin, No. 81, No. 82, No. 83, Oct. 6, No. 85, Oct. 13, 1782, Archives des Affaires Etrangères, *Espagne*, Vol. 609 (Stevens Transcripts); Doniol, V, 203–216.

[6] Urtasún, *Historia diplomática, op. cit.*, II, 769; Dánvila, *Reinado de Carlos III, op. cit.*, V, 381.

[7] Doniol, V, 212.

[8] Shelburne to the King, 1.30 P. M., Nov. 20; the King to Shelburne, 9.42 A. M., Nov. 21, 1782, *Correspondence of King George the Third*, VI, 158, 159.

Time passed as the negotiators studied these several combinations. George III prorogued Parliament until the 5th of December, hoping to be able to announce a general peace at the opening. Vergennes was willing in the last analysis to give up Guadalupe and Santa Lucia and even Martinique (by way of an exchange) if Great Britain would surrender Gibraltar to Spain,[9] France to recoup by some Spanish possession in the East or West Indies, presumably Santo Domingo, a possibility of French aggrandizement which was not attractive to Shelburne. When news reached London of the American preliminaries, Shelburne encountered more resistance to the exchange of Gibraltar. Vergennes and Aranda became alarmed at the possibility of Parliament overthrowing the Shelburne Government and with it all chances of a satisfactory peace. Rayneval reported, on his third trip to London, that the war spirit was running higher and that the British Government could raise funds for another campaign, something which it was exceedingly doubtful if the French could do. When Parliament convened, without a Continental peace, Shelburne sent up a trial balloon and discovered great opposition to the cession of Gibraltar, the gallant defense of which had fired the nation. He began to hesitate about the exchange offer. Finally he sent notice through Rayneval that Spain might retain Minorca and have all Florida, east and west, and Great Britain would keep Gibraltar. Aranda, after showing to Vergennes his instructions of November 23, took it upon himself to accept this.[10] He feared that British possession of French islands in the West Indies would fetter Spain's American empire in the future. He believed, too, that French public opinion would be so outraged by such a cession to redeem Gibraltar that it would touch off the ever-imminent revolution which he saw threatening the French monarchy itself. Thus he justified to his superiors the extraordinary responsibility which he had assumed. Vergennes was astonished but delighted at this decisive concession, glad that France did not

[9] *Ibid.*, p. 181. For Gibraltar, see the instructions to Fitzherbert, *British Diplomatic Instructions, op. cit.*, pp. 202–215.

[10] For this phase of the negotiation, see Urtasún, *op. cit.*, II, 754–776; Dánvila, *op. cit.*, V, 373–390; Doniol, V, 202–281.

have to cede the islands, and happy in the thought of peace at last and the perfect triumph of his great combinations.[11]

They signed the Anglo-French preliminaries on January 20, 1783, at Versailles, in Vergennes's office. *Ipso facto* the Anglo-American preliminaries went into effect and the secret contingent article about the boundary of Florida dropped away because that province went to Spain. At the same moment the Anglo-Spanish preliminaries [12] were concluded, and a general armistice took place. The Spanish Government without enthusiasm ratified the articles, and Floridablanca avoided any expression of appreciation to Aranda.[13]

Hostilities thus ceased among all the belligerents, for the Netherlands were included in the general armistice of the same date, although preliminary articles of peace had not yet been signed between Great Britain and the United Provinces. With a general peace certain, Shelburne had been unwilling to offer to the Dutch the advantageous terms which Fox held forth in April, 1782.[14] Vergennes, his great ends accomplished, France, aching

[11] Doniol, V, 239.

[12] During the latter phases of these Anglo-Spanish negotiations, Don Ignacio Heredia was sent to London by Aranda to confer directly with Shelburne. He also was concerned in the negotiations preceding the definitive treaty. Dánvila, *op. cit.*, V, 385–391; Archivo Histórico Nacional, *Estado, leg.* 4220 (Library of Congress photocopy).

[13] The King nevertheless conveyed to Aranda his satisfaction with his services, when finally the definitive treaty was signed. R. Konetzke has depicted Aranda's part in the negotiation in *Die Politik des Grafen Aranda*, pp. 162–172. In his notable memorial to Carlos III, a defensive summary of his administration and of his policies, dated October 10, 1788, Floridablanca stated, anent Aranda's signature of the preliminaries of January 20, 1783, that "it is not right to say that the Count de Aranda secured the utmost possible in conformity with the instructions and orders which Your Majesty commanded me to send to him." *Obras originales . . . de Floridablanca*, ed. by Antonio Ferrer del Rio, in *Biblioteca de Autores Españoles*, Vol. 59 (Madrid, 1867), pp. 317–318.

[14] In April, Fox proposed to take advantage of repeated Russian offers to mediate between Great Britain and the Netherlands and offered peace on the basis of the Anglo-Dutch treaty of 1674. To establish an entente with Russia at this critical time the Cabinet voted, June 26, to propose an open recognition of the principles of the Armed Neutrality. Fox also solicited the support of Frederick the Great for such a Dutch treaty, on the ground that he could not afford to see Great Britain destroyed as a power in European affairs. *Correspondence of King George the Third*, V, 427; Russell, *Memorials and Correspondence of C. J. Fox, op. cit.*, I, 333, IV, 333–337; *Diaries and Correspondence of Lord Malmesbury*,

for peace and free from any treaty obligations to the Netherlands, would not really insist on British recognition of the Dutch demands for the restoration of colonies still held by British arms. Nor would he press effectively for the recognition in the Dutch treaty of the principles of the Armed Neutrality, which had been so convenient to French diplomacy during the war. But the French at least promised to deliver back to their Dutch associates the recaptured colonies in Asia, Africa, and America, the holding of which during the past several months had served to keep the Netherlands from making any separate peace.[15]

While the plenipotentiaries of Great Britain and the Netherlands continued their endeavors at Paris, supplementary parleys went on between Great Britain and the other belligerents concerning new articles, proposed by one side or the other for incorporation into the definitive treaties. In the case of France and Spain these resulted in only minor adjustments.[16] In the case of the United States they led to no alteration of the preliminary articles. This phase of the negotiations was carried on by the new Fox-North coalition which had meanwhile succeeded the Shelburne Government. These two curious political enemies and bedfellows had crystallized feeling against Shelburne when the preliminaries had been announced, and had brought about the overthrow of his Government, but they never succeeded in bettering Shelburne's preliminaries. They could not, because England was sick of the war. Parliament itself had insisted on the peace and was responsible for it for better or worse. It already had once turned out the North Government on the issue of continuing the

I, 484; Précis of negotiations between Great Britain and the Netherlands, March 4 to October 29, 1782, Shelburne Papers, Vol. 72.

[15] Vergennes to Vauguyon, No. 9, May 25, 1782, Archives des Affaires Etrangères, *Correspondance Politique, Hollande,* 549, 67 (Stevens Transcripts).

[16] Long-drawn-out Anglo-Spanish negotiations finally defined the boundaries within which British log-cutters and settlements were to be confined on the Honduran coast.

In equally voluminous exchanges and correspondence Great Britain evaded the demand of Vergennes to grant, specifically, "exclusive" fishery rights on the treaty coasts, and finally adopted a formula which somewhat ambiguously defined fishing rights as they were before the war. Some declarations and counter-declarations as to commerce and India completed the settlement. These were affixed to the definitive treaty.

American war.[17] Fox had always opposed that war. He and North could not undo the peace by which Shelburne had got his King and country out of the war.

Fox, again Foreign Secretary, replaced Oswald at Paris with a man of somewhat similar temperament, the eccentric and philosophical David Hartley, member of Parliament and another old friend of Franklin. It was this same Hartley whom we have already observed during the course of the war in correspondence with Franklin, harping on the idea of "sweet reconciliation" by means of a federal union *within* the Empire. Now he accepted the task of attempting to bring about a federal union *without* the Empire.

It was Hartley's business to arrange, *ad referendum,* certain dispensations in favor of British fur-trading interests caught unexpectedly south of the new boundary line.[18] Next he was to negotiate, also subject to approval at home, a treaty of commerce on the principle of reciprocal freedom of trade and navigation by each party in all the dominions of the other, except that American ships could not be permitted to carry into any British port other than the produce of their own country.[19] These arrangements having been perfected, Hartley purposed—and his oral instructions from Fox seemed to sanction the project—negotiations that would establish a *succedaneum* (the word is Fox's) for the old colonial connection, a substitute to consist of a federal alliance to be erected between the United States and Great Britain on the ruins of the Franco-American alliance. As revealed by Hartley's letters to Fox,[20] this scheme comprehended: first, mutual defense

[17] "When one country announces that it will fight no longer, the other country may get almost any terms it desires," notes a recent Canadian historian (professor in an American state university) in giving the first reason why Oswald and Strachey could not get a better boundary line at Paris for Canada. Burt, *Province of Old Quebec, op. cit.,* pp. 333–334.

[18] Eunice Wead, "British Public Opinion of the Peace with America," *Am. Hist. Rev.,* XXXIV, 525; Wayne E. Stevens, *The Northwest Fur Trade, 1763–1800* (Urbana, Illinois, 1928), p. 71. See above, pp. 234–238.

[19] No reciprocal injunction against British ships engaging in the American carrying trade appears to have been suggested.

[20] The papers of David Hartley, including copies of his official correspondence, formerly in the private library of Mr. Joseph Leiter, Washington, D. C., are now in the W. L. Clements Library at the University of Michigan. They are well calendared by Hugh Alexander Morrison, *The Leiter Library, a Catalogue*

of the American dominions of each party; secondly, the British navy to defend and protect the United States, in return for which the United States should continue to support and strengthen it by naval material and seamen. This, thought Hartley, "would be nothing more or less than the restoration of the old system," for he would add an article that in case the respective territories of the contracting parties should be attacked on land by any foreign enemy they should assist each other with military succor; such would be "an article of equal reciprocity and in effect no more than a stipulation of perpetual peace between themselves." The naval article, he explained, would give Great Britain a right to claim great naval equivalents, for instance a supply of a certain number of American seamen (we wonder whether by impressment?) to serve on board British men-of-war during the life of the treaty.

This ingenious project failed, partly because Hartley and the commissioners were unable to agree on his proposed additional articles for the definitive treaty, and because a British order-in-council, issued behind Hartley's back, July 2, 1783, cut off all American participation in the commerce of the British West Indies. It was thus apparent to the commissioners that no such commercial treaty as Hartley proposed would be ratified by his government. Franklin, Jay, and Adams also brought out for inclusion in the definitive treaty counter-articles which Fox found "captious," namely: adoption of maritime articles similar to those of the Franco-American treaty of commerce and the Armed Neutrality, with further liberal provisions devised by Franklin for the protection of private property at sea in time of war; these amounted to the immunity of all innocent private property, with provision for the preëmption rather than the confiscation of contraband, defined as "arms, ammunition, and military stores of all kinds." The commissioners also proposed that Great Britain extend protection to American ships against the Barbary pirates in the Mediterranean, and even admit American citizens to some

. . . (Washington, 1907), pp. 345–365. For a more detailed summary of these Hartley negotiations see my sketch of John Jay in *The American Secretaries of State and Their Diplomacy*, I, 209–226. See also Guttridge, *David Hartley, op. cit.*, pp. 294–317.

share in British log-cutting privileges on the Honduran coast. And John Adams had ready an article, which he had thought of as early as March, 1782, for prohibiting the fortification of the northern boundary and forbidding the introduction of armed vessels on the Great Lakes by either side.[21]

When no agreement on these points was possible it was at least premature to broach too positively the articles of the grand plan. Hartley finally signed for Great Britain the definitive treaty, embodying nothing more than the preliminary articles of November 30, without the separate Florida article.[22] He also assisted at the exchange of ratifications of the preliminaries. He accomplished nothing more than this, though he persisted in conversations with the American Commissioners until he was peremptorily recalled.[23]

We have said that these negotiations for the elaboration of the Anglo-American peace settlement took place during the interim between the European preliminaries of January 20 and the signature of the definitive treaties of peace on September 3, 1783. During that same time negotiations continued between the Fox-North coalition and the other quondam belligerents. Before the Dutch could arrive at any agreement with the British, the other parties had long since arranged final terms. In vain the Dutch, with only perfunctory support from the French, were clamoring for the restitution of all captured colonies, for outright recognition of the principles of the Armed Neutrality by Great Britain, and for damages for captures during the war in violation of

[21] The American proposals, together with exchanges with Hartley, may be found scattered throughout Wharton, VI, notably pp. 470–472, 601. I am indebted to Professor Helen Dwight Reid for a note on Adams's project for neutralization of the northern river-and-lake boundary, which is embodied in a project in his writing, entitled "T. of 1783," in the collections of the Massachusetts Historical Society.

[22] The West Florida article remained out by its own terms when Great Britain did not retain that province in the Spanish treaty. The Anglo-American definitive articles were signed at Hartley's lodgings, Hotel de York, Paris, and were thus completely outside the nominal mediation of Austria and Prussia whose representatives signed the definitive Anglo-French and Anglo-Spanish treaties at Versailles the same day.

[23] By the Marquess of Carmarthen, the Foreign Secretary of the new government of the younger Pitt, which succeeded the Fox-North coalition in December, 1783.

them. The British on their part firmly demanded either Trinco-
malee, on the island of Ceylon, or Negapatam, on the southeast
coast of India opposite; the right to navigate freely among the
Dutch possessions of the East Indies; and the humiliating salute
of the British flag on the high seas by all Dutch vessels, as before
the war. Finally Vergennes notified the Dutch plenipotentiaries
that he could wait no longer for the relief from financial expenditures that would come to France with a final peace, that France
and her allies would sign the definitive treaties on the 3d of
September.

The Dutch were forced to capitulate. Here Great Britain won
one of the greatest advantages of the whole negotiations: she
excluded the obnoxious principles of the Armed Neutrality from
any general [24] recognition in the final peace settlement, a diplomatic victory which was to be of value to her during the next
cycle of maritime wars with France and Napoleon. Acquisition of
Negapatam gave a *point d'appui* for British smuggling trade to
the populous island of Ceylon; the right to trade and navigate
freely among the Dutch East Indies opened highways for later
British aggrandizement in Malaysia.[25] When the Anglo-French
and Anglo-Spanish preliminaries were signed, Rayneval wrote
exultantly from London to a colleague in the Foreign Office at
Versailles: "So at last we have peace, my dear friend. It renders
infinite honor to our respected Minister. England has been plucked
all over; but to pluck the bird without making her squawk, *voilà
le grand art!* That is what our chief has done, and he is veritably
honored here in this country." [26]

[24] The Anglo-French treaty renewed the treaties of Utrecht between the two
parties. Articles XVII–XX of the treaty of commerce of Utrecht contained the
principles of the Armed Neutrality of 1780 (except for blockade) and specifically
excluded foodstuffs, naval stores, and other raw material from the contraband
list. But this bound only Great Britain and France, and would go by the board
when the next war should break out between the two. (Actually in 1793 Russia
joined Great Britain in throwing overboard the principles of the first Armed
Neutrality.) The British successfully avoided similar articles in the treaties
with the other enemy powers, who were likely to be neutral in future wars.

[25] Elder, *Dutch Republic, op. cit.,* 233–246, briefly summarizes the Dutch
negotiations. Colenbrander, *Patriottentijd op. cit.,* I, 218–306, gives full details.
The Dutch preliminaries were made definitive by the treaty of May 20, 1784.

[26] Rayneval to Hénin, London, January 26, 1783. Bibliothèque de l'Institut,
Paris, Vol. 1275, fol. 52 (Library of Congress photostat).

Had Vergennes really stripped England so bare as Rayneval put it? As we spread out the final texts of the French and the Spanish treaties, we do not find that Great Britain, once accepting the inevitable loss of the American Colonies, fared so badly. She was required to cede the relatively unimportant island of Tobago to France, but she received back all the other conquered possessions: Grenada and the Grenadines, Dominica, St. Christopher, Nevis, Montserrat. She yielded to France the slave-trading preserve of the Senegal River, but retained one on the Gambia. She allowed France to keep St. Pierre and Miquelon for fishing bases in the Gulf of St. Lawrence, but clouded the title with declarations making it difficult to fit them for naval bases. She continued French fishing rights on stipulated coasts of Newfoundland, but in doing this she was recognizing, in new waters, no more than France already had possessed in others before the war. In India the articles of peace were astonishingly favorable to Great Britain. France gained no more than she had before 1778.[27] In fact the British were able to conclude peace on the principle that they first proposed, the independence of America and the treaty of Paris of 1763 as a fundamental basis, with a few exchanges, and minor cessions in North America and the eastern Mediterranean. To Spain Great Britain gave up Minorca and the two Floridas, and agreed that the British wood-cutting settlements on the "Spanish Continent" [28] should be restricted to a certain portion of the Honduran coast, between the Belize and Hondo rivers, and this without derogation to Spanish sovereignty there; but George III retained Gibraltar and with it control of the entrance to the Mediterranean, so valuable in those future wars when that sea was to be of vast importance to the preservation of the British Empire.

[27] See a balancing in parallel columns of provisions of peace of Paris of 1763 and peace of Paris of 1783, in regard to India, which concludes: "Under these [unfavorable] circumstances a peace has been made in India equal, if not superior to the Peace of Paris of 1763 when the British navy and land forces were triumphant in every quarter of the globe." Shelburne Papers, Vol. 87, p. 237.

[28] This phrase was a loophole for later chicane in which the British contended that Central America was not the "Spanish Continent" but the American Continent.

Shelburne,[29] confronted with a mighty combination of victorious allies and hostile neutrals,[30] and after his own Parliament had overthrown the preceding North Government by publicly declaring that Great Britain would not fight any more for the Colonies, had wriggled out of a bad situation with the loss of only Florida, Minorca, three small islands in America, and some unimportant territory in equatorial Africa. To balance these losses he acquired a valuable new smuggling post in India and a gateway of entrance to the islands and realms of the Far East. Dutch ships still had to salute the British flag as it sailed by. The King of Great Britain continued to call himself King of France. But the American Colonies were gone—gone forever. There was the victory of France and of the United States.

During the months of discussion and negotiation which had preceded the final peace settlement both sides had eluded the assiduous efforts of Russia and Austria to mediate. Great Britain feared to commit her interest in any way to Austria, an ally of France, if only nominally; and France herself distrusted the disinterestedness of Austria as a mediator. Both distrusted the stability of Catherine II. The repeated offers of these powers were therefore unacceptable and were politely evaded. But after the belligerents themselves had arranged the terms of their peace without expensive brokers they solemnly accepted the mediation of Austria and Russia. The definitive French and Spanish treaties were signed at Versailles, September 3, 1783, over the names of Austrian and Russian plenipotentiaries, with an explicit if empty statement by each that the treaty was the result of the mediation of his august sovereign.[31] The Anglo-American definitive treaty,

[29] In the definitive treaties the Fox-North Ministry ratified with little change what Shelburne had already settled in the preliminaries, and in the Dutch articles it took only what Shelburne had already won in the preceding negotiations.

[30] In Shelburne Papers in W. L. Clements Library, Vol. 87, pp. 200–239, is a collection of rough notes in which Benjamin Vaughan, Oswald, and Shelburne frankly assessed the precarious military and naval situation and the compelling factors which controlled the negotiations. These notes form a valuable English commentary on the peace and deserve more space than we can give them here.

[31] The several preliminaries, and the definitive treaties, may be found in G. F. de Martens, *Recueil des principaux traités de l'Europe* (Gottingue, 1779–1786), Vol. II. See also J. Adams to the President of Congress, Paris, September 5, 1783, Wharton, VI, 674.

signed in Paris the same day, escaped the mediation entirely, as was intended by the British plenipotentiary. John Adams regretted afterward that the Anglo-American definitive articles had not also been signed by the mediators, so that Russia and Austria would thus have finally recognized the independence of the United States.

Reviewing the diplomatic history of the period of the American Revolution we perceive that bitter international rivalries of the eighteenth century had built up such a situation, grievous but not abnormal for Europe, that once the American insurrection broke out it precipitated a combination of factors and set in motion a train of events that engulfed the whole world in war.[32] But for those hateful rivalries the struggling republican Colonies would not have found an ally. Great Britain would have suppressed their revolt. The French alliance, let it never be forgotten, brought independence, but it brought also its involvement within the baleful realm of European diplomacy of the eighteenth century. When the peace negotiations came, this same strife, these imbroglios of shifting European political structures, presented to the United States its opportunity. Perspicaciously the American Commissioners divined the situation. Resolutely they broke away from the bridle which Congress, from the hands of a sophisticated ally, had trustfully imposed upon them. With sure genius they took advantage of Europe's quarrels to cut their country from them. Congress promptly and gladly ratified the treaty.[33]

The historian now privileged to read documents unknown to the members of the Continental Congress can have nothing

[32] This is not an exaggerated statement when one remembers that the occupation of the western powers prepared the scene for the War of the Bavarian Succession and the later hostilities between Russia and Turkey. All overseas possessions of the maritime powers were involved. China and Japan at that time did not come within the purview of world politics, and Australia was scarcely known.

[33] Every one of the nine States whose delegates were present voted for it with alacrity, and every member of Congress present in the chamber. Some members would have voted to rebuke the commissioners for signing preliminaries without Vergennes's advice, particularly when they learned that Marbois, the French *chargé*, had commented on the impropriety. La Luzerne's intimate, Robert R. Livingston, Secretary of Foreign Affairs for Congress, expostulated with the commissioners that their distrust of France had been "unnecessary." (Livingston to the Peace Commissioners, March 25, 1783, Wharton, VI, 339.) A resolution proposed in Congress to this effect soon dropped out of sight.

but praise for the work of their plenipotentiaries at Paris.

Their action was the first decisive step to loose a new nation from Europe's bonds and Europe's distresses, so that their people after them might have freedom to expand, and to develop a new continent, to rise to surpassing power, and to do this during that century and a half which was to follow before the industrial and scientific revolutions of our own times united the nations of six continents in the embrace of a dynamic civilization and its political perils, placing them far closer to each other than the six great European powers stood in the days of Catherine II, Frederick the Great, Kaunitz, Floridablanca, George III, and the Comte de Vergennes. The greatest victory in the annals of American diplomacy was won at the outset by Franklin, Jay, and Adams.

APPENDIX AND BIBLIOGRAPHICAL NOTE

*Preliminary Articles of Peace. Articles to be inserted in and to
constitute the Treaty of Peace (with separate article which was
not ratified), signed at Paris November 30, 1782. Original in
English. Ratified by the United States April 15, 1783. Ratified
by Great Britain August 6, 1783. Ratifications exchanged at
Paris August 13, 1783. Proclaimed April 15, 1783.*

Articles agreed upon, by and between Richard Oswald Esquire, the
Commissioner of his Britannic Majesty, for treating of Peace with
the Commissioners of the United States of America, in behalf of his
said Majesty, on the one part; and John Adams, Benjamin Franklin,
John Jay, and Henry Laurens, four of the Commissioners of the said
States, for treating of Peace with the Commissioner of his said
Majesty, on their Behalf, on the other part. To be inserted in, and
to constitute the Treaty of Peace proposed to be concluded, between
the Crown of Great Britain, and the said United States; but which
Treaty is not to be concluded, untill Terms of a Peace shall be agreed
upon, between Great Britain and France; and his Britannic Majesty
shall be ready to conclude such Treaty accordingly.

Whereas reciprocal Advantages, and mutual Convenience are found
by Experience, to form the only permanent foundation of Peace and
Friendship between States; It is agreed to form the Articles of the
proposed Treaty, on such Principles of liberal Equity, and Reciprocity,
as that partial Advantages, (those Seeds of Discord!) being excluded,
such a beneficial and satisfactory Intercourse between the two Countries, may be establish'd, as to promise and secure to both perpetual
Peace and Harmony.

ARTICLE I.ˢᵗ

His Britannic Majesty acknowledges the said United States, Viz!
New Hampshire, Massachusetts Bay, Rhode Island and Providence
Plantations, Connecticut, New York, New Jersey, Pennsylvania,
Delaware, Maryland, Virginia, North Carolina, South Carolina and
Georgia, to be free Sovereign and independent States; That he treats

with them as such; And for himself, his Heirs and Successors, relinquishes all Claims to the Government, Propriety, and territorial Rights of the same, and every part thereof; and that all Disputes which might arise in future, on the Subject of the Boundaries of the said United States, may be prevented, It is hereby agreed and declared that the following are, and shall be their Boundaries Viz!

ARTICLE 2.ᵈ

From the north west Angle of Nova Scotia, Viz! that Angle which is form'd by a Line drawn due north, from the Source of S! Croix River to the Highlands, along the said Highlands which divide those Rivers that empty themselves into the River S! Laurence, from those which fall into the Atlantic Ocean, to the northwesternmost Head of Connecticut River; thence down along the middle of that River to the 45.ᵗʰ Degree of North Latitude; from thence by a Line due West on said Latitude, untill it strikes the River Iroquois, or Cataraquy; thence along the middle of said River into Lake Ontario; through the middle of said Lake, untill it strikes the Communication by Water between that Lake and Lake Erie; thence along the middle of said Communication into Lake Erie, through the middle of said Lake, untill it arrives at the Water Communication between that Lake and Lake Huron; thence along the middle of said water communication into the Lake Huron; thence through the middle of said Lake to the Water Communication between that Lake and Lake Superior; thence through Lake Superior northward of the Isles Royal & Phelipeaux, to the Long Lake; thence through the middle of said Long Lake, and the water Communication between it and the Lake of the Woods, to the said Lake of the Woods, thence through the said Lake to the most Northwestern point thereof, and from thence on a due west Course to the River Missisippi; thence by a Line to be drawn along the middle of the said River Missisippi, untill it shall intersect the northernmost part of the 31.ˢᵗ Degree of North Latitude. South, by a Line to be drawn due East, from the Determination of the Line last mentioned, in the Latitude of 31 Degrees North of the Equator, to the middle of the River Apalachicola or Catahouche; thence along the middle thereof, to its junction with the Flint River; thence strait to the Head of S! Mary's River, and thence down along the middle of S! Mary's River to the Atlantic Ocean. East, by a Line to be drawn along the middle of the River S! Croix, from its Mouth in the Bay of Fundy to its Source; and from its Source directly North, to the aforesaid Highlands which divide the Rivers that fall into the Atlantic Ocean, from those which fall into the River S! Laurence; comprehending all Islands within twenty Leagues of any part of the

Shores of the united States, and lying between Lines to be drawn due East from the points where the aforesaid Boundaries between Nova Scotia on the one part and East Florida on the other shall respectively touch the Bay of Fundy, and the Atlantic Ocean; excepting such Islands as now are, or heretofore have been within the Limits of the said Province of Nova Scotia.

ARTICLE 3.ᵈ

It is agreed, that the People of the United States shall continue to enjoy unmolested the Right to take Fish of every kind on the Grand Bank, and on all the other Banks of Newfoundland; Also in the Gulph of S.ᵗ Laurence, and at all other Places in the Sea where the Inhabitants of both Countries used at any time heretofore to fish. And also that the Inhabitants of the united States shall have Liberty to take Fish of every kind on such part of the Coast of Newfoundland, as British Fishermen shall use, (but not to dry or cure the same on that Island,) and also on the Coasts, Bays, and Creeks of all other of his Britannic Majesty's Dominions in America, and that the American Fishermen shall have Liberty to dry and cure Fish in any of the unsettled Bays Harbours and Creeks of Nova Scotia, Magdalen Islands, and Labrador, so long as the same shall remain unsettled; but so soon as the same or either of them shall be settled, it shall not be lawful for the said Fishermen to dry or cure Fish at such Settlement, without a previous Agreement for that purpose with the Inhabitants Proprietors or Possessors of the Ground.

ARTICLE 4.ᵗʰ

It is agreed that Creditors on either side, shall meet with no lawful Impediment to the Recovery of the full value in Sterling Money of all bonâ fide Debts heretofore contracted.

ARTICLE 5.ᵗʰ

It is agreed that the Congress shall earnestly recommend it to the Legislatures of the respective States, to provide for the Restitution of all Estates, Rights, and Properties which have been confiscated, belonging to real British Subjects; and also of the Estates Rights and Properties of Persons resident in Districts in the Possession of his Majesty's Arms; and who have not borne Arms against the said United States: And that Persons of any other Description shall have free Liberty to go to any part or parts of any of the thirteen United States, and therein to remain twelve months unmolested in their Endeavours to obtain the Restitution of such of their Estates, Rights and Properties as may have been confiscated; And that Congress shall also earnestly recommend to the several States a Reconsideration and Revision of all Acts or Laws regarding the premises, so as to render the said Laws or Acts perfectly consistent not only with Justice and Equity, but with that spirit of Conciliation which on the Return of the Blessings of Peace should universaly prevail. And that Congress shall also earnestly recommend to the several States, that the Estates Rights and Properties of such last mention'd Persons shall be restored to them; they refunding to any Persons who may be now in Possession the bonâ fide Price, (where any has been given,) which such Persons may have paid on purchasing any of the said Lands, Rights, or Properties since the Confiscation.

And it is agreed that all Persons who have any Interest in confiscated Lands, either by Debts, Marriage Settlements or otherwise, shall meet with no lawful Impediment in the prosecution of their just Rights.

ARTICLE 6.th

That there shall be no future Confiscations made, nor any prosecutions commenced against any Person or Persons, for or by reason of the Part which he or they may have taken in the present War, and that no person shall on that account suffer any future Loss or Damage either in his Person, Liberty or Property; and that those who may be in confinement on such charges, at the time of the Ratification of the Treaty in America, shall be immediately set at Liberty, and the Prosecutions so commenced be discontinued.

ARTICLE 7.th

There shall be a firm and perpetual Peace, between his Britannic Majesty and the said States, and between the Subjects of the one and the Citizens of the other, Wherefore all Hostilities both by Sea and Land shall then immediately cease: All Prisoners on both sides shall be set at Liberty, & his Britannic Majesty shall, with all convenient speed, & without causing any Destruction or carrying away any Negroes, or other Property of the American Inhabitants withdraw all his Armies Garrisons and Fleets from the said United States, and from every Port, Place, and Harbour within the same; leaving in all Fortifications the American Artillery that may be therein: And shall also order and cause all Archives, Records, Deeds and Papers belonging to any of the said States, or their Citizens, which in the

Course of the War may have fallen into the hands of his Officers to be forthwith restored and delivered to the proper States & Persons to whom they belong.

ARTICLE 8.th

The Navigation of the River Mississippi from its Source to the Ocean, shall for ever remain free and open to the Subjects of Great Britain and the Citizens of the United States.

ARTICLE 9.th

In case it should so happen that any Place or Territory belonging to Great Britain, or to the United States, should be conquered by the Arms of either, from the other, before the Arrival of these Articles in America, It is agreed that the same shall be restored, without Difficulty, and without requiring any Compensation.

Done at Paris, the thirtieth day of November, in the year One thousand Seven hundred Eighty Two

RICHARD OSWALD	[Seal]
JOHN ADAMS.	[Seal]
B FRANKLIN	[Seal]
JOHN JAY	[Seal]
HENRY LAURENS.	[Seal]

[On the page of the original next after the above signatures, is the following, the brackets being in the original:]

Witness
The Words [and Henry Laurens] between the fifth and sixth Lines of the first Page; and the Words [or carrying away any Negroes, or other Property of the American Inhabitants] between the seventh and eighth Lines of the eighth Page, being first interlined

CALEB WHITEFOORD
Secretary to the British Commission.
W. T. FRANKLIN
Sec^y. to the American Commission

[On the last written page of the original appears the separate article, which was not ratified.]

SEPARATE ARTICLE.

It is hereby understood and agreed, that in case Great Britain at the Conclusion of the present War, shall recover, or be put in possession of West Florida, the Line of North Boundary between the said Province and the United States, shall be a Line drawn from the Mouth of the River Yassous where it unites with the Mississippi due East to the River Apalachicola.

Done at Paris the thirtieth day of November, in the year One thousand Seven hundred and Eighty Two.

Attest	RICHARD OSWALD [Seal]
CALEB WHITEFOORD	JOHN ADAMS. [Seal]
*Sec*ᵧ. *to the British Commission.*	B FRANKLIN [Seal]
Attest	JOHN JAY [Seal]
W. T. FRANKLIN	HENRY LAURENS. [Seal]
*Sec*ᵧ. *to the American Commission*	

BIBLIOGRAPHICAL NOTE

France, Spain, and the United States

The documentary sources for the beginning of the diplomatic history of the United States, and for the French alliance, are in general very rich. Much of the material has already been published or made available through transcripts for study in the United States and has been worked up by scholars both in Europe and America. Important and voluminous selections of French material, mostly from the archives of the foreign office, were printed in Henri Doniol's monumental *Histoire de la participation de la France à l'établissement des Etats-Unis d'Amérique,* 5 vols. (Paris, Imprimerie Nationale, 1884–1892). To use Doniol without being misled requires much critical application. After carefully reading the five stout folio volumes (plus a supplementary shorter sixth volume), with the great volume of interspersed but selected documents, and after perusing masses of other diplomatic correspondence not given in Doniol (if only for lack of space), one is forced to conclude that what appears at first as a monumental work of great objectiveness is really dominated by strong national bias. Doniol's admiration for the way in which Vergennes retrieved the position of France after the great defeat of 1763 leads him to hold that minister up as a model for the one who would resurrect French power after the prostration of 1871 (see preface to the fifth volume). This patriotic feeling colors the great work. The author regards Vergennes's despatches uniformly as statements of fact, whereas they were constantly and studiously couched for the purposes of putting desired ideas into the minds of the foreign governments near which his envoys were stationed. Doniol in his narrative comment utilized such printed foreign sources and studies as had then been published, such as Jared Sparks's editions of the works of Franklin and Washington, the *Grantham Papers,* Cornélis de Witt's *Thomas Jefferson; étude historique sur la démocratie américaine* (Paris, 1862) ; and de Circourt's *Histoire de l'action commune de la France et de l'Amérique pour l'indépendance des Etats-Unis,* 3 vols. (Paris, 1876), which was a translation of the pertinent volumes of George Bancroft's *History of the United States,* with additional matter for the preparation of which the author made use of Bancroft's copious transcripts from French, English, Dutch, and Prussian archives, transcripts which now repose for perusal in the collections of the New York City Public Library.

Some of the documents in Doniol, with additional matter selected from Loménie's *Beaumarchais,* were published in English translation by John Durand, *New Materials for the History of the American Revolution* (New York, 1889). Doniol had no access to Spanish archives and was mistaken in believing they would reveal little to change the outlines of his narrative. Dr. J. F. Yela Utrilla's *España ante la independencia de los Estados Unidos,* 2 vols. (Lérida, 1925), is a one-volume monograph accompanied by a volume of documentary matter, which includes, among other documents already printed in America, selections from previously printed correspondence between the Spanish Ministry of Foreign Affairs and the ambassador, the Count de Aranda, at Paris. Yela's work is so far the best in that part of the field, and his documents may be regarded as the Spanish supplement to Doniol.[1] In the Division of Manuscripts of the Library of Congress is a great quantity of typed transcripts, made before 1926, from the Spanish archives at Simancas, containing correspondence between the Spanish Foreign Office and its representatives at Paris and London during the American Revolution. Its nature is indicated on pages 20–25 of W. R. Shepherd's *Guide to the Material in Spanish Archives Relating to the History of the United States* (Washington, 1906).[2] This matter has mostly been worked over by Yela, *op. cit.,* and is cited by him; significant documents are printed in his appendix.

The British and French archives both have been ransacked for material in facsimile representation of original documents, in B. F. Stevens's *Facsimiles of Manuscripts in European Archives Relating to America, 1773–1783,*[3] a collection of great value, about one third

---

[1] Yela supersedes M. Conrotte's *Intervención de España en la independencia de los Estados Unidos* (Madrid, 1920).

[2] A check of these typescripts with the originals shows that the selections were not competently made, nor the copying perfectly done. It is understood that for this reason the Library discontinued the service. Later (1928) the Library of Congress installed photocopying apparatus in Spain, with its own trained staff; and the photocopies now include most of this material.

[3] E. S. Corwin's brilliant monograph, *French Policy and the American Alliance of 1778* (Princeton, 1916), is based on Doniol (for the study of which it is an incalculable aid) and the Stevens *Facsimiles,* together with available other printed materials, except the Spanish sources. P. C. Phillips, *The West in the Diplomacy of the American Revolution* (Urbana, Illinois, 1913), goes behind Doniol into French archives, but he also does not touch the Spanish sources; nor does C. H. Van Tyne in his illuminating articles, based on French archival investigations, in *A.H.R.,* XXI, 528–541, XXXI, 20–40. In my own *The Hussey-Cumberland Mission and American Independence* (Princeton, 1931) I have analyzed further the rôle of Spanish diplomacy during the American Revolution from documents in Spanish and other European archives, which were not available to these authors. John J. Meng, *The Comte de Vergennes, European Phases of His American Diplomacy (1774–1780)* (Washington, 1932), touches on Vergennes's European problems. A more comprehensive diplomatic history of the

of which is concerned with the diplomacy of the Franco-American alliance. It includes the secret service papers of the undersecretary, William Eden (later Lord Auckland), from the Auckland Papers. The Stevens *Transcripts Relating to the French Alliance,* in the Library of Congress, consist of carefully collated and indexed copies of the series *Correspondance Politique, Etats-Unis,*[4] from the Ministère des Affaires Etrangères, Paris; there are also in the Library of Congress more recently made facsimiles of the series *Mémoires et Documents, Amérique,* and *Etats-Unis,* for this period. These several series may be said to have been completely duplicated by the Library from the original documents. The Jared Sparks Transcripts at Harvard College Library contain, in addition to matter included in the Stevens *Facsimiles,* the correspondence of Lord Grantham, British Minister at Madrid, 1776–1778. The publication in London in 1927 of *The Correspondence of King George the Third,* Sir J. Fortescue, editor, makes available a most valuable set of source material. Unfortunately it does not print many important enclosures referred to in covering documents.

On the American side the official correspondence was first printed nearly a century ago by Sparks, *Diplomatic Correspondence of the American Revolution,* 12 vols. (Boston, 1829–1830),[5] a series for many years most valuable but not edited in accordance with present-day canons, and now superseded by Francis Wharton's *Revolutionary Diplomatic Correspondence of the United States,* 6 vols. (Washington, G.P.O., 1889). Though this edition leaves out numerous documents, it purports to print the correspondence left in the official custody of the State Department (now transferred to the Library of Con-

American Revolution is Valentín Urtasún's *Historia diplomática de América, Primera parte, La emancipación de las Colonias británicas, tomo primero, La Alianza Francesa,* 2 vols. (Pamplona, 1920 and 1924). These two volumes are the first volumes of what is suggested by the title to be an ambitious work. While the author has covered a far wider range of non-Spanish printed sources and monographs than has Yela (who does not mention Urtasún) and has a more supple and pretentious style, he has not had sufficient access to manuscript sources (except for the Stevens *Facsimiles*), even to those of Spain. Corwin and Phillips are unknown to him.

An important contribution in the shape of a study of national psychologies and the interplay of French and American culture, which supplements the strictly political studies, is Bernard Faÿ's *L'Esprit révolutionnaire en France et aux Etats-Unis à la fin du XVIII⁰ siècle* (Paris, 1925).

[4] Volumes I to XIX inclusive, from 1778 to Dec. 30, 1781, of this series have been calendared in English, in *Report of the [Canada] Archives Branch,* for the years 1912, pp. 162–214, and 1913, pp. 152–206.

[5] J. B. Scott has reprinted some articles published by Jared Sparks on the French alliance in the *North American Review* in 1830, and in the *National Intelligencer* of Washington in 1847: *The United States and France; Some Opinions on International Gratitude* (New York, 1926).

gress), as well as other matter previously published and unpublished (see enumeration on p. viii of Wharton, I), and it, too, may be considered sufficiently definitive for anything except the most detailed study of the diplomacy of the Revolution. There is a narrative introduction. The papers of Silas Deane have been published in *N.-Y. Hist. Soc. Collections,* 1896, in five volumes; Franklin's papers have been published, in selections, in numerous editions and works of which that of A. H. Smyth (New York, 1906) is the best. The Franklin Papers of the American Philosophical Society at Philadelphia have been calendared by the Society: *Calendar of Franklin Papers,* 5 vols., (Philadelphia, 1906). So have the Franklin Papers of the Library of Congress (Government Printing Office, 1905), except for the diplomatic correspondence which is printed by Wharton. The best biography of Franklin is by Bernard Faÿ, *Franklin, the Apostle of Modern Times,* (Boston, 1929). The original Arthur Lee papers were whimsically divided in three parts and placed in the libraries of the University of Viriginia, Harvard College, and the American Philosophical Society. The several collections are calendared. The *Life of Arthur Lee,* with papers, published by R. H. Lee (Boston, 1829) prints most of these papers. Lee is still an historical mystery, who may never be satisfactorily known. The Library of Congress edition (Hunt, Ford, Fitzpatrick and Hill, editors) of the *Journal of the Continental Congress* (Washington, G.P.O., 1904–1931) supersedes all earlier editions. Of major importance for the opinions and debates of Congress is Edmund C. Burnett's edition of *Letters of Members of the Continental Congress,* now (1935) carried in seven volumes through the year 1784, and still in process of publication (Washington, Carnegie Institution of Washington, 1921–). The editing is as near perfect as humanly possible.

The Netherlands and the Armed Neutrality

H. T. Colenbrander, *De Patriottentijd,* 3 vols. (The Hague, 1897), covers the foreign relations of the United Provinces of the Netherlands, 1776–1787, in a comprehensive and masterly manner, based primarily on investigations in Dutch, German, English, and French archives. There are three particular studies of Dutch-American relations during the War of American Independence. Friedrich Edler, *The Dutch Republic and the American Revolution* (Baltimore, 1911), is based largely on the transcripts made by George Bancroft from manuscripts in Dutch, English, French, and Prussian archives, now in the collection of the New York Public Library (a collection which was most meagerly used by that historian in his *History of the United*

States), and on Wharton's *Revolutionary Diplomatic Correspondence of the United States* (*op. cit.*), together with secondary material. Edler's work is valuably supplemented by F. W. van Wijk's *De Republiek en Amerika, 1776–1782* (Leiden, 1921). The lack of familiarity with foreign sources shown in this book is somewhat compensated by exploitation of contemporary Dutch pamphlets and newspapers and the C. W. F. Dumas collection, as well as other manuscripts in the Rijksarchief at The Hague. Francis P. Renaut's *Les Provinces-Unies et la guerre d'Amérique, 1775–1784*, 2 vols. (Paris, 1924, 1925), and *La politique de propagande des Américains durant la guerre d'indépendance, 1776–1783*, 2 vols. (Paris, 1922, 1925), duplicate [6] each other to some extent; they are based on French and Dutch archival studies, but in many cases documented inadequately, a fault, however, which is more glaring in this author's earliest than in his latest volumes. The French archives are more thoroughly used, albeit with a strong national bias, in Paul Fauchille's *La diplomatie française et la ligue des neutres de 1780 (1776–1783)* (Paris, 1893), which captured the Doniol Prize, offered in 1889 by the Académie des Sciences Morales et Politiques. Doniol's volumes, already alluded to, are of great value. P. J. van Winter, *Het Aandeel van den Amsterdamschen Handel aan den Opbouw van het Amerikaansche Gemeenebest*, Vol. I (The Hague, 1927), is an exhaustive monograph on the contribution of the Amsterdam trade to the foundation of American nationality, in which the author has utilized, in addition to the conventional American and Dutch collections, many previously unknown manuscripts illustrative of Dutch-American business relations.

There are three documentary histories of the Armed Neutrality of 1780. J. B. Scott, *The Armed Neutrality of 1780 and 1800* (New York, 1918), contains in addition to a selection of documents, none of which antedates 1780, excerpts (with lacunæ) from the principal publicists, in English translation when necessary. Sir Francis Piggott and G. W. T. Omond, *Documentary History of the Armed Neutralities, 1780 and 1800* (London, 1919), was also compiled during the World War. It presents a limited number of documents carefully and purposefully selected, as an argument against the principles of the Declaration of Paris. August Hennings, *Sammlung von Staatsschriften die, während des Seekrieges von 1776 bis 1783, sowol von den kriegführenden, als auch von den neutralen Mächten öffentlich bekannt gemacht worden sind; in so weit solche die Freiheit des Handels und der Schiffahrt betreffen*, 2 vols. (Altona, 1784), is a most valuable publication. No mention need be made of any of the voluminous literature

---

[6] Both are also duplicated in the same author's *Les rélations entre la Russie et les Etats-Unis, 1776–1823;* Vol. I, *Catherine II et les insurgents, 1776–1783* (Paris, 1923).

on the Armed Neutrality of 1780 which appeared before Carl Bergbohm's *Die Bewaffnete Neutralität* (Dorpat, 1883), because it is completely and critically enumerated in, as well as altogether superseded
by, that brilliant monograph. Bergbohm however did not have the
advantage of direct archival study, though he utilized a pretty representative printed collection of Russian documents, as well as the
classic *Diaries and Correspondence of Sir James Harris, First Earl
of Malmesbury,* 4 vols. (London, 1844), which, it is remembered,
represents a selection made by the grandson editor. Three later historians, already cited, supplement Bergbohm, because they have had
access to archival material not used by him: Doniol, Fauchille, Colenbrander. To them must be added the significant contribution of Thorvald Boye, *De Væbnede Neutralitetsforbund et Avsnit av Folkerettens
Historie* (Christiania, 1912), who has gone through the relevant
Scandinavian and English archival matter.

For earlier bibliographical data the reader is referred to the chapter
by E. J. Lowell on the relations between the United States and Europe
during the Revolution, in Volume VII of Justin Winsor's *Narrative
and Critical History of America* (Boston, 1888), together with the
editor's critical notes on authorities.

The Negotiations for Peace

An unusual mass of source material for the peace negotiations of
1782–1783 is available in print, transcript, or facsimile. The official
diplomatic correspondence of the American Commissioners has been
pretty well printed in Wharton, *op. cit.,* from the original papers of
the Continental Congress reposing now in the Library of Congress.
Wharton has interspersed a good deal of other relevant documentary
material which had been turned up before his publication. Certain
selections only from the papers of John Jay have been printed by
H. P. Johnston, *Correspondence and Public Papers of John Jay,* 4
vols. (New York, 1890–1893); and fragments of a diary kept during
the peace negotiations have been printed by Frank Monaghan,
Diary of John Jay (Sterling Memorial Library, Yale University,
1934). A supplementary volume of hitherto unprinted Jay correspondence is being prepared by the same editor. More copious selections of
Adams's papers, including apparently complete entries of his diary
for the period of the peace negotiations, have been presented by Charles
Francis Adams, *The Works of John Adams,* 10 vols. (Boston, 1850–
1856); but biographers and historians so far have had to content
themselves (except for the small Jay collection in the New York
Historical Society) with those portions of the Jay and the Adams
papers which the families have chosen to publish. The principal body

of each [7] of these original collections is understood to be preserved in special family archives and forbidden to the scrutiny of historians. I have already commented on the Franklin papers, printed and unprinted, which have long since been completely available to historians. E. E. Hale and E. E. Hale, Jr., in *Franklin in France,* 2 vols. (Boston, 1887), print significant original documents from French and English archives, notably the official papers of Oswald.[8] Francis Wharton prints other material of the same nature in the appendix to Vol. III of the *Digest of the International Law of the United States* (Washington, 1887). The Laurens papers are available in the archives of the South Carolina Historical Society and were utilized by David D. Wallace in *The Life of Henry Laurens* (New York, 1915). Shelburne's public papers are now in the possession of the W. L. Clements Library of the University of Michigan, where they are available to qualified scholars (for catalog [under Landsdowne] see Part I of Appendix to *5th Annual Report of Royal Historical Manuscripts Commission*), These have been exploited and to a limited extent reproduced by Baron Fitzmaurice, *Life of William, Earl of Shelburne,* 2d ed., 2 vols. (London, 1912).[9] Volume 70 of the Shelburne papers, which contains Oswald's instructions, commissions, despatches, and journal, is to be found in transcript in the Franklin papers, transferred from the Department of State to the Library of Congress, under title of "Oswald's Journal; Peace Commission, 1782." Two volumes of the papers of Thomas Townshend dealing with these negotiations exist in the Clements library. The papers of Henry Strachey, insofar as they remained in the possession of the Strachey family, are extensively calendared in the *Appendix* to the *Sixth Report of the Royal Commission on Historical Manuscripts* (London, 1877), pp. 399–404; and also in *Report of the Public Archives for the Year 1921* (Ottawa, 1922), pp. 207–281. The principal despatches of Fox on the American negotiation are printed in Lord John Russell's edition of the *Memorials and Correspondence of Charles James Fox,* 4 vols. (London, 1853–1857). Of major importance here is Sir John Fortescue's edition of the *Correspondence of King George the Third,* already

[7] An exception must now be made in the case of the Jay papers in the possession of a descendant, Mrs. Arthur Iselin, who has permitted Frank Monaghan to examine them for his biography now under preparation. He informs me that there is among these papers nothing of great importance for the history of the peace negotiations that is not already published.

[8] The papers of Oswald's secretary, Caleb Whitefoord, are printed in *The Whitefoord Papers* (Oxford, 1898).

[9] The late Clarence Walworth Alvord extolled the character and services of Shelburne in an interesting lecture, in 1925, "Lord Shelburne and the Founding of British-American Goodwill," printed in *Proceedings of the British Academy* for 1926.

cited. The Royal Historical Society has published (London, 1934) in the 7th volume of *British Diplomatic Instructions, 1689–1789,* those relating to France (Part IV), 1745–1789, in selected form. The official and private papers of David Hartley have already been mentioned. The W. L. Clements Library possesses also a valuable collection of photostats of the papers of Benjamin Vaughan, assembled from several repositories of the originals. Very valuable selections and excerpts from the despatches and memoranda of the French Foreign Office are reproduced in Doniol, *op. cit.* (A supplement to Vol. V was published seven years later, in 1899). A few Spanish documents are given by Yela, *op. cit.*

The archives of England, France, Holland, and Spain have been searched by Jared Sparks, George Bancroft, B. F. Stevens, Randolph Adams, and the European Mission of the Library of Congress (by myself and later Worthington C. Ford) for documents bearing on these negotiations. The most notable and comprehensive of the collections of transcripts is the B. F. Stevens *Transcripts Relating to the Peace Negotiations of 1782–1783,* now in the Library of Congress. It includes a vast body of documentary material from the archives of the several foreign offices of England, Holland, and France. It has been interlarded and supplemented with more recent acquisitions of transcripts and facsimiles relating to the same subject. One should also consult, in the same library, the voluminous *B. F. Stevens Transcripts Relating to the French Alliance,* above mentioned.[10] The European Mission of the Library of Congress (1927–1932) has also furnished a large volume of photocopies from Spain and Holland which are classified separately. I have already alluded to the voluminous Bancroft Transcripts in the New York Public Library, which cover this period, together with de Circourt's publication printing selections of them. The Jared Sparks Transcripts, in the Harvard College Library, contain a complete copy of the official correspondence of Oswald.

The W. L. Clements Library has been securing facsimiles from England and France, supplementary to the Shelburne basis of its collections, and it is understood to contemplate extending this work to other countries. Dr. Randolph G. Adams, the watchful librarian of that institution and Miss Edna Vosper, its custodian of manuscripts, are compiling a comprehensive documentary history of the peace negotiations. The late Mr. Clements kindly allowed me to have access to the documents so far collected on the subject, and Dr. Adams and

---

[10] For the years 1778–1781 inclusive, these are calendared, incompletely, in the *Report of the Work of the* [Canada] *Archives Branch* for 1912 and for 1913 (Ottawa, 1913, 1914).

Miss Vosper helped in making them more accessible during my visits to Ann Arbor.

Special studies of a secondary nature are Doniol,[11] Corwin, Phillips, Yela, Dánvila, and Urtasún, already cited above. To these should be added the older but notable narrative by John Jay (the grandson), *An Address on the Peace Negotiations of 1782 and 1783,* before the New York Historical Society (New York, 1884), later revised in Vol. VII of the *Narrative and Critical History of America* (Boston, 1888), edited by Justin Winsor, who consulted English archives and also had available the Stevens, Bancroft, and Sparks Transcripts. (His citations to *Jay MSS* are presumably to a set of his own notes and not to the first John Jay's original papers). On the whole the most satisfactory and comprehensive narrative is that of Urtasún, but curiously enough he did not utilize the Spanish archives.[12]

[11] See also Doniol's "Tentatives de l'Angleterre en 1781 et 1782 pour amener la France à traiter de la paix," in *Rev. d'hist. diplomatique,* XIV (1900), 161–198.

[12] The citations in this volume are always to printed material, when it is printed, rather than to manuscripts presumably unavailable to the reader. Manuscripts are cited only when not printed. As explained in the preface, I have occasionally made reference to originals in European archives where such material if not available in the United States.

INDEX
(by Dr. Philip C. Brooks)

INDEX

Adams, John, on European wars, 12-13 n.; for independence and trade, 30; on committee for treaty plan, 45; named plenipotentiary, 101; brusqueness arouses Vergennes, 104; on treaty of Aranjuez, 109; seeks Dutch accord, 156; mission to Netherlands, 168-170; instructions to, 174-176; methods on mission to France, 176-178; sees through mediation scheme, 186; independent reply to Vergennes, 186-187; on peace commission, 189; Shelburne to sound, 194; favors Canadian cession, 200; insists on independence, 201 n.; delayed in Holland, 203; insists on recognition, 213 n.; reinforces Commissioners, 232; breach of instructions, 234; on disarmament of boundary, 251; regrets escape from mediation, 255; and diplomatic victory, 256; signs preliminary articles, 263-264. *See also* United States; Peace negotiations; Alliance with France.

Adams, Samuel, opposed to France, 176-177.

Aiguillon, Armand, Duc d', French foreign minister, 17 n.

Aix-la-Chapelle, Lee–de Neufville negotiations at, 156-160.

Alberoni, Julio, Spanish minister, 14.

Allen, Anthony, correspondence with Deane, 59 n.

Alliance with France, original plan of Congress, 46; United States shrinks from, 48; proposals of American commission (1777), 52-53; terms, 61-65; effect on British policy, 66; ratified, 67; and territorial guarantee, 100 n., 217; limitations of, 176; England demands termination, 180; Vergennes would evade, 181-183; and Anglo-American agreement, 240; principles in Anglo-American discussions, 249-250; evaluation, 255; material on,

265-268. *See also* France; Vergennes.

Almodóvar, Marquis of, ambassador to England, 78; offers mediation, 79-80; and British reply to ultimatum, 82, 84.

Amsterdam, munitions shipped from, 121 n.; importance, 117-118, 127-128; merchants oppose British plan, 141; French privileges to, 143-145; merchants wish American alliance, 157-158.

Andrew Doria, American ship saluted at St. Eustatius, 122.

Apalachicola River, as boundary, 96, 218-219, 264.

Aranda, Pedro, Count of, Beaumarchais reports to, 37 n.; zealous for war on England, 42, 76; comments upon Grimaldi, 56 n.; reports on peace in Germany, 79; instructions on subsidies, 92 n.; favors recognition of United States, 108; discusses boundaries, 215-220; records of Paris mission, 221-222 n.; accepts British offer, 246-247. *See also* Spain; Floridablanca.

Aranjuez, Convention of, provides Spanish entry into war, 79-80; terms, 84-86; violated by Spain, 105; secret article, 109.

Archangel trade, British ships in attacked, 151.

Arcon, Chevalier d', bombards Gibraltar, 230 n.

Arkansas Post, Spanish expeditions from, 102.

Armed Neutrality, outgrowth of neutral rights problem, 113; derived from Hübner plan, 151, 154; rules of proclamation, 154; Russian invitations accepted, 155-156; an "Armed Nullity," 161; evaluation, 162-163; principles of in peace parleys, 244 n., 247 n., 248, 251-252; material on, 268-270. *See also* Catherine II; Hübner; Bernstorff.

MIDLAND BOOKS

(continued on next page)